# CHAMPAGNE SUPERNOVAS

## KATE MOSS, MARC JACOBS, ALEXANDER MCQUEEN, AND THE '90S RENEGADES WHO REMADE FASHION

### MAUREEN CALLAHAN

**SIMON &
SCHUSTER**

London · New York · Sydney · Toronto · New Delhi

A CBS COMPANY

First published in Great Britain by Simon & Schuster UK Ltd, 2014
A CBS COMPANY

1 3 5 7 9 10 8 6 4 2

Simon & Schuster UK Ltd
1st Floor
222 Gray's Inn Road
London WC1X 8HB

www.simonandschuster.co.uk

Simon & Schuster Australia, Sydney
Simon & Schuster India, New Delhi

A CIP catalogue record for this book
is available from the British Library

ISBN: 978-1-47113-698-6
ISBN: 978-1-47113-787-7 (Trade Paperback)
ISBN: 978-1-47113-700-6 (ebook)

Printed and bound by CPI Group (UK) Ltd, Croydon, CR0 4YY

*To the children of the '90s*

*"We don't wake up for less than $10,000 a day."*
—Linda Evangelista, supermodel, 1990


*"Trash is future luxury."*
—Nicolas Ghesquière, designer, 2013

# CONTENTS

CONTENTS

# CHAMPAGNE SUPERNOVAS

INTRODUCTION

# THIS NEW KIND OF BEAUTY

EVERY LONG-HELD NOTION OF beauty and fashion—and the way these things were created and consumed—had begun to change, forever, in 1992. That was the year a scrawny, short, flat-chested unknown named Kate Moss was signed as the face of Calvin Klein, demolishing the reign of Amazonian supermodels and saving the house in the process. That was the year Alexander McQueen, a pudgy vulgarian from the East London projects, showed his thesis collection at Central Saint Martins, London's famed design school. He called it "Jack the Ripper Stalks His Victims," and it was twisted and warped and witty and sent the London press into paroxysms of outrage. And that was the year an emerging young design star named Marc Jacobs, three years into his job as VP of design at Perry Ellis, got an unusual phone call.

The man on the other end of the line was Nick Egan, a graphic artist from London with an impressive rock 'n' roll pedigree. Egan had worked with the Clash, the Ramones, Malcolm McLaren and Vivienne Westwood, and staged some of Marc's early shows. Now Egan was directing music videos, and he needed a favor.

Would Marc let him use his space at Perry Ellis? Egan was working with a band called Sonic Youth—Marc wasn't overly familiar—

and they needed a place to shoot. Also, could they use this collection that Marc was about to show, maybe even film some models walking in the pieces?

Marc was dubious. He was under enormous stress, and this collection that Egan wanted to use—it was unprecedented, Marc knew it. But at twenty-nine, he was a good generation removed from the girls he was designing for. Marc had come of age at clubs like Studio 54 and Hurrah, places that didn't even exist anymore, and this collection mainlined a new kind of cool, one that a major designer had yet to interpret. Marc knew it could be the defining collection of his young, sun-kissed career: Like nobody else in American fashion, he understood this moment in youth culture. There was a smash-and-grab sensibility, a rummaging through thrift shops and discards, and an embrace of dispossessed beauty. It was a pulverizing, almost moralistic rejection of every excess wrought in the 1980s.

Marc had been struggling to establish an identity at Perry Ellis, to move the house, sclerotic in its preppy tastefulness, forward—if not ahead of the times, at least on track with them. With this work, which would come to be known as "the grunge collection," he'd cracked it. But Marc was also self-conscious: Would the buyers and critics get what he was doing? Would the girls he was designing for get it? Was it sublime or sacrilege to buy a flannel shirt on St. Mark's Place for two dollars, then ship it off to Italy to have it remade in silk? To turn a utilitarian thermal undershirt into a luxury good made of cashmere? Marc was equally aware that this collection might make him just another great pretender in the pantheon of fashion design, cannibalizing a subculture he knew little about.

And what was this band Sonic Youth about, anyway? Why had they zeroed in on him, at this critical time in his professional life? Did they actually like Marc's clothes, or were they trying to mock his studied blend of high and low fashion? As it turned out, Sonic Youth was intimidated by him, and he was intimidated by them, and this was a small example of the larger feeling among kids on the fringe: Nobody felt cool enough. "Was I going to be used," Marc said later, "as sort of a Seventh Avenue designer who has exploited grunge?"

Marc didn't know it, but in 1992 he had a kindred soul in Lee McQueen, then a student at Central Saint Martins. McQueen, too, was an upstart, bored senseless with what was considered fashion. He was a fan of avant-gardists Rei Kawakubo, Martin Margiela, Jean-Paul Gaultier, and Helmut Lang and that was about it, really. McQueen was a happy warrior of dark arts, and he longed to infuse fashion with the things he was most interested in: sex and death, mutilation and contamination, perversion and harm.

"He always had these horrible Victorian pornography books that he carried around," says his old friend Alice Smith. "I don't know where he got them—they were these little fat books that he got in a junk shop or something and they were horrible pictures—he thought they were amazing—of women wearing ball gags and cages over their heads, over-the-top S&M, and he'd be going, 'Isn't that lovely? Look at this woman in these leg irons!' He had quite a distinct idea."

McQueen was gifted, and, as the best designers often are, a hustler and a showman. The press always covered the yearly thesis collections shown at Central Saint Martins, and he was determined to stand apart. "That show was their launchpad," says Bobby Hillson, who established the MA fashion course at Central Saint Martins and was McQueen's mentor. "The students were written up all over the world."

It wasn't enough for McQueen to be written up: His collection had to be the one to electrify. He went to Hillson with his concept: Jack the Ripper. His models were to be the victims, their clothes badges of bloody struggle; Hillson thought it was a shaky idea at best, but she wanted to help.

"He was doing terrible things to the fabric, and I said, 'You can't do this with the cheap fabric you've got.' And he said, 'I can't afford anything else!'"

And so Hillson went to her cupboard and removed "terribly expensive, rich fabrics that had been donated to us. And I said, 'Take some of these.' You know, somebody would've died if they saw what he did with them."

McQueen was slashing and ripping, printing and staining. He was chopping off locks of his hair and sewing them into the clothes, a riff on a Victorian tradition among lovers, who would buy and exchange the locks of prostitutes. He was obsessed by the latter notion, and for as long as he could sewed his own hair into his label.

"Jack the Ripper Stalks His Victims" was shown in 1992, and it changed McQueen's life forever: In that crowd was a peculiar, fashion-mad English aristocrat named Isabella Blow.

She went by "Issie," and was so overcome that she told McQueen she wanted to buy the whole collection. She'd pay in installments, £100 per, until she owned all six pieces. She told McQueen she'd do whatever she could to help; Issie was averse to the nine-to-five, but she had deep connections in the industry and a strong affinity for mongrels and misfits.

First, she said, McQueen must change his name. Issie told him that Lee, his first name, was too common for high fashion. She suggested his middle name, Alexander: It was majestic, had some weight and dignity to it. He agreed. It wasn't hard for him to make that change: McQueen would do whatever it took.

Marc and McQueen weren't the only designers on the bubble in the summer of 1992.

Calvin Klein, who'd built the ultimate 1980s status brand, was on the verge of bankruptcy by the beginning of the '90s, his name diluted through careless and diffuse licensing deals. To save his house, Klein had to become relevant again, and this meant going younger, less crisp and arch—almost dirtier. Klein, approaching fifty, trusted his team, who were in their early to mid-twenties and dialed into what was happening on the streets of London and downtown New York: art director Fabien Baron, creative head Neil Kraft, senior art director Madonna Badger, and consultant Carolyn Bessette.

"Everything was up for grabs," says Badger. The central conundrum facing the brand, she says, was how to reframe its overtly sexual DNA in the age of AIDS.

The team considered the women they'd pinned to their inspiration board as potential new faces of Calvin Klein: women as disparate as Rosie Perez, the short, curvy, Nuyorican actress hot off Spike Lee's *Do the Right Thing*, and the lithe, elegant supermodel Linda Evangelista, whose arrogance ultimately worked against her. "We don't wake up for less than $10,000 a day," she'd said in 1990, and even for a supermodel, such a comment seemed deliberately contemptuous to the rest of the Western world, living, as it was, through a recession and the aftermath of the Gulf war. Evangelista didn't make it past the first round.

For a moment, Perez was the front-runner. "I remember Carolyn Bessette shooting that down," Badger says. "She wanted it to be modern and fresh." Klein trusted Bessette's taste; she was a muse, and he would eventually charge her with casting all his CK shows. In mid-1992, this moment of grunge and grit and '70s regression, Bessette was nothing like the minimalist glamazon she became after marrying John F. Kennedy, Jr.: These days, she wore Egyptian musk and no makeup and had competitions with female Calvin staffers to see who could go the longest without washing her hair. Bessette coolly knocked back her own patrician beauty, spurning perfectionism for a warmer, no less artful dishevelment; at heart, she was a downtown girl who loved vodka, Parliaments, and partying at Save the Robots till six in the morning.

"We were half-hippie, half-natural," Badger says. "It was a total sea change, the opposite of the '80s." The question was: Could Calvin Klein make squalor sophisticated?

There were two other contenders on the inspiration board: Both were European, small and slight, and had an understated, off-kilter beauty. There was Vanessa Paradis, a French actress and pop star best known in the States for dating Lenny Kravitz. The other was Kate Moss, who had just begun appearing in a UK style bible called *The Face*.

For all the physical resemblance—egg-shaped faces strafed with stratospheric cheekbones; china-doll physiques; doe eyes and jagged teeth—the two girls represented the diverging path of high fashion. Paradis, says Badger, "was the one that had that *look*." She'd just starred in ads for Chanel, as a chanteuse in a birdcage, yet the concept itself was already outdated: Putting a young girl in a cage, initially as terrified as any Hitchcock heroine, calmed by a splash of Chanel and unaware of the threat posed by the fluffy white cat alongside her perch—it was an atonal choice for 1992, made by an eighty-two-year-old house. Having Paradis watched over by the ghost of Coco Chanel only underscored the campaign's mustiness.

But the shots of Kate were radical. Most of them were by an un-known British photographer named Corinne Day, and were unlike anything that would have been classified as fashion. Day favored black-and-white over color, wastrels-as-models with hangover pal-lors, the clothes falling apart, too big or too small, pillaged from thrift stores and bedroom floors. Her settings were outdoors and down-market, all natural light and awkward poses. Day's work was as considered and manipulated as that Chanel ad, but the effect was the opposite: druggy, filthy, exuberant.

"Corinne was just attracted to youth culture and wanted to docu-ment it," says Corinne's husband, Mark Szaszy. "Because you don't get any idea of what youth culture is doing from *Vogue*."

The image that the Klein team kept coming back to was one of

Day's, the July 1990 cover shot of Kate from *The Face*: the sixteen-year-old in close-up, a smile so wide it smushes her eyes nearly shut and reveals almost all the imperfect teeth in her mouth, a spray of freckles visible on the bridge of her nose. As a cover, it broke all the rules. It was black-and-white; Kate wasn't making eye contact with the viewer; she was barefaced. Three years earlier, such imagery would never have reverberated beyond its subculture. In 1992, it was stunning.

But Paradis was the known quantity, and she got the offer first. She turned it down, so Klein and his team turned to their second choice: Kate.

As the final decade of the millennium dawned, there would be no greater expression of the cultural, economic, and social revolutions to come than fashion. What rock 'n' roll was to the '50s, drugs to the '60s, film to the '70s, and modern art to the '80s, fashion was to the '90s: the fuse, then the filter.

Much of it had to do with the long-escalating interplay between art and fashion, which had existed since the Italian designer Elsa Schiaparelli collaborated with Dalí, Cocteau, and Man Ray in the 1930s. The cross-pollinating continued through the modern age, from the founding of Andy Warhol's *Interview* in 1969 to the insurrectionism of Helmut Newton, Vivienne Westwood, and Malcolm McLaren in the '70s and Keith Haring, Cindy Sherman, and Jean-Michel Basquiat in the '80s. And there was the electrifying emergence of hip-hop, which brought with it a whole new style.

"Fashion as a significant cultural phenomenon in the '90s had to do with an increasing popular awareness in fashion, and the increasing interchanges between fashion and art," says Valerie Steele, director of the Fashion Institute of Technology. All that had come before allowed someone like Alexander McQueen to be recognized as "sui generis—a phenomenon recognized for being a fashion designer and an artist," she says. "Fashion was increasingly seen as something that penetrates."

Alternative culture was simmering by 1991, yet in so many ways, society hadn't moved on from the 1980s: Michael Jackson had just been signed to Sony in a $1 billion deal. The year's biggest acts ranged from the polyester pop of Color Me Badd and New Kids on the Block to the cartoonish hair-metal of Poison, Skid Row, and Extreme. *Terminator 2: Judgment Day*, the sequel to the 1984 Arnold Schwarzenegger original, was the year's top-grossing movie. The year's overarching question was, "Will Charles leave Di?" A divorced future king, let alone one remarried to his longtime mistress, was unthinkable.

Politically, it felt very 1980s too: George H. W. Bush was still in the White House, his reelection a given. The Clarence Thomas–Anita Hill hearings broke open a long-delayed discussion about sexual harassment; public opinion polls showed a wide majority of Americans believed Thomas. And in fashion, the trends of the 1980s had yet to give way: shoulder pads, shellacked makeup, and a brittle, sequin-encrusted *Dynasty* glamour; Lycra and leg warmers as daywear; neon and bulky knits paired with stirrup pants; high-waisted jeans, side parts and suspenders and high-top sneakers—all of it prevailed, all of it long past modern. Big houses like Armani and Versace, Ralph Lauren and Bill Blass, dominated the marketplace; beauty was defined by glamazons like Cindy Crawford, Naomi Campbell, Linda Evangelista, Claudia Schiffer, and Christy Turlington—who, in 1991, was signed to a record-breaking $800,000 contract with Maybelline, requiring only twelve days' work per year. "We realize the power we have," Turlington said in a 1991 *Time* magazine cover story. "We're making tons and tons of money for these companies, and we know it." According to Karl Lagerfeld, supermodels were the new movie stars: "For me, the really great girls today . . . are like goddesses from the silver screen," he said. "They sell dreams."

*       *       *

But whose dreams? Fashion was supposed to be *for* the young and *by* the young, yet it hadn't been that way since the London youthquake of the '60s and '70s, since Twiggy and David Bailey and Mary Quant and the mods, since Westwood and McLaren and the punks. The supermodels of 1991 may have been in their early twenties, but with their height, their proportions, their peculiar expressions—they often looked angry about being so beautiful—they seemed so much older and harder, haughty and remote, the clothes they wore so matching and mature. The young found no haven here, no place of hope or worship. That was not the way it should be, and even designers felt it.

"That was a time in fashion where all of a sudden, there was this great division," Marc Jacobs said. "There was that old-school mentality of what fashion was, but then there was this far more interesting, far more subversive side of fashion, which was cool in spite of itself."

Bubbling under at the end of 1991 was a collective hunger for change. Outlier Bill Clinton was gearing up to run for president of the United States. Magic Johnson became the first major American sports star to announce he had AIDS. The Soviet Union collapsed. And a band from the Pacific Northwest whose major-label debut, in its first week of release, ranked #144 on *Billboard*'s Top 200, would set the tone for a new era: Four months later, on January 11, 1992, Nirvana's *Nevermind* became the #1 album in the country, knocking Michael Jackson's *Dangerous* out of its slot and becoming a cultural and generational rallying call. The '90s would be a leaching-out of all that had come before.

"I remember being in Berlin the year the Wall came down," Marc said, "and I was in some bar, and 'Smells Like Teen Spirit' was on the radio, and I just thought, 'Wow, this has really crossed over.' I started to feel like, 'This is the way I felt a very long time ago, and now it seems to be acceptable.' The idea of imperfection, girls like

Kate Moss. There was this new kind of beauty that was starting to be recognized."*

A revolution happened in the '90s, and no one noticed. This is the story of that fleeting yet hugely influential time—the moment when the alternative in fashion and beauty became mainstream, and the mainstream became big business—as told through the stories of three of its leading luminaries: Kate, Marc, and McQueen.

---

*"Smells Like Teen Spirit" was released in the US on September 10, 1991; the Berlin Wall fell in the fall of 1989.

CHAPTER 1

# THE MAYBE DRAWER

HER PICTURE WAS STASHED in "the maybe drawer," where the agency kept the common girls. Later, lore would have Kate Moss an obvious star, Sarah Doukas, the agent who discovered her, raving that Kate "had an ethereal quality about her" and that "I saw her and knew instantly I'd struck gold." Yet here Kate was, stuck with the duds.

Corinne Day was a model turned struggling photographer on the hunt for subjects, and had shown up at Storm, Doukas's fledgling agency, unannounced. Corinne was looking for girls to shoot; surely Storm had some who'd work for nothing. Corinne was granted grudging access to the lower-tier girls and, while sifting though the drawer, gravitated to the out-of-focus Polaroid of the girl with the dishwater hair and alien face: eyes set wide and high atop sharply angled cheekbones, kind of like E.T.

Day turned to one of the bookers. "Who's this?"

The booker took a look. "Um . . . I think that's Kate Moss."

It was late 1989. Something was happening in London. There were new synthetic drugs and illegal warehouse parties and freezing, crumbling squats in Shoreditch where all the art-school kids were living. Nothing seemed more romantic or glamorous.

"I'd like to meet her."

In many ways, Kate Moss was the epitome of a typical teenage girl. She lived in Croydon, a middle-class suburb of London, in a modest, well-kept house with one bathroom—hardly the rough area she'd later claim. She had a brother, Nick, two years younger. She went to high school not far down the road. She was of average height and weight and had no particular style.

But things were much darker than they appeared. Her parents were separating. Kate's mother, Linda, had just taken up with another man. Kate was rarely home, often at the pub up the road, or partying till three in the morning, or cutting school and getting high under the bleachers. At fourteen she had recently lost her virginity.

Kate clung to one thing: A year earlier, in the summer of 1988, she'd been spotted at JFK airport by a model agent. Her father laughed and her mother was shocked; she said Kate wasn't all that pretty, definitely not photogenic. Even Kate, says a family friend, "was confused. She thought she was pretty, but she didn't think she was a model." Like every other girl her age, she compared herself to the supermodels of the day—Cindy, Christy, Linda, Naomi—and found herself lacking.

Still, Kate wanted to try; what else did she have to aspire to? Linda took her daughter on go-sees once.

"At the end of that first day," Kate said, "my mum said, 'If you want to do this, you're on your own, because I'm not traipsing around London like that ever again. It's a nightmare.'"

"Kate's relationship with her mother was always strained," says a friend. Kate spent her teenage years, and beyond, looking for a second mother.

Initially, Kate clung to Sarah Doukas, the agent who discovered her at JFK, but Doukas wasn't much better. Her agency, Storm, was very new. Doukas didn't have time to babysit girls like Kate, whom she saw booking catalog work but not much else, and she didn't have time to check out photographers either.

Only fourteen and very much on her own, Kate was determined to become a working model. She had no interest in school. She wasn't a big reader, had no discernible talent or skill. She liked boys and beer and cigarettes and rock 'n' roll and hanging out, nothing more. At least with modeling she had a shot at making some money, buying a car or someday a house. Her parents thought it was ridiculous and her mother refused to help, but Kate had to try—even if, as a friend says, "she didn't like it. She felt like a piece of meat. The photographers were pervy."

"I went to this guy's house in North London, and he was in his bedroom," Kate said, recalling one of her earliest assignments. "He asked me to take my top off." She did. "He asked me to take my bra off." She wouldn't. "There were other girls who had taken theirs off and were just lying there on the bed." Kate left. He wasn't a photographer. "He had just phoned the agency," Kate said, "and they didn't check him out."

On October 26, nearly two months to the day that Doukas found Kate at JFK, she sent her new find off for test shots with a photographer named David Ross. He was underwhelmed.

"I didn't get it," he says. "Kate was a child. She wasn't anything to write home about." There was no wild style happening, no staggering beauty: She was a plain girl with brown hair and hazel eyes wearing a knit top under an old coat. When Ross answered his bell and saw her, he didn't think this was the model he'd been waiting on—he actually asked her if she was lost, "like you would any child in the street."

Kate corrected him, and he felt sorry for her. She obviously didn't have what it took to be a model, but besides that—who would send a young girl off to be photographed by a strange man? "I said, 'Look, don't be angry, but I can't photograph you by yourself. I'm not going to ask you to come back with your mum, but at least come back with a friend.'"

Ross's politeness masked his irritation; he thought Sarah Doukas was jerking him around. "I thought, 'Really?'" Ross says. "You have to remember, this is 1988. The power woman was peaking. The super-model was peaking. They were at every party, they were hanging out with George Michael. Sarah had promised to give me really juicy models, girls who were really on the way up. And, um, you know . . . Kate was so far away from that."

As was Corinne Day. At twenty-eight, she had retired from a modest career as a model: She was fine for catalogs and ad work, but when it came to high-end editorial, Day was too short, too thin, her features too fine and subtle. She got work in Japan, Australia, and Italy, but she was never going to be a star, and she resented the industry's myopic definition of beauty. She'd gone back to London with her boyfriend, Mark Szaszy, also a former model. Together, they decided to pursue photography, but only Corinne had a vision.

"Corinne was quirky, skinny, waifish," Mark says. "And, you know, that's not what it was about in the '80s. She was rejected from many jobs." Day took those rejections hard. "She thought: 'Why should big mean best? Why can't other female body shapes be accepted as beautiful? Why is it this way *all the time?*' "

Then she found Kate in that drawer.

"The first thing that Corinne liked," Mark says, "was that Kate was the opposite of the Amazonian models. The biggest challenge was to make the opposite of what was fashionable, fashionable. And Kate resembled Corinne: 'You're me, and I'm going to make you famous.' "

Corinne's affinity for Kate went beyond their physical similarities. Corinne, too, appeared to have been a lost girl. Her father was a bank robber and her mother ran a brothel, and when Corinne was five, she and her brother went to live with her grandmother for good.

Corinne quit school at sixteen, and once her brief modeling career was over, she turned to photography, shooting smudged-up, off-duty models in their hotel rooms, surrounded by stuffed-up ashtrays and the remnants of room service: This, to Corinne, was glamorous. Along with photographers Nick Knight, Nigel Shafran, and David

Sims, Corinne was working out a new kind of lingua franca in fashion photography, one that was a little bit hard to look at. The idea of contrast, of placing elegant women in decaying sites, was nothing new to fashion—Avedon had been doing it since the late 1950s—but Corinne sought to expand that idea, demanding such realism extend to models. Nan Goldin was Corinne's idol, and while she didn't want to be derivative, she wanted to shoot like that: documentary-style images of uncommon, slightly ruined beauties in their natural habitats.

When Corinne found Kate, she felt she had her avatar, the dissident who could potentially disturb the industry in ways Corinne couldn't. Kate was so unformed, though—she didn't know how to pose, to hold herself, to shake off her self-consciousness. Corinne began taking Kate over to her grandmother's house, where they'd do test shots together in the back garden while Corinne's nan made them tea and sandwiches.

This felt, to Kate, almost wholesome. Her experience might have been limited, but she trusted Corinne, who was becoming more of a second mother to her than Sarah. Several months later, Kate moved in with Corinne and Mark, and they became a little family.

Corinne had a plan. She knew there was no way she'd ever get British *Vogue* or *Harper's Bazaar* or any big fashion glossy to look at her work, but there were a couple of independent magazines that were all about youth culture: the right clubs and the right drugs, more interested in street style than the fashion industry.

*The Face* and *i-D* were both founded on the tail end of the punk movement, and they took their cues from forerunners such as *Interview* and *Punk* and the original *Details*—magazines that celebrated subcultures and freaks while attracting the right kind of celebrity. The motto at *i-D*: "Style isn't what but how you wear clothes." The kids they shot on the street were goths, punks, New Romantics, rockabilly, and rave kids.

"I wanted to get out the concept that we don't lay down the rules about what you wear, the idea of 'in-out' fashion," said founding editor Terry Jones. But just like *The Face*, *i-D* had its ideas about "in-out" fashion: Anything in *Vogue* and the like was out, *i-D*'s outsiders in. The London scene was so small that, for a time, *Face* editor Sheryl Garratt's roommate was *i-D*'s editor. No other UK magazines, with the exception of *Blitz*, which arrived a bit later, "would be interested in whatever it was we would be fretting about," Garratt says.

Both publications had distinct mandates. "*i-D* was a sort of fashion fanzine and *The Face* was very much a music magazine," says Garratt. "But they both evolved into this thing that was much bigger than that, and they evolved very much in tandem."

In their way, *The Face* and *i-D* were as exclusive as *Vogue*. Not just any outsider would make it into *i-D*'s pages: You had to be the *right* kind of outsider. You had to be cool. Everyone else was shunned, and this philosophy attracted a strain of celebrity that shared the magazine's DNA. *i-D*'s 1985 fifth-anniversary issue featured a who's who of the magazine's coups—Morrissey, John Galliano, Paul Weller, Leigh Bowery, Adam Ant, and two who would go on to be key players in London's coming Britpop scene: Patsy Kensit and Jeremy Healy.

To quote one disgruntled letter to the editor: "You are a stupid lot of wanking ignorant trendies."

Then there was *The Face*, as old as *i-D* and, in 1989, undergoing an identity crisis. "It was a thing of faded magnificence," says Sheryl Garratt. She sat down with her new art director, Phil Bicker. They both felt something was happening in London, and they not only wanted to reflect it but to push the culture forward, to claim the decade as their generation's own.

"We had this quite young team, me and Phil being key to that," says Garratt. "We talked a lot about how we wanted it to be. I talked about how, in clubs in the '80s, it was all about being cool and posing and pouting and looking sharp, and suddenly there are all these kids sweating in fields and smiling. Suddenly, being in a club was now all about a great big sweaty hug from somebody. And I wanted the magazine's fashion to reflect that."

Bicker agreed. He had come from small publications such as *Miss London* and *City Limits*, and taking over *The Face* gave Bicker his best shot at putting his stamp on this cultural groundswell. His first edict: Ban anyone—photographers, models, stylists—who was established.

"People were sending in portfolios and stories to *The Face* that I was refusing to run," Bicker says. "I said, 'Why do we want to run pictures of Linda Evangelista or Tatjana Patitz when we need to cut out our own thing, for our own audience?'" This stance, Bicker says, was as much about rebellion as resentment. On the one hand, high-end fashion photographers were happy to use *The Face* as a dumping ground for editorials that were too experimental for mainstream fashion magazines, yet *The Face* couldn't get access to designer clothes or afford to commission those very photographers.

"Fashion had become very protective of itself. It had become: 'Fashion is this. This is what fashion is,'" Bicker says. "And anything outside was beyond its power and it wasn't interesting."

*The Face* had no budget and didn't attract fashion advertising, which gave the magazine a unique advantage: It meant they could shoot whatever clothes they liked without having to include pieces that belonged to advertisers. The magazine became an outlet for hungry young photographers and stylists and models who had their own ideas about what constituted fashion.

Corinne lasered in on *The Face*. She got an appointment with Phil, who was looking for a model to brand the magazine for the '90s— a new face of *The Face*. For that first meeting, Corinne brought along a bleary Polaroid of Kate. Bicker recognized where it had been shot— on the main high street in Ickenham, the working-class London suburb where Bicker had grown up. "You couldn't tell where it had been taken unless you'd been there," Bicker says. "When Corinne showed me that picture, I was like, 'This is it.'"

Corinne's husband, Mark, doesn't recall it that way. "Corinne was really pushing Kate," he says. "She was so decisive. She knew how to photograph, how to style. There was no stylist or hairdresser or makeup artist interfering. The average male photographer wouldn't feel comfortable without all those people—he'd be depending on some crazy stylist who couldn't make up his mind about what to put the girl in."

Just as *The Face* was struggling with the pluses and minuses of outsider status, so was Corinne. There were very few female fashion photographers of that era. Ellen von Unwerth was the most famous, but she was working out of the Helmut Newton playbook, a sinister, Germanic kind of eroticism, S&M glossed up in black-and-white. On Corinne's tier were Peggy Sirota and Sylvia Plachy, both of whom shot for *Sassy* in the US. Both were interested in realism, but neither was working in fashion.

Corinne wasn't just the lone female fashion photographer in London; she was the only one defining a new kind of beauty with a girl who defied all its prevailing notions. What Corinne and Kate were doing—creating a no-logo, anti-glam aesthetic that took sex out of the equation—could never have been done by a male photographer, even if he had a Kate. It wasn't just down to Corinne's gender: It was the curious alchemy between these two, with their damaged souls and optimistic perseverance.

Bicker decided to give Kate a cover try. He assigned the job to a male photographer, Marc Lebon, himself a product of London stylist Ray Petri's Buffalo style, which, in the 1980s, was a precursor to what was about to explode: the elevation of the street over high style and the embrace of a post-punk, multiethnic, androgynous look.

Corinne was outraged.

"Why take Corinne's girl and do that?" Mark says. "But he did. And the cover was crap."

It was. Even Bicker admits it. *The Face*, Garratt says, was "determined" to do a football-themed issue, since the sport was "just getting reclaimed from hooligans" and turning into part of this entire youth movement. Lebon gave Kate a football and had her hold it up to her face.

"That wasn't a great cover," says Bicker. "Kate really isn't herself."

Bicker asked Corinne if she'd be up for shooting an editorial with Kate for the very next issue. The theme was "The Third Summer of Love"—a document of the emerging British subculture of soft drugs, fuzzy pop music, and, as *The Face* would put it, "football thugs with flowers."

It was an organic rejection of Thatcherism and corporate culture, of anything that felt top-down and too clean, and it was peaking in 1990. Kids were referencing the flower children of the late '60s, but this really was a culture of their own invention. There were all-night raves held in abandoned warehouses and fueled by ecstasy; all-day rock festivals in muddy fields, where the Stone Roses and the Happy Mondays, the leaders of the neo-psychedelic Madchester scene, would play to hooligans and hipsters alike; a sense that this generation was looking to root itself in inclusiveness and authenticity, that everything from fashion design to the dance floor should be democratized. It was happening in the US, too, with acid house in Detroit, raves in New York, grunge in the Pacific Northwest. The indie rock kids were partial to heroin, the rave kids to ecstasy. The effects of both were largely the same: a rush of calm and euphoria, a cushioned membrane of warmth. But heroin turned all that feeling inward, while ecstasy had the opposite effect, giving rise to sweaty group hugs in fields and nightclubs.

Corinne had seven pages and no budget to photographically articulate this entire generational revolution, one that hadn't even congealed yet. But she did have Kate and possibly a shot at the cover.

Meanwhile, Sheryl Garratt and Phil Bicker were working on a

backup plan. Maybe the cover could be conceptual? They considered using a crowd shot from one of the festivals. They had an image of the alt-comedienne Sandra Bernhard by Herb Ritts, another donation. Ritts was a star fashion photographer, working in black-and-white with a heavy bent toward old-Hollywood glamour. He'd moved into directing music videos for the biggest pop stars of the day—Madonna, Janet Jackson—but there was a formalism to his work that felt off. He made his subjects look unreachable, as erotic as marble.

"If you're saying, 'This is the start of the '90s'—a Herb Ritts image of an American comedienne is not the way to go," Garratt says. "Phil was just like, 'This is not right.' And I kind of knew he was right."

It was out.

Meanwhile, Corinne had taken Kate and a tiny crew down to the beach at Camber Sands in East Sussex—they picked that spot so Kate could meet up with her boyfriend after the shoot. And even though Corinne's concept was to do something totally lo-fi and natural, she put as much effort and consideration and manipulation into her work as Ritts did. But you'd never be able to tell by looking, and that was Corinne's great gift.

Her stylist was Melanie Ward, a cool girl who'd done a year at Central Saint Martins and wound up working in the fashion under-ground after a stylist spotted her at a party: she liked Ward's look and offered her a job, simple as that.

"What we were doing was really the antithesis of what was going on at the time," Ward said. "Everything else was maximalism—women who were very polished and untouchable and Amazonian. We were living a very different way. People would pass food down to us on the fire escape and we would count our pennies to be able to afford to take photos. Kate was our muse. She was this fresh, beautiful girl."

Corinne and Melanie conceived the Summer of Love shoot to-gether. "It was just about a young girl at the beach," Mark says. "Just being a young girl, playing."

Kate was into the concept, until Corinne asked Kate to take her top off. It was March and it was freezing, but also: What? Kate was self-conscious about her small breasts, and Corinne knew it.

"I see a sixteen-year-old now, and to ask her to take her clothes off would feel really weird," Kate said later. "But they were like, 'If you don't do it, we're not going to book you again.' So I'd lock myself in the toilet and cry and then come out and do it. I never felt very comfortable about it. There's a lot of boobs. I hated my boobs! Because I was flat-chested. And I had a big mole on one. That picture of me running down the beach—I'll never forget doing that, because I made the hairdresser, who was the only man on the shoot, turn his back."

In the finished editorial, called "The Daisy Age," Kate looks alternately disaffected—in one shot, she's leaning against a cement wall, in white jeans and a macramé top, smoking a cigarette with all the panache of a middle-aged pensioner—and exuberant. Here she is, a neo-hippie flower child in an Indian headdress, little makeup, raggedy hair, and no top, throwing back her shoulders and smiling.

Sheryl Garratt hated it. She wondered if they should be showing such a young girl topless, or smoking a cigarette. But mainly, she thought the pictures were ugly. "I'd like to say I was sitting there thinking, 'We've just encapsulated the spirit of the '90s,'" Garratt says. "But did I think that at the time? No. I thought, 'Is this fashion at all? She's wearing bloody sandals on the beach!'"

Bicker not only disagreed, but he thought that Kate, in close-up and Indian headdress, should be the cover: He fought Garratt, who had no other option in her back pocket. "I was saying, 'It's a great photo. We should put it on the cover. It sums up this moment perfectly.'"

There was another problem: Only one other person had been on the cover of *The Face* more than once in one year, and that was Madonna. Should such a distinction go to some unknown teenage model who had no glamour, no figure, bowed legs and jagged teeth and one eye that was slightly off-center?

The answer was yes.

## CHAPTER 2

# THE PINK SHEEP
# OF THE FAMILY

AS HELLIONS GO, HE was among the nicest. Lee McQueen loved the legend that had him, as a young apprentice on Savile Row, stitching the words *I am a cunt* into a jacket he was making for the Prince of Wales. That the people who knew McQueen best still debate whether he did it testifies to his gift for self-mythologizing.

McQueen liked it when people either feared him or underestimated him (both were best) and he took everything that, in lesser hands, could have been a weakness—his looks, his weight, his lack of money or education or connections—and leveraged it hard. He made posh people feel like they were inferior. He inverted the entire psychology of the industry: He made fashion people aspire to be fluent in poverty and struggle, to possess the ingenuity required to do more with less. His attitude masked his own insecurity—after all, what business did a chubby, unattractive, uneducated boy from the council estates have here anyway?—and it usually worked. Plum Sykes, the *Vogue* contributor who began as an assistant to future McQueen muse Isabella Blow, recalls the first time she met the designer.

"He came into the office wearing, like, jeans falling off his bottom and a checkered lumberjack shirt," she says. "He looked like a complete yob, and that was the image he was cultivating." He refused to do the double air-kiss or acknowledge common social graces. "I was intimidated by the fact that he was a working-class boy, like a rough 'n' tough Cockney. Like a Dickens character. He was from the East End of London. I'd never been to the East End of London."

While McQueen exploited his less-than-fashionable qualities, he was also ashamed of them. He was self-conscious about his weight. He hated his face, and for the first few years of his career would only be photographed with his head wrapped in cling film or gaffer's tape, saying that he was still on the dole and couldn't get caught. His teeth were a mess. He'd smashed the front ones diving into a pool when he was nine, and his parents couldn't afford to have them fixed until Lee was sixteen. Even then, the most they could buy were cheap caps. The lack of proper dental care would cause him horrible tooth pain for much of his life. McQueen's former boyfriend Andrew Groves recalls one night in 1994 when McQueen, by now fairly well known, was in so much agony that he had to go to the emergency room. McQueen always made a show of brushing off his humiliations, or turning them into commentary: "It was really amusing to him," says Groves, "to have a tooth missing and to have to go to a meeting at *Vogue*."

That tooth fell out while McQueen was biting into a Big Mac. He was twenty-six and a rising star.

He would rarely, if ever, articulate his more tender feelings; he made it clear that the fashion world was silly, superficial, and he carried himself as though he was far too talented to be concerned with manners or proper grammar or missing teeth. He was, in fact, too talented for that, but still he felt so on the outside of this world he loved, this world of beauty so extreme it seemed pornographic. He would never be beautiful.

"He always had imposter syndrome," says Alice Smith, a friend who represented McQueen in his early years. "He felt like he shouldn't be there." Smith recalls going to see McQueen receive the award for Best British Designer in 1996 at the Royal Albert Hall. She was seated in the mezzanine with all the other people on McQueen's team, watching as the evening's honorees filed in below. "We were looking down into this giant pit going, 'Oh look, there's Anna Wintour,' and suddenly we saw this little chubby fellow arriving, and he had his ticket, and he was showing it to people as if to say, 'I'm allowed to come in.' "

Lee Alexander McQueen, born March 17, 1969, was the youngest of two boys and three girls and his mother's favorite. At the time, the family lived in Lewisham, a South London district with its own gothic history: Lore had it that the area had been founded in the sixth century by a pagan member of a Germanic tribe known as the Jutes. In 1944, during World War II, the town was hit with a V-1 flying bomb, and more than three hundred residents were killed. It took nearly ten years for the town to rebuild and recover, and in December 1957, Lewisham was the site of another catastrophic event when a packed passenger train missed a signal and crashed into an idle train, killing ninety people. That rail disaster is considered one of the worst in Britain's history.

Before Lee had his first birthday, the family moved to a council estate—the equivalent of the projects in the US—in Stratford. Though the McQueens struggled financially, it was nothing compared to the emotional and psychological torment wrought by Lee's father, Ronald. He was a taxi driver, a rough man who suspected, from the time Lee was a toddler sketching Cinderella on his older sister's bedroom wall, that his youngest son was gay. Ron didn't like it. He wanted Lee to grow up and have a job worthy of a man, as a plumber or an electrician. Instead, his son was a freakish boy who worshipped Calvin Klein so much that he'd tacked a piece of paper with the designer's name to his bedroom wall. Ron largely ignored Lee. Much later, Lee would say that his father had less of an issue with his son's sexuality once he became famous and "solvent," though friends recall a more complicated relationship. In the early days, it was Ronald who would drive his taxi off-hours to wherever Lee was working, helping to transport his clothes from studio to showroom. On those occasions when his father would attend one of Lee's fashion shows, he would stand in the back, while Lee's mother, Joyce, always sat front row.

As a child Lee was highly sensitive, and although he would later refer to himself as "the pink sheep of the family," he clung to his mother. Joyce, a bookish woman with her own artistic bent, encouraged her youngest to pursue his interest in clothes, which was evident from the time Lee was four or five, unhappy with whatever outfit Joyce had picked for him to wear to school. "Mum!" he'd say. "I can't wear that! It doesn't go, it doesn't go!"

"I always, always wanted to be a designer," he later said.

Lee would spend many afternoons sitting contentedly with Joyce and her sisters, drinking tea and sketching his earliest designs. Or he'd listen to Joyce as she explained what she'd newly learned about their ancestry, a fascination that Lee shared and one that would later work its way into his most famous collection, "Highland Rape."

When Lee was sixteen, Joyce went back to work, teaching night courses in social studies and genealogy. Despite all he had in common with his mother, an interest in books—unless they had to do with fashion—and traditional learning was not among them. He had a hard time in school anyway; some of the other kids bullied him and called him "McQueer." He found solace in the outdoors, became obsessed with bird-watching and swimming, and despite the solitary nature of these two hobbies, Lee joined both the Young Ornithologists' Club of Great Britain and his school's synchronized swimming team. His ability to conform, however, was limited: He was nine when he joined the swim team, and he probably would've been kicked out for insubordination—he preferred swimming freestyle underwater—had he not smashed his front teeth against the concrete lip of the pool during a back flip gone awry. This was the injury that would go uncorrected by his parents and cause him lifelong pain.

Later, when he had money and had been embraced by editors and socialites and the CEOs of multibillion-dollar global corporations, he'd have his teeth properly capped. He would tell friends that he was surprised it didn't make him feel any better about himself.

"I don't think he was happy with how he looked physically," Groves says. The more money he'd go on to make, the more cosmetic work McQueen would have done, and the unhappier he'd become.

McQueen was, unsurprisingly, exceptionally gifted at finding women who wanted to take care of him. "I think he really knew how to work people," Groves says. "That drive reminded me of Madonna." In 1990, McQueen showed up at Central Saint Martins, the most prestigious fashion institute in Europe, without an appointment. He was a high-school dropout from the council estates, yet Bobby Hillson, the department chair, let him in the program anyway. "He had no money and he looked a mess," she says. She was in "amazement," she says, "that he had the nerve to come and see me, just like that . . . We did attract, clearly, the mad ones."

Hillson helped him get work so he could pay tuition. The rest of the money came from his aunt Renee, his mother's sister, who loaned him $7,500. Hillson thought McQueen was so brilliant that he'd either wind up a superstar or a casualty, but nowhere in the middle. She was right about both.

There was another woman who would have as much impact on McQueen's future as Hillson. She would be second only to Joyce in McQueen's affections, and she was, in many ways, his soul mate: Isabella Blow, otherwise known as Issie. They called themselves "lovers without the sex."

Isabella Blow was an eccentric aristocrat who was cash-poor and always on the hustle. Her childhood was as traumatic as McQueen's, if not more so; her family history gothic. Her paternal grandfather, Sir Jock Delves Broughton, was a clotheshorse and a party boy, and was only in his thirties when he ran up $70 million in gambling debts. To pay them off, he sold most of his family's 34,000-acre estate. In November 1940, just months after divorcing his first wife, Vera, Jock, fifty-six, married twenty-six-year-old Diana Caldwell; weeks later, Diana was very openly carrying on an affair with the Earl of Erroll, Joss Hay.

The earl and the Broughtons were all part of the same decadent social group known as "the Happy Valley set." Drunkenness, debauchery, and intra-scene adultery were common and accepted, but Jock was enraged by his new bride's affair. Sometime early in the morning of January 24, 1941, the earl was shot to death, at point-blank range through the head on a road in Nairobi, Kenya, where the set had decamped. Jock became the prime suspect. The wealth and fame of the parties involved, the sexual jealousy, the cold-bloodedness of the crime—the Jock Delves Broughton trial was the O. J. Simpson case of its day. A servant had testified that he'd seen Jock with two guns on the night of the murder, and the next morning, another eyewitness said Jock was washing out his own bloody clothes. He was found not guilty. Jock returned to England in 1942 a pariah, checking into Liverpool's Adelphi Hotel, and committing suicide by shooting himself up with Medinal, a barbiturate, fourteen times. Most took this as proof Jock was guilty, and the case remained such a source of fascination it became the subject of James Fox's famous 1987 book *White Mischief*.

After Jock's death, Issie's father, Evelyn, was left with just a thousand acres of the original Broughton plot and began downsizing, selling off most of his father's possessions and turning the bulk of the land into a working farm. In 1955, after one brief marriage, Evelyn, at forty, married a twenty-five-year-old commoner named Helen Shore. She was descended from greengrocers.

Helen and Evelyn moved into what had been the gardener's shack on the Delves Broughton estate, and three years later Helen gave birth to Isabella. Her father was disappointed to have a girl. In 1961 Helen gave birth to another daughter, Julia, and one year later she finally had a son. They named him John Evelyn.

Helen was pregnant again in September of 1964, when John, then two and a half, choked on a small piece of food, fell into the family swimming pool, and vomited. He was asphyxiated before he could drown. As Issie remembered it, Helen had asked her to look after John that day, and the guilt stuck with Issie always.

Issie never forgave her mother, though it's hard to know if John's death is solely to blame. Issie may not have grown up with money—in fact, her father was so cheap he refused to fix her teeth, and his own friends joked that her homeliness meant she'd be great in bed—but like many aristocrats, she was still a snob. She hated that her mother had common origins, but in fairness, that hate might have been molli-fied had Helen actually been more interested in being a mother.

She and Evelyn, like Jock and his wives before them, had a dif-ficult marriage, riven by grief and resentment. After Evelyn met the next Lady Delves Broughton on vacation while his wife was having surgery, Helen left. She assembled her children on the lawn and shook their hands goodbye.

Her brother's death became the defining trauma of Issie's life. In her later retellings—like McQueen, she liked making people squea-mish, and would often pull this story out to strangers at cocktail parties—she had her mother off in the house reapplying her lipstick while little John toddled into the pool, choking on the canned food they were forced to eat on the nanny's day off.

For Issie, who forever felt like an ugly duckling, this was revenge: blaming her brother's death on her mother's vanity while garnishing a tragedy with what, for her, was a Dickensian flourish.

"That explains my obsession with lipstick," Issie would say, and even her own husband, Detmar Blow, after hearing conflicting ac-counts of what happened that day, suspected that the lipstick detail was fake, that Issie, like McQueen, had a gift for cultivating her own creation myth.

"I am a force of nature," she'd often say to Detmar.

She had much else in common with McQueen: They both hated their teeth. Of McQueen's, Issie would say, "They're like Stonehenge," but she could get away with it because she called her own crowded buckteeth "combine harvesters" and "yellow fangs." By the time Issie saw a dentist—as a young woman living in New York City, with enough connections to see the very one who treated Frank Sinatra—she was crushed to hear it was too late. Though she would tell all those shocked strangers and acquaintances that she smeared lipstick all over her face and teeth in gory homage to her mother's fatal carelessness, the truth was banal: She did it because she hated her mouth more than any other feature—and she hated all of her facial features, hiding behind hats and veils.

"A cheaper and less painful form of plastic surgery," she would say.

But this was long before Issie and McQueen each succumbed to despair, to drugs, to self-sabotage and, finally, suicide. Before they ever met they were on parallel tracks, and even when their friendship broke apart, corroded by jealousy and anger, on parallel tracks they stayed.

Not long after dropping out of high school at sixteen, McQueen saw a TV program about Savile Row's apprenticeship program. It was a perfect fit for him: Most tailors wanted inexperienced young people because they were easier to train, and Lee would get paid to learn, £100 a week.

In 1985, Lee was hired at the Row's Anderson & Sheppard, which counted Prince Charles and Mikhail Gorbachev among its clients. In a picture from this time, Lee is seen in the workroom with his fellow apprentices. They are all neatly put together, wearing earth tones and soft expressions. Lee, off to the left, stands out: He is the tallest in the room by at least a head, and chubbier. His hair is cropped close on the sides and curly on top; he is wearing tight blue jeans, especially so at the crotch, cinched high at the waist with a thick, brass-buckled brown belt. His bright-red dress shirt is tucked in and buttoned up all the way to his throat, and his smile is awkward—a square that could easily be mistaken for a grimace. His hands are stuffed into his pockets. He is not alone in seeming uncomfortable, though he was more so than most. Even here, he would be teased about his sexuality, with some of the girls repeatedly asking Lee if he had a girlfriend. They'd snicker; he'd blush. They'd tease him about his love of house music. He could not find a place to fit in anywhere—he didn't even belong in the gay clubs, where he stood apart from all the other buff, good-looking men, so confident and preening.

So he kept to himself.

Lee would show up every morning at eight, turn on Radio 2, and get to work. Like all the other apprentices, he was paired with a mentor. "I sat for two months padding collars, and two years learning how to make a jacket," he said. His training here was militaristic: Knowing how to properly affix a button was as important as being able to make a bespoke suit itself, and the tiniest flaw required ripping up and starting over. He was the shop's most gifted apprentice, mastering the construction of a "forward"—the scaffolding of a jacket—in thirty months. It usually takes thirty-six.

Lee apprenticed at Anderson & Sheppard until sometime in 1987, and accounts of his departure—most from the primary source—vary: Lee alternately claimed that his mother had been sick, that he had outgrown his training, that a shopkeeper across the street was leering at him. Anderson & Sheppard say they fired him.

Later that year, McQueen was hired by Gieves & Hawkes, just a few doors down the Row. He was nineteen years old, and here he concentrated on perfecting the art of the trouser. On his twentieth birthday, he quit, claiming that here, too, he was mocked for being gay, and it's quite possible; despite their seeming gentility, the shops on Savile Row engaged in their own coded brutality. Andrew Groves says that McQueen felt extremely class-conscious at both houses, and that it's the employees themselves, not the posh patrons, who are the bullies. It's soft violence, both domestic and directed at the customer, who by current prices is charged a minimum of £3,500 for a bespoke suit. "On Savile Row—it's self-mythologizing, but they say things," Groves says. "They'll take the measure of you and they'll say, 'Oh, it's a 46FC,' which is 'fat cunt.' Or if you say something that applies to you—say, 'Those cakes are large'—they'll whistle, which means . . . you're large as well."

After leaving Gieves & Hawkes, McQueen went freelance. He was hired to work on costumes for productions of *Miss Saigon* and *Les Misérables*, which later informed the theatricality of his fashion shows. He also got a gig as a pattern cutter for the London-based Japanese designer Koji Tatsuno, where he learned to drape and cut on the body. But he quickly plateaued and, as Groves says, the minute McQueen felt he'd mastered something, it was "on to the next."

A colleague at Tatsuno suggested Lee meet designer John McKitterick, who worked at a small label called Red or Dead.

"He was a very shy man, very unassuming," McKitterick says. But he was impressed by Lee, and hired him to work as a pattern cutter and machinist. As he'd been at Savile Row, Lee was at Red or Dead: always on time, highly focused, very quiet. "He rarely talked about any ambition he had or anything," McKitterick says. He and McQueen wound up getting along very well, even if McQueen remained an enigma. "I didn't know anything about his private life," McKitterick says. "I knew he came from the East End, I knew his family lived there, and I remember he was always quite hard up. He never had any money."

It was clear to McKitterick that Lee McQueen had talent but, counter to myth, his genius was not evident from the beginning. McQueen was doing everything he could to push himself forward, and when McKitterick told McQueen he was leaving Red or Dead to set up his own shop, McQueen knew he had to make a move.

It was 1990. McQueen told McKitterick he wanted to do the same thing: He, too, wanted to be a fashion designer. He was thinking that Milan was the place. London was dead; there hadn't been a significant fashion movement there since the punk era, and that was well over a decade ago. London Fashion Week was such a joke that McQueen and his friends called it "London Fashion Weekend."

McKitterick was surprised. "I didn't think Lee had that ambition," he says. "Normally, when people want to be a fashion designer, you know about it—because they talk about it all the time, they're trying to put themselves forward and get into the business any way they can. He came to me out of the blue."

McKitterick had worked in Milan and happily gave McQueen his contacts list—editors, talent agents, designers—though privately, he remained skeptical. "Even to go to Milan with [a] contacts book and try to make it is a big risk," McKitterick says. "It's extremely hard to get a job." McQueen was also going with a one-way ticket, no money, and an underwhelming portfolio: so far, he'd only executed others' work. He'd designed nothing himself.

McQueen later said the book he took to Milan was "the worst portfolio you've ever seen." But he was hired at Romeo Gigli, and later would recall the moment with such cinematic melodrama that even his friends were skeptical: McQueen claimed he was promptly turned away for being fat and ugly, and as he ambled down the street, with his sad little portfolio and vanishing prospects, he heard a young woman yelling behind him. "This girl came up to me screaming like a madwoman: 'Stop, stop, stop. Romeo wants to see you. He wants to see you tomorrow.'"

McQueen was put to work as a packing cutter. He was happy to pay his dues and brought with him not just a strong, blue-collar work ethic but a jolt of British youth culture: acid house and ecstasy and rave, kids dressing in baggy jeans and footballers' tops, looking for little more than the next party, the next high, the next hug. McQueen was never much of a raver himself—he was more of a sawdust-pub kind of guy, not into drugs or alcohol, really—but still, he recalled showing up for work at Gigli "dressed like a nutty little raver . . . in my denim patchwork flares and happy, happy smiley T-shirt. It freaked a lot of people out, all these dressy fashion students and PR people, but Romeo seemed to like that."

He wound up rooming with Lise Strathdee, a colleague at Gigli, and two other people. He was trying to become more social, but it was a process. Most evenings after work, the housemates would commune in the kitchen and cook and drink and gossip; sometimes Lee would join them, sometimes not. When he was around, Lee would make cutting remarks about gays, the kind he was subject to at home and at school and on Savile Row, and so Strathdee was shocked one night when the housemates were comparing Milanese nightspots and Lee "named every single gay club. It was evident he was a frequent patron." They were fascinated: "It was quite a revelation and a mystery as well." She remembers feeling relieved to know he had friends.

After about six months, Lee's contract at Gigli was up, and he returned to London in the fall of 1990. He went back to work at Red or Dead, and found himself attracted to the collection he was working on, which was highly sexual and dark, informed by S&M and fetish wear. Once again, McQueen said it: He wanted to be a designer. He wanted to go to Central Saint Martins. And again, he asked McKitterick for help: He needed cash, and did McKitterick have any connections at Saint Martins?

McKitterick, who by now was doing clothes for pop stars of varying coolness—Erasure, Dead or Alive, Kylie Minogue—hired McQueen to work a couple of days a week and then sent him to see his very good friend Bobby Hillson, founder and chair of the master's program at Central Saint Martins.

"I said to him, 'Go and speak to Bobby, see what she can do. You never know.'"

\*     \*     \*

As impressed as Hillson was, she had reservations. Lee was talented, but so rough. He was a high school dropout. He didn't know how to behave in a group. He had no manners.

But she took him. The current student body was too heavy on "nice middle-class girls who wouldn't say boo, people who wanted the nice easy life working for companies like Jaeger or whatever. That wasn't exciting to me." As rare as they were, she wanted renegades like John Galliano, who'd graduated Saint Martins in 1984 and who was the last great student the school produced. McQueen had potential to be the next.

"All the other staff said, 'He's trouble,'" Hillson says. "And I said, 'Yes. But we've got to take him.'"

Lee McQueen was the first student ever admitted without having the proper credentials or going through the proper channels. He showed up for his first day of school in late September of 1990 looking so startled and out of place that Simon Ungless, who was in the same class, mistook McQueen for one of the instructors' kids.

"I thought he was fourteen or fifteen," Ungless says. "He didn't look like a typical fashion student on the first day of school." McQueen showed up in what Ungless calls "a Summer of Love rave outfit": flared blue jeans with frayed cuffs and an old baseball shirt. He often wore an Indian headdress.

Ungless and McQueen bonded quickly; they both felt they were more talented than their peers. "I remember Bobby asking a student who her client was"—the kind of girl she was designing for—"and she said, 'Kylie.'" Kylie Minogue had been one of John McKitterick's clients. "We just found that really funny and started laughing unbelievably."

Among the students, Ungless alone was charmed by McQueen; others streamed in and out of Hillson's office to complain about him. "They'd say, 'He's a pain in the ass, why did you take him?' They explained that he couldn't shut up—that when they had people in to lecture, Lee would talk right through them."

Hillson knew what was going on: Lee wasn't being obnoxious for the sake of being obnoxious, or a rebel, or out of a need to elevate himself. He was scared.

"I realized he was out of his depth," Hillson says. "He'd left school at fourteen." She felt that if anything, Lee was too eager to participate, and his lack of formal schooling meant that he didn't know how. But she didn't want to share that with the students and ostracize McQueen any further. "I just said to them, 'Oh, you know, he'll settle down. Or he'll leave.'"

Ungless and McQueen became inseparable. They were both from a working-class background—McQueen's urban, Ungless's rural. They couldn't understand where the bulk of their peers were coming from: They all idolized the house of Versace, which epitomized "'80s excess, a dinosaur, then," says Ungless—while he and McQueen were more compelled by the abstract minimalism of Helmut Lang and Martin Margiela. They'd go out dancing a lot: Fruit Machine on Wednesday, Love Muscle on Saturday, Trade all day Sunday. "Rave was done for us by then," he says. "It was all dance music and house." He remembers McQueen as a "total lightweight" who'd have half a cider and who, like Ungless, felt a misfit everywhere, even among his tribe.

"We were gay men who didn't fit in," he says. "We'd go to the clubs where everyone had their shirts off, Muscle Mary—and we certainly weren't that."

For all their closeness, Ungless knew little about McQueen's family. "I knew of his mum, and his sister Janet," he says. "I was vaguely aware that he had these brothers." McQueen opened up more to Hillson, perhaps because she was so familiar to him: an older woman, a maternal figure who gave him the preferential treatment he felt he deserved. When McQueen couldn't afford the fabric he needed, she'd crib the good stuff from her cupboard. She passed along names and numbers of designers who needed freelance help so McQueen could pay his rent. She was his advocate when other professors attempted to humiliate him—one knocked Lee down to a BA course as punishment, something Hillson knew was ridiculous. She told McQueen her office was open to him anytime, and that he could talk to her about anything. He responded in kind.

"He was really open," Hillson says. "He didn't get on with his father. He made that quite clear. His mother adored him and he was very close to her. But the father—he just couldn't come to terms with his gay son, you know?"

Ungless thinks the hardship made McQueen that much better: "He would try harder, work harder, because of needing to," he says. "You just kind of got on with it. It makes you more adaptable."

In his eighteen months at Central Saint Martins, McQueen focused, and as he began to come to terms with his sexuality, he began to explore the things he was truly attracted to: the violence of nature. The dark aspects of sex. His complicated view of women, which toggled between victimhood and inviolability. These themes, which were to be lifelong obsessions, were funneled through his graduating thesis collection, inspired by Jack the Ripper.

As he worked on it, Hillson had one serious critique: He could not put this collection together in any meaningful way using the cheap fabrics he was buying in East London. The effect McQueen was going for, slashing and printing and staining the clothes, required high-quality fabrics that could take the abuse. His market report, a requirement of his thesis, was done his way. He wasn't interested in math or demographics or trends: Instead, he claimed that he had traced his ancestry back to one of Jack the Ripper's victims.

His teachers were skeptical. "Well," said McQueen's former instructor Louise Wilson, "he always had a story to tell."

Among McQueen's materials were pieces of his own hair, locks sewn into clear pockets in each of the six garments. The gesture was a nod to the Victorian tradition of prostitutes selling their own hair for lockets, which lovers would give to each other. This, too, was to become a motif in his work for the rest of his life. McQueen called the collection "Jack the Ripper Stalks His Victims," and it was shown at the Kensington Olympia in July 1992. The clothes were unlike anything his graduating classmates had come up with: a pink Victorian tailcoat riven with thorns and bloodstains; a navy jacket with two knee-length daggerlike panels in front and a structured plume above the bum; an asymmetrical coat that clung tight to the body and covered only one breast; another figure-hugging white organza gown with a sheer top and inlaid rose petals that read as pooled blood. This was fashion as shock-art, but McQueen was also a careerist, and he knew a collection this aggressive would get attention. He was right.

Squeezing into McQueen's show at the last minute was Isabella Blow. She had been working as a stylist at British *Vogue* since 1990, having been fired from *Tatler* for running up stratospheric expenses—£50,000 on one editorial—for setting most shoots at her country estate, and for being easily distractible. That she knew Galliano "back when he was selling clothes on the street for £10" had long worn thin. She'd dabbled in heroin, dated Jean-Michel Basquiat, befriended Warhol, and done time with Anna Wintour at American *Vogue* before getting fired from there, too. Still, Issie had an eye; everyone in fashion knew that. Except Lee McQueen.

After his presentation, Issie reached out to him. She would later say that first collection was about "sabotage and tradition—all the things, I suppose, the '90s meant." She was so knocked out she wanted to buy the whole collection.

"Three fifty, love," McQueen told her. "Take it or leave it."

Issie took it, but, ever cash-poor, she had to pay in installments. She would make it up to Lee in the meantime: She had people he should meet, a place for him to live and work for free. Later, McQueen would tell people that he'd charged Issie £5,000 for his thesis collection, an outrageous sum that a graduating student would never have commanded. But Issie never corrected him. She understood what it was to build a myth.

## CHAPTER 3

# FIFTEEN-YEAR-OLDS
# DON'T GO TO NIGHTCLUBS

MARC JACOBS'S MOTHER, JUDY, was just nineteen years old when she had him, a teenage bride fresh off a shotgun wedding. Her husband, Steve, was ten years older, handsome and sophisticated, a nightclub agent for the William Morris Agency. Judy had been working at William Morris—her uncle was the president of the company and got her a low-level job—and, right out of high school, she set her sights on Steve. Her parents begged her to go to college, to explore and expand, and she did, for two weeks. She came home. She couldn't live without him.

Judy and Steve moved into an apartment at the Buxley, then a brand-new high-rise on Sixty-Fifth Street and First Avenue on Manhattan's Upper East Side. They looked like a golden couple, their youth and beauty disguising how sick both of them were.

Steve was chronically ill, at times requiring hospitalization for the ulcerative colitis he'd had since he was a teenager. Judy was prone to sharp mood swings, and eight days after Marc's birth, she had what her brother, Jeffrey Weisbord, calls her "first postpartum" episode, at Marc's bris. She became so distraught that someone called 911. An ambulance came and took Judy to the nearby Gracie Square Hospital, but they weren't equipped to treat her. Judy was then transferred to Mount Sinai, where, according to Jeffrey, she remained in a catatonic state for six months, leaving Steve to care for Marc. Eventually, courses of electroshock therapy brought her around. For a time.

"Judy was beautiful, and when she was well, she had a fabulous personality," Weisbord says. But this was a time when little was understood about mental illness, and when Judy was unwell, she required intensive inpatient treatment. She was given a dual diagnosis of schizophrenic manic depression, or, as it's known today, schizoaffective disorder. In patients who suffer from this, the markers of schizophrenia (hallucinations, paranoia) and of bipolar disorder (extreme highs followed by major depressive episodes) are equally present.

For a teenage mother in 1963—even one like Judy, whose family had means and access to the best doctors in New York City—there was very little that could be done. Antipsychotic medication had only been in use in the United States since 1956, with lithium and Thorazine the most common treatments.

By the time his mother was released from Mount Sinai Hospital, Marc was less than one year old. She was foreign to him, and Judy had a hard time coping: Her husband was battling his own chronic illness, and he was hardly ever home—out most nights tending to his clients, superstar comics such as Joey Bishop and Joan Rivers—leaving a precarious Judy alone with her new baby.

Judy and Steve went on to have two more children: three years after Marc, they had a daughter, and a son quickly followed.

Her family was alarmed. "A marriage made in hell," says Weisbord.

When Marc's little brother was fifteen months old, Steve Jacobs entered the hospital, his ulcerative colitis worsening. Steve spent the last three months of his life in that hospital. "My sister was twenty-six years old, with three kids," Weisbord says. The support Judy received from family and friends—Joan Rivers loaned the Jacobs family her summer home on Fire Island to grieve and recuperate—was genuine and constant, but it was no match for the enormity of her illness.

Marc was seven when his father died.

It was a lonely time. He was a sensitive boy, artistic, unathletic, and interested in the wrong things—clothes, jewelry, arts and crafts. He was different, and the other kids knew it too. It was hard, Marc said, "being the only kid in a big group that doesn't want to play football and buy stereos and drive cars. When I went to sleepaway camp, I just kind of wanted to sit there and make an ashtray or do a lanyard necklace or paint my jeans. And to stand there and not be chosen for a baseball team—it's like, force me to do something and then don't choose me to do it. Okay, what am I supposed to enjoy about that process? How am I supposed to feel good about myself with all that going on?"

Marc resented his mother, in her lucid moments, for going out, for seeming to have fun, for choosing time with strange men over him. Years later, after he'd lost people too, struggled with drugs and self-loathing, he tried to articulate his complicated feelings about her.

"I hate the term 'bad taste,' but my mother wasn't a very chic person," he said, and for a fashion designer, this may be the meanest thing you can say about someone. "Jane Fonda in *Klute* was definitely one of her role models, much to my father's dismay. But when I'd watch my mother getting dressed up to go out on dates and she'd be putting on three rows of false eyelashes and some hideous fox-trimmed brocade coat with a wet-look miniskirt and knee-high boots, I thought she was fabulous."

By the time Marc was fifteen, Judy had remarried twice, first to Milton Franks, the editor of *Redbook* magazine. He came with a big house on the water in Huntington, Long Island, and four kids of his own. The marriage didn't last long.

Her next husband lived in Teaneck, New Jersey, and she picked up the kids and moved out there. All of the children were wildly neglected.

"My sister went off on a cruise and left the kids with the housekeeper," Weisbord says, "who was having parties." Social services intervened.

Marc eventually decided to go live with his paternal grandmother, Helen, on New York's Upper West Side. Helen had no interest, however, in Julie or Paul; Weisbord thinks that Helen may have been trying to replace her late son with Marc. His younger brother and sister were sent to a foster home in New Jersey, where they were raised together.

"That's when Marc stopped communicating with his sister and brother," Weisbord says, and Marc's estrangement continues to this day. After Marc went to live with his grandmother, Weisbord and his wife, Louise, were able to maintain a relationship with Marc for a little while, though he was already pulling away. The Weisbords blame Helen.

"She did everything she could," Weisbord says, "to alienate him from everybody." Marc was so traumatized that he told his teachers at New York's High School of Art & Design that his parents had been killed in a car crash. Marc's mother spent the bulk of her life in and out of mental institutions, at one point, Weisbord says, spending "many years in a private hospital." He recalls one of the last times he saw his nephew: Marc was around fifteen, and Weisbord drove him to Paramus, New Jersey, to visit Judy, who was in a psychiatric hospital called the Pines.

He doesn't remember talking to Marc much about Judy, or what was wrong with her, or how Marc felt about seeing her. He remembers being struck by how "uncomfortable" Marc seemed. "Judy was fun, talkative—well-dressed," Weisbord says. "But he was coming from Helen, who was always dressed fashionably. To the nines."

\*       \*       \*

Like Alexander McQueen, Marc Jacobs knew from a very young age that he wanted to be a fashion designer. With Helen's encouragement, he enrolled in the High School of Art & Design on East Fifty-Sixth Street, an elite and academically rigorous vocational school for the creatively inclined. (Calvin Klein went there, as did fashion photographer Steven Meisel.) Helen let her grandson do whatever he liked: travel across the country and come back with tattoos—as he did on a trip to Venice, California, when he was sixteen—go clubbing at Studio 54, date older men. Despite receiving the same liberties from his grandmother as he had at home from his mother, Marc didn't interpret this as disinterest or neglect. He felt that Helen, unlike his mother, was stable. Physically and emotionally, she was always there. She trusted his judgment.

"No one ever said no to me about anything," he said. "No one ever told me anything was wrong. Never. No one ever said, 'You can't be a fashion designer.' No one ever said, 'You're a boy and you can't have long hair.' No one ever said, 'You can't go out at night because you're fifteen and fifteen-year-olds don't go to nightclubs.' No one said it was wrong to be gay or right to be straight."

Marc had learned about shopping from Helen—which department stores were best for what—but was most excited by the small boutique under construction down the street, on Columbus and Seventy-Second. It was another branch of the cult uptown shop Charivari, which stocked international designers such as Yohji Yamamoto and Azzedine Alaïa; Jackie O and Andy Warhol shopped there. The first Charivari, which opened on April 1, 1967, on Eighty-Sixth and Broadway, startled that area's more genteel shoppers with its opening-night salvo: a live go-go dancer in the window.

This was clearly the place.

In late-1970s New York City, there were only a few clubs that mattered. Uptown, there was the champagne-and-cocaine decadence of

Studio 54, of course, where a young Marc was a habitué, toting along his high school textbooks so he could leave the club in the morning and head straight to class. But he was conflicted about his attraction to the scene: "It gave me an unhealthy curiosity about subcultures and anonymous sex," he said. Far more enthralled with Studio 54 was another beautiful, aspiring fashion designer: Tom Ford. "I was so dazzled by all of it," Ford said. He spent nights there following Calvin Klein around, "because I thought he was so handsome," but Klein never noticed him. In from Long Island came another regular named Isaac Mizrahi, then just fourteen years old. "I would work all week on a crazy outfit to wear to Studio 54," Mizrahi says. "We were gorgeous, so cute, and we got right in. It was a crazy old place. Seeing Truman Capote was fabulous. Seeing Halston was fabulous, or Bianca Jagger, who was there every time I was."

Downtown, there was Max's Kansas City, which attracted such punk bands as the Cramps, Suicide, and the Patti Smith Group, and avant-garde performers like Klaus Nomi. There was an entirely different hierarchy emerging below Twenty-Third Street, this one built on avant-gardism, hustling, filth, and noise.

These were places for "suburban refugees who had run away from home to find a new family," said performance artist Ann Magnuson. They were like-minded kids who worshipped "Devo, Duchamp, and William S. Burroughs, and . . . hated the things we hated: disco, Diane von Furstenberg, *The Waltons*."

"Those clubs were so vital," says veteran nightlife reporter Michael Musto. "This was before the Internet, when, to have human interaction, you'd have to go out every night. They really were like the town halls for cool kids."

Marc was electrified by these scenes, but he feared he'd be revealed as an imposter. These were true believers; he was more of a dilettante. He later described how he'd put himself together for a night out and never feel like he'd nailed it:

"I like romantic allusions to the past . . . what I wore during my experimental days in fashion, when I was going to the Mudd Club and wanted to be a new wave kid or a punk kid but was really a poseur. It's the awkwardness of . . . feeling like I was in, but I never was in."

Marc began dating Robert Boykin, one of the co-owners of Hurrah. Boykin was gorgeous: thin and blond, with fine features and exquisite taste. He lived in a huge, white, art-filled apartment in the Dorilton, an extravagant Beaux Arts building on Seventy-First and Broadway, and Marc moved in after living with his grandmother only a short time.

"I met Robert in '79, at an opening Dianne Benson was giving," says artist Addison Parks, and despite all the downtown art stars in the room, Boykin and Marc were the most magnetic. Parks stumbled upon them lying in Benson's bathtub, Robert "smiling like a Cheshire cat," Parks says. "It was Robert and Marc that clicked, like there was a light shining on them." Marc was much younger than his boyfriend, still in high school, yet he carried himself as though he were five to ten years older. He was friendly and open yet enigmatic and so very beautiful, with long black hair nearly to his waist, thick brows, a strong nose and chin. He looked equal parts boy and girl and seemed preternaturally comfortable that way. "Marc was anointed early on," Musto says. "He always radiated success, but he never seemed full of himself."

Marc had heard that his hero, Perry Ellis, was going to the opening-night party for the new Charivari, and he comfortably crashed it. Helen was friendly with Selma Weiser, the owner, and Selma liked Marc too. "I remember I was talking with Perry," says Weiser's son Jon, "and Marc was standing behind me, and he stuck his arm under my arm and pushed his way out in front of me and shoved out a piece of paper to get Perry's autograph." Ellis obliged.

"I told him I wanted to be a designer and that he was my favorite American designer," Marc said. Ellis told him that if he was really serious, he should enroll at Parsons School of Design.

"So I went to Parsons."

CHAPTER 4

# JUST ANOTHER
# COMMON BITCH

BY JULY OF 1990, Kate Moss had been on the cover of *The Face* twice, but little else was happening. She'd dropped out of high school and left home at fifteen to pursue this very iffy career fulltime. She was in league with Corinne Day, who was a mentor and an older sister, and stylist Melanie Ward. Unlike Moss and Day, Ward came from a stable, middle-class home in a suburb east of London; her mother was a fashion-mad bookworm, and Ward absorbed the idea, early on, that fashion was as valid as literature.

What Ward had in common with Moss and Day was the elemental feeling, from a very young age, that "I was always the odd one out."

One night, fresh out of school, Ward was at a warehouse party in London, wearing one of her customized pieces: a man's suit jacket worn as a minidress, the sleeves altered to look more feminine, nothing underneath. A woman who worked for L'Oréal approached Ward and said she loved her look and asked her if she'd like to be a stylist.

At the time, Ward had no idea what a stylist was. Her naïveté was to Ward's great advantage: Because she didn't know that stylists borrowed clothes from designers, who then advertised in the magazine for a cross-branding effect, she was, without knowing it, introducing a new way of styling. Ward's reflexive aversion to head-to-toe designer was radical, and it wasn't an affectation.

"It was very instinctual, very organic," Ward says. "At the time, what was going on in fashion was very manicured and manipulated . . . The models were very Amazonian, untouchable. And I think we were feeling, for some reason, the polar opposite, in our guts."

After Ward's first shoot, she was signed to London's Z Agency, which also represented up-and-coming photographer Juergen Teller. She crossed paths with photographers Corinne Day, David Sims, and Nigel Shafran; fellow travelers in a small scene, they began collaborating.

"We were very young and enthusiastic, and we'd show people our work, and they would generally be confused," Ward says. "Nobody would book us for advertising. They'd be like, 'Why are you showing me this? These are documentary photos of teenagers.'"

Day and Ward were usually able to place their fashion editorials in only two publications: *i-D* and *The Face*. But it wasn't until they found Kate that they had something alchemical.

Ward remembers first seeing Kate in a candy shop, just before a formal appointment scheduled with her later that afternoon at the Storm offices. "We were in our early to mid-twenties, and Kate was fourteen, fifteen," Ward says. She and Day responded as much to Kate's look—small, slight, subtle—as to her demeanor. "I think Kate just reminded us of how we were when we were that age," Ward says. "She had confidence and a little attitude."

Day and Ward weren't alone in taking note. In 1989, six years out of Central Saint Martins, a then thirty-year-old John Galliano hired Kate to walk in his show. Galliano, too, was another outlier, a broken genius of sorts: His thesis collection for Central Saint Martins was bought, in its entirety, by a London boutique owner, one of several fates that would presage Lee McQueen's career. Before the decade was out, he would be on the verge of bankruptcy.

Galliano cast Kate in his spring/summer 1990 show, her biggest break yet. He felt drawn to Kate, this elfin girl who worked her ass off—for nothing!—who didn't fit in among the other models and wasn't at all what editors and critics would expect. Kate's fittings took more time than those of any of the other models: She was so small and thin that hours were spent reworking the clothes, but she never complained.

It was refreshing. Galliano himself was feeling fragile, a onetime wunderkind gone bust: In 1987, he'd been named British Designer of the Year, and by 1989 he was broke and on the verge of collapse. His humiliation was high-profile, and he was struck by the poignancy of Kate's otherness: She'd come for fittings in her thrift-store finds and beat-up boots, her long hair hanging in strings, each day surrounded by world-famous warrior models plated in Versace and Chanel, who made it quite clear they thought this plain little foundling did not belong.

"We were looking for new girls, and she was cast as a wild child," Galliano said. "I think she came up to the studio—we were in the New Kings Road—and, wow, I'd found my little rough diamond."

At the time, Kate considered herself "feral," but Galliano chose Kate, whom he called his "Lolita," to open the show. She hadn't eaten all day and was terrified of walking the runway. She'd later say she felt like she "was up there on my own," and when the show was over, Kate went to the after-party and guzzled so much whiskey that she missed her flight the next day. She finally made it back to London that Wednesday.

She was hungover and disoriented and intimidated and she loved it. Her entrée into this new world, however long it was meant to last, had already meant a higher class of party with a higher class of people: Galliano's DJ, Jeremy Healy; music manager and all-around scenester Fran Cutler; fellow model Lucie de la Falaise. She was no longer interested in hanging out at the low-ceilinged local pub, knocking back swarmy, lethal concoctions of cider and lager. Soon she'd be training her palate at the Hemingway Bar at the Ritz in Paris, where she began drinking fizzy cocktails made of gin and champagne.

"When I used to come back to Croydon and get into our car, which wasn't air-conditioned—and a house with no pool—I was like, 'I'm not staying here forever,'" Kate said. "I never had that feeling of, 'That's your lot.'"

Walking for Galliano was promising, but Kate's life hadn't changed in any meaningful way since then. Her parents were unimpressed and emotionally divested. She had no other aspirations. Kate was getting bits of work for teen magazines and trade publications, and otherwise partying and taking pictures with Melanie and Corinne, with the occasional bookings in Paris and Milan. Things really could go either way.

It was Corinne who had the idea that Kate should come live with her and her boyfriend, Mark, in their dilapidated Soho apartment on Brewer Street.

Corinne and Mark were poor. They'd come back to England from Milan, where Mark had supported them as a model while Corinne began her autodidactic approach to photography, doing free shots for off-duty models. "Corinne would take their clothes—what they had and what she had—and she would create looks," Mark says. No stylist, no hair or makeup artist, just Corinne and the model. Her favorite setup was to shoot the girls in their dingy hotel rooms, wrung out from fourteen-hour days on set, messy hair and faded makeup, surrounded by drained coffee cups and stubbed-out cigarettes, unmade beds and piles of fashion magazines. This was Corinne not just breaking the seal, showing the world what these avatars of perfection really looked like: This was her codifying a new kind of glamour, one informed by imperfection, lassitude, vice, decay. Her girls were the photonegative of the images proliferating in mainstream fashion magazines, the purge to the binge.

"She would photograph them and make them look good and fashionable and interesting," Mark says. "And they would get work. And the modeling agencies realized this and suddenly they were sending Corinne loads of girls."

Her aesthetic was trickling up.

"It wasn't about 1980s glamour; it was about the street," Kate said. "Everyone was saying, 'Let's get off our tits and have a laugh. Be more real and not have to grow up so quickly. And have fun.'"

Day's friend, the actor Vincent Gallo, saw that those images transcended fashion and augered a generational shift. "It was just as exciting to see those pictures of Kate," he said, "as it was the first time I went to Max's Kansas City or the Mudd Club."

"The images of Kate Moss by Corinne Day . . . really changed fashion," Marc Jacobs said. "That was a moment when we looked at beauty and glamour in a different way." The "Summer of Love" shoot in particular was resonating with Marc, helping him identify the kind of girl he'd like to dress.

"If I had been a teenager when Kate Moss came out, I would have been so happy," he said. "She's not some statuesque Amazon, perfectly formed. There was this amazing kind of warmth and real coolness, without any effort."

Novices, too, were seeking out Corinne and Kate—one, another young model turned photographer named Mario Sorrenti, the other, aspiring hairdresser James Brown. Both had talent, and both were opportunists. They liked Corinne but knew Kate was the one.

Brown, a squirrely little fellow with a narrow face and coils of reddish brown hair, was charming and effervescent, super-fun to be around, and Corinne invited him to move into Brewer Street: She and Mark were having trouble making rent every month, so Mark built Brown a sleeping bunk and Brown kicked in.

"He made a beeline for Kate," Mark says. "He knew what he was doing. It was an ideal situation for him because he was living with Corinne and getting Corinne's editorial."

And then there was Sorrenti, on sets, at parties, in the small loft on Brewer Street, asking Corinne for advice on composition and technique. He began seeing Kate, whom he later described as "an aesthetic shock . . . the most beautiful woman I'd ever seen." His profile rose. "Via Kate, suddenly he was in the social scene," Mark says. "I could see what he was up to."

Corinne and Kate, though, were oblivious. They were too enthralled with each other, Corinne taking Kate to the Camden and Portobello markets, teaching her how to sift through piles of nubby sweaters, matted shearling, faded nightgowns, and all manner of scrap to emerge with a thrashed glamour all her own. At Brewer Street, Kate spent hours working out her sartorial algorithms: a limpid black Martin Margiela skirt, rolled up to hit midcalf, paired with battered red Adidas; a blush-pink vintage silk nightgown repurposed for evening with a chunky black boot. To Corinne and Melanie, Kate was their little dress-up doll, and Kate felt safe here: Corinne and Mark, Melanie and James and Mario, they all saw something in her, even though she'd been told by working professionals that she was nothing but a silly hopeful who thought she had what it took. One photographer in Paris actually told Kate that she had no chance at all, that she was "just another common bitch."

Kate Moss, at fifteen, looked at him with disbelief. And she laughed.

## CHAPTER 5

# I AM THE '90S

IT WAS ISSIE WHO convinced Lee his name was too common for his ambitions—or so she said. McQueen would later insist that using his middle name was all his idea, that he was scamming his way on the dole and needed different public and private identities.

The truth is probably somewhere in the middle. Isabella insisted on addressing him as Alexander, even as it became a sign of one's closeness, real or imagined, to refer to him as Lee, the name he preferred. Later, when his own mother called him Alexander, he'd beg her to stop.

"He was Lee to us," says Alice Smith, his first publicist. "When he became 'Alexander McQueen'—it was very odd to suddenly say, 'Alexander.' But if you said 'Lee,' people thought you were being pretentious."

It was the first concession to upward mobility that would distort McQueen's interior and exterior lives beyond recognition, even to himself.

In 1993, McQueen had a meeting at Denza, the international fashion recruitment company where Smith worked. She was struck by his talent level. "He was brilliant," she says. "A genius. Even at that stage."

She put him forward for a job at Alberta Ferretti, the high-end Italian designer known for her balmy chic. Smith says he showed up wearing "a three-piece suit from Savile Row—a gray suit, with a waistcoat and everything." It was a classic case of overcompensation; most fashion people traffic in reverse affectation, dressing down to show how little they need to prove. McQueen had no way of knowing this. Where he came from, if you wanted a good job, you showed some respect and dressed up.

"He looked like a little hamster," Smith says. "Everyone else came in jeans and a T-shirt—all the other designers. But he was not used to the normal design world."

When he didn't get the job at Ferretti, Smith wasn't surprised, despite having such belief in him she'd drawn a star on his résumé. "I'm sure it was the way he looked," she says.

McQueen decided to abandon the traditional approach: Get hired by an established house, work your way up, and maybe, someday, become head designer or get backing for your own line. Why did it have to be that way? He'd do it on his own, and not just because he wanted to, but because he had to. Because the establishment was making it clear there was no room for the likes of him.

"The fashion world was so remote to us," Andrew Groves says. "It was Linda Evangelista and Versace and supermodels. I think he knew he had nothing but his ability and his talent. And a big part of that talent was to make people do what he wanted them to do."

McQueen's genius, like Isabella Blow's, extended to subterfuge. These were two people who knew how to get their way—often by doing what they wanted and dealing with the consequences later—and who, because of the way they looked, were relegated to the fringes of this world they loved so much. They feasted on this rejection, used it as fuel, this idea of themselves as trespassers: Issie, a lover of art, drugs, and horses in the hallway mounted by naked houseguests, would make herself the English eccentric nonpareil. McQueen, with his intrinsic belief that he was the best and most original British designer of his generation, would devote himself to elevating the grotesque. "He was really clever back then," Groves says. It was 1992, and McQueen's nascent friendship with Isabella was already proving beneficial: That July, British *Vogue* assigned writer Eve MacSweeney and photographer Oberto Gili to do a story on Issie and Detmar, who lived up in Gloucestershire in their prefab pile called Hilles. It sat on nine hundred acres and had been built by Detmar's grandfather in 1913, but was meant to look like it was four hundred years old. Hilles was Issie's great love: As she once said to a friend, "I'm not marrying a man; I'm marrying a house."

For that momentous shoot, Issie asked Alexander to make them each something. For Detmar, McQueen made a light pink waistcoat embellished with rose petals; for Issie, a pink-and-black coat in the shape of a beetle. McQueen had just left Saint Martins three months prior, and already, his work was about to be seen in *Vogue*—as was the work of another Issie protégé, Philip Treacy, a haberdasher who, like, McQueen, was treating his medium as art. The two were a bit rivalrous, especially when it came to their patron. "It was like Issie having two lovers," Treacy said. "I was the first one, and now there was a second."

McQueen couldn't be bothered with jealousy. He was getting somewhere between £30 and £40 per week on the dole, working out of the council flat he shared with Simon Ungless, his friend from Central Saint Martins. McQueen thought it was hilarious that although his clothes had already been featured in *Vogue*, he couldn't afford a rack; instead, he'd pile his pieces in bins or on the floor. He'd rummage through the fabric shops on Berwick Street and steal as much as he could, shoving it into his empty Tesco bags, then head over to Smith's offices and cause some havoc.

"While we were desperately trying to make calls to Burberry and Louis Vuitton and make the place look serious," Smith says, "he'd sit in our office and eat biscuits and tell us stories of his lurid gay exploits."

Smith and her business partner, Cressida Pye, loved it. Unlike just about every other young, aspiring fashion designer kissing their asses, trying to get invited to the right parties and carrying themselves with borrowed hauteur, Lee McQueen was a brute. On a very deep level, he knew it was part of his charm. As was his tenacity.

To be told no, to be turned down for jobs at Ferretti and, later, Jil Sander—McQueen knew how gifted he was. That he was going to churn counterclockwise, to impose himself on a self-selecting establishment, made him gleeful. "I think he was absolutely, blissfully happy with what he was doing," Ungless says. "He was creative and completely ecstatic. Those were difficult times, because of finances and things like that, but personally, I think he was really happy."

In early 1993, less than one year out of Central Saint Martins, Lee McQueen decided to show during the dismal London Fashion Weekend. All these young designers were, in the words of McQueen's peer Fabio Piras, "fashion desperados," by both choice and circumstance. "You had no money, and a certain synergy grows out of a recession. People said, 'Fuck it—we're going to have a show.' And of course, the first person to do that from my generation was Alexander McQueen."

"He was reaching," says Groves. "There were all these people from Saint Martins with no day jobs. The idea of putting on a fashion show was the same as putting on a party in a nightclub."

McQueen was beginning to work out his creative process: First, he'd imagine the kind of show he wanted to mount, the scale and the setting, then the characters, and finally, what those characters would wear. The clothes would always come last.

He called his first collection "Taxi Driver," and years later finally admitted it was inspired as much by his father as by Martin Scorsese's film of the same name. McQueen staged the show at the cavernous

Bluebird Garage on King's Road in Chelsea; seventy years old, abandoned, and in disrepair, it was a cheap and ideal setting. He couldn't afford to rent chairs, so his audience was forced to stand. Among those in attendance were Bobby Hillson and Katy England, fashion director of the upstart magazine *Dazed & Confused*, a three-person operation housed in the apartment below Corinne Day and Kate Moss in Soho.

"We're in this filthy warehouse," Smith says. "There are no seats; we're all just standing around. It was very dark, and no one knew what was going to happen." This was a first: a fashion show that felt dangerous. Up came the drum 'n' bass, then the lights, and finally, the models. "They all looked like they'd been in a fight," Smith says, "and the clothes looked like they'd all been dragged through a hedge. But *fabulous* clothes, right from the start."

"It was very romantic, as opposed to the aggression one later could see in his work," Hillson said. "This was very ethereal and strange. Everything was in white, and the models walked the runway in bare feet."

As much as "Taxi Driver" was about beauty, it was also about death and decay; McQueen swathed some of his models in transparent latex, giving the effect of bespoke body bags. "It was completely mad," Smith says. After the show, McQueen and Ungless took a cab to Man Stink, and stashed the bagged collection behind garbage cans to beat coat-check. Those pieces were lost forever.

No matter, though. Editors had walked out of that first show disgusted, and that was exactly what McQueen wanted. He knew they'd be back.

"Taxi Driver" was meant to be a throwdown, less a challenge to the working order than an announcement that those days were numbered. While most other London designers were showing floaty, minimalist pieces set to ambient, romantic music—in line with the dictates of British *Vogue*, which had declared, in its August issue, that this gentle and gauzy look was "the new silhouette"—McQueen was mounting a grisly revolution.

Not for him were the pronouncements of fashion editors, all in league with the houses anyway, each fanning the other to sell clothes and ad pages. McQueen was a visionary, and he knew there were girls out there who had no use for what British *Vogue* had to say. He could see it in the streets, feel it in the clubs, look at it in *i-D* and *The Face*, in the spirit of this new model named Kate Moss, who was emerging as the grunge goddess of the UK.

"*Vogue* had decided that they were going to dictate what women wore, but it didn't work," says Beauregard Houston-Montgomery, then a writer for *Details*. That publication was a New York analogue to *i-D* and *The Face*, chronicling a seedy yet dazzling subculture populated by drag queens, club kids, independent actors, musicians, and designers such as Marc Jacobs, a *Details* pet. What these magazines had in common, says Houston-Montgomery, was that they "realized that you can't dictate what people wear—you have to reflect it. They understood it from a sociological perspective."

So did McQueen. He was working on a new kind of tailoring: what McQueen called "the bumster," a slim-fitting pant slung low on the hips, revealing a good two inches of the wearer's crack. It was widely interpreted as hip-hop inspired, though it actually sprang from McQueen's own culture and tastes; he found the line from the lower spine to the top of the ass the most erotic part of the body.

"I asked him, 'What's the idea behind it?' " says Alice Smith. "And he said, 'The idea is to make the legs look shorter and the [torso] look long. I said, 'Is that what you want?' And he said yes. That's what he thought was beautiful. He said to me that that was the classic gay silhouette." It was also his way of making women foreboding. "It was an art thing, to change the way women looked, just by cut, to make a longer torso," he said. "But it was taking it to an extreme. The girls looked quite menacing, because there was so much top and so little bottom."

McQueen wasn't just operating in the tradition of punk. He was at the vanguard of wound culture, the exploration of physical and psychological trauma that would come to dominate much of the fashion, film, art, photography, and music of the '90s. It was aborning in Kurt Cobain's scabrous howl, in the seductive malevolence of David Lynch's *Twin Peaks* and Jonathan Demme's *The Silence of the Lambs*, the containment of maggots feasting on a cow carcass in Damien Hirst's *A Thousand Years*. Just as the late eighteenth century's Romantic movement was, in many ways, a reaction to the industrial revolution, this new fin de siècle disarticulation of beauty, our collective sway toward the narcotic and necrotic, was an expression of millennial anger and dread, the fear that sex could equal death and that technology might soon subsume humanity.

"There's beauty in anger," McQueen said. "Anger, for me, is a passion. . . . How can you move something forward if you are not confrontational?"

As a provocateur and a showman, however, McQueen was indebted to a few who came before. In 1977, Claude Montana showed a collection widely interpreted to be enamored with neo-Nazism. In 1984, Thierry Mugler closed a runway a show with a reenactment of the Virgin Mary giving birth; it cost $1 million. That same year, Jean-Paul Gaultier put men in skirts, and in his boutiques repurposed pissoirs as changing rooms. Vivienne Westwood once put her models in stockings covered in prints of penises, though she did not see McQueen as a kindred spirit. "His only usefulness," she once said, "is as a measure of zero talent."

McQueen didn't care. He thought Westwood was irrelevant. But he reveled in the attention, in how threatened his predecessors were. He tried to incite a feud on his own, announcing, "John [Galliano] was the '80s. And I am the '90s."

McQueen loved Galliano, his ability to swing between baroque romanticism and androgynous postmodernism. "We grew up in the '80s and saw John's ascent at Saint Martins, so when Lee went to Saint

Martins, John was his blueprint," says Andrew Groves. "And I think he also thought: 'I'm taking this over.'"

McQueen was "obsessed by him," says friend John McKitterick. "He was the one to beat."

In the meantime, Lee McQueen spent his nights at gay bars on Old Compton Street in Soho and his days working on his next collection. He soon set up shop in a grand, decrepit town house provided by Isabella Blow, who also had him up to Hilles all the time, giving him a majestic old bedroom with a four-poster bed and a sink and piles of books. And she, struggling financially herself, paid off many court judgments against him for defaulting on bills.

"Issie loved protecting him," says Detmar Blow. "So much."

McQueen, in turn, wanted to protect the women he loved in the way he knew how.

"I want people to fear the women I dress," he said. He made allusions to having seen some of the women in his life suffer at the hands of their boyfriends or husbands. He was working through his own trauma, but it was going to take him a while to realize just what he was up to, and why.

CHAPTER 6

# A CULTURE PERSON
# IN THE FASHION WORLD

IN 1981, MARC JACOBS graduated from the High School of Art
& Design and enrolled at Parsons, considered the Harvard of art
schools. Anna Sui had already been through there, and among Marc's
fellow students were Isaac Mizrahi, who was two years ahead, and
Tom Ford, who was majoring in architecture. The tuition was $6,495 a
semester, and though the design training was intensive—once a week,
seniors would have class at the Metropolitan Museum of Art's Costume Archive—there was little business training, even though most
of these students didn't want to go work for an existing label. They
wanted to establish their own houses.

The fashion department was chaired by Ann Keagy, who was
described by fashion eminence Eleanor Lambert as the "brisk, handsome, fresh-skinned and firm-jawed" keeper of a "Domesday Book,"
which contained the contact information for every student since 1947.
Keagy banned jeans on campus—"If they're going into the industry,
they must learn to look put-together"—and kept her students at a remove. "There are no cozy rap sessions during school hours," she told
Lambert, "and none of those silver-cord relationships."

"On our first day, she gave us a big speech that we had to live, eat, sleep, and drink fashion," says designer Tracy Reese, Marc's closest friend in the class of '84. "If that wasn't for us, then we were in the wrong place. She laid down the law that first day and we knew we were doing something really serious. If you had three absences, you failed . . . The list went on and on."

By Keagy's design, the program was so small that most everyone knew everyone else, or at least of them. Decades later, Marc would recall how "incredibly talented" everyone at Parsons thought Mizrahi was, Mizrahi included. In fact, by the time he was a junior, Mizrahi had been offered two jobs: one by Perry Ellis himself, and another with Milo Morrow, head of the costume shop at the New York Shakespeare Festival. Unlike Jacobs, Mizrahi wasn't a devotee of Ellis's crisp American sportswear, but if he wanted to be a designer, this was the job to take. He remembers Keagy telling him to go with the costume shop: "God knows what's going to happen to Perry Ellis," she said.

For Jacobs, the Perry Ellis he'd met years before at Charivari—so casual, so undone, so gorgeous—remained the ultimate: "He didn't wear a suit like the other Seventh Avenue designers," Jacobs later said. "He wore jeans, long hair and smoked pot. He just seemed really so much cooler than everyone else."

Jacobs wanted to be a new kind of American designer, one who served the girl overlooked by the industry: cool yet awkward, young but sophisticated.

Mizrahi, too, had a feeling. He went with Ellis and never regretted it. "He taught me everything," Mizrahi says. Nonetheless, it was Marc who was the star at Parsons.

"It was obvious that he was going to go all the way," Reese says. "He was already well connected. His boyfriend at the time owned nightclubs. He got me a job with the Charivari people." Reese recalls meeting celebrities through Marc and having no idea who they were, only that they were important and that Marc knew them and was very much liked by them. "I was just some kid from Detroit," she says. "I [didn't] feel like, 'I have to move in those circles.' But he naturally did, and he was very comfortable. He had a lot of drive. A lot of drive. It was important to him to be well liked and accepted, and he was always reaching higher, pulling himself to the next level."

Marc maintained a close relationship with the Weisers at Charivari; Selma, the owner, took him along on business trips to Hong Kong, where he learned about sourcing fabric and overseeing production. He also did a summer at Parsons in Paris. "I had to take out a student loan to come, but then I went to class maybe twice," he said. He spent his time partying, and what was meant to be a four-week course turned into ten weeks of lost time. "I ended up on someone's boat in Saint-Tropez," he later said. "I swore I'd never go back to the States." On the flight home, he wept.

The Paris experience Marc had as an undergraduate—blowing off almost every class to party, going missing for another six weeks after he was due home, returning to no real consequences—encapsulated a scenario Marc, to his great peril, would repeat throughout his career. That he was able to return to Parsons in New York and flourish is remarkable, though he benefited from Keagy's retirement in 1982.

For his thesis collection, Marc had been working on a line of oversize sweaters embellished with large polka dots and smiley faces. It referenced the childlike jubilance of Keith Haring's street art, the work of British op-art painter Bridget Riley, and presaged the totems of the rave scene. Charivari stocked those sweaters, becoming the first shop to sell Marc Jacobs, and they sold so well that Bill Cunningham, the venerable street style photographer for the *New York Times*, shot a series of everyday women wearing them on New York City sidewalks. This, Marc would say, was "sort of the beginning of my career."

That collection also won Marc the Perry Ellis Golden Thimble Award, the Chester Weinberg Gold Thimble Award, the Student of the Year Award, and the attention of the man who would launch Marc Jacobs as a designer. His name was Robert Duffy, and he was a very unhappy executive at Ruben Thomas. Desperate to keep him, the company gave Duffy carte blanche to hire any designer he'd like and create a new line. He took meetings with everyone he could think of, including Stephen Sprouse, another of Marc's idols, but no one clicked. He went to the Parsons graduation dinner, where all of the thesis collections were shown.

"I saw Marc's three sweaters on the runway, and I knew immediately this was the person," Duffy said. "Hand-knit by his grandmother with really awkward proportions and shapes: It was everything I loved—the friendliness, the color. It was really grunge back in 1985."

Duffy asked Marc to come design for Ruben Thomas's Sketchbook label. Duffy was twenty-eight, Marc twenty-one. Years later, Duffy would tattoo "1984" on the inside of his left wrist, to mark the most momentous year of their lives. "We literally shook hands that day," Duffy said. "It was what I dreamt of: If I could find a designer who I could really relate to, it would be a tremendous adventure."

He had no idea.

Marc wasn't that dissimilar from his closest friends at Parsons—Tracy Reese, Susan Martin, Chris Isles: "The inseparable overachievers," Marc called them. They were all obsessed with the filth and fury of downtown New York and felt that Seventh Avenue, the traditional headquarters of high-end fashion in the city, had nothing to offer their generation.

Marc alone, however, had star power. Even if he wasn't the most innovative designer—he was more of a curator, a recombinator of pop culture—he had cachet as an established denizen of the downtown club scene. It was the smaller, cooler publications who picked up on Marc first: *Paper*, the *East Village Eye*, and especially *Details*, then a stapled-together indie magazine that was as exclusive, in its way, as

*Town & Country. Details* editor Annie Flanders had a standing table at Max's Kansas City and a skeleton staff that ran on coke.

Everyone who was interested in what was happening in downtown New York City read *Details*, *Paper*, the *East Village Eye*, *Interview*, and *7 Days*. *Details* was the most buzzed about, the one Condé Nast was already eyeing as an acquisition, and their most favored designer was Marc Jacobs.

"Marc was *Details*'s little pet," says former contributor Beauregard Houston-Montgomery. "He had a lot of problems. He got noticed, but he wasn't getting backing from Seventh Avenue. *Details* really helped put him over by showing his work." In the July/August 1984 issue, *Details* named Marc Jacobs "student designer of the year."

Over at *Paper*, they were not as impressed. "In those days, I used to give Marc a hard time," says longtime editor in chief Kim Hastreiter. "He was inconsistent." She also felt he was overtly copying other designers, other lines; even as he progressed and gained fame, she'd see Geoffrey Beene one season, Biba the next. "It wasn't design to me," she says. "It was styling. Marc went into the fashion world, but he was really a culture person."


Dianne Benson, who, like Selma Weiser at Charivari, sold avant-garde clothes by Japanese and French designers in her eponymous Manhattan boutiques, remembers trying to hire Marc when he was still a teenager. She took him for a drink at a bar on Prince Street in SoHo and spoke about her vision: The Dianne B. boutiques were expanding, and with the backing of superstar Japanese designer Rei Kawakubo, Benson had just opened a massive new store in SoHo, on the same street as the Mary Boone and Leo Castelli galleries. Art and fashion were organically, enthusiastically commingling: Jenny Holzer, Keith Haring, Kenny Scharf and the graffiti artist Kano all began using clothes as canvas. SoHo shops were designed to look like art galleries, all stone and cement and bare white walls, garments doubling as installations.

In 1982, when *Artforum* put an Issey Miyake dress on its cover, fashion was finally, controversially, equated with art. "The very definition of art," the editors wrote, "needs to break down to affirm its strength."

Benson herself was collaborating with Robert Mapplethorpe and Cindy Sherman, running into them at clubs and art openings and asking them to do stuff for her shops, simple as that. "Part of the idea of going downtown was that people didn't have managers and stylists," she says. "It was a different time."

In that spirit, she pursued Marc. She'd known him from the time he was thirteen or fourteen, when he'd come into her first shop on Madison Avenue and try on all her latest shipments. "I see him in this Claude Montana dress," Benson says. "He was a kid full of life." She knew him, too, through her friend Robert Boykin, Marc's boyfriend. She saw his talent and gave him the hard sell. Marc took it all in, then told Dianne that he needed to think about it.

A couple of days later, Marc got back to her. "He said, 'It's just not good enough,'" Benson says. "'It's just not big enough. I want a bigger challenge.'"

In 1985, the *New York Times* critic John Duka reviewed Marc's debut spring line for Sketchbook, calling it "one of the freshest in some time" and "as up-to-the-minute as you can get." Marc cited his influences as a mash-up of the extravagant romanticism of *Amadeus* and Prince's *Purple Rain*. Most unusual was his bold play with proportion: an ample, shruggy below-the-knee dress with a shrunken trompe l'oeil vest tugged over a silk chiffon blouse; a white top, roomy as a painter's smock, paired with bicycle shorts made of cotton damask and modest black flats. Even at her earliest, the Marc girl was never about sex, and this conceit alone set him apart.

"Actually intelligent, but seems not to have a care," was his description of the Marc Jacobs girl. "I have no respect for people who don't do anything, but I think it's magical to seem as if you live to have fun." He stressed that he wanted to design for the modern girl, which should only necessitate two collections per year—the old ways, the old luxury, was not for him. "The idea of a separate wardrobe for a vacation—the next time I'm on an ocean liner with twelve pieces of hard luggage, I'll let you know," he said.

As early as 1985, *Women's Wear Daily* had declared Marc Jacobs at the forefront of "the new American look," a breezy, unpretentious approach that was reinvigorating an entire subset of the fashion industry. "I'm not in the designer market," Marc said. "I don't want to be as intimidating as Calvin Klein or any of those people."

Yet before the year was out, Ruben Thomas fired Marc Jacobs— "the boy wonder," according to *WWD*—and Duffy would later admit that Marc's rampant drug use sank him. "Everyone I knew at that time who was twenty to twenty-five was taking drugs," Duffy said. "But at a certain point I stopped, and other people stopped, and Marc wasn't stopping . . . I just kept thinking, 'There are a lot of high-functioning drug addicts.'"

Duffy was also one of the very few who knew how emotionally desolate Marc's upbringing was, how profoundly unworthy of love he felt. "He was just trying to escape," Duffy said. "I knew he had an unhappy childhood. I knew he was unhappy. I knew he hated himself. I knew all of this. We talked about it."

Marc's identity as a fashion designer, a prodigy, was really all he had, and Duffy knew that for all his instability, Marc Jacobs had limitless potential. He quickly found Marc a Canadian backer named Jack Atkins, who just as quickly dropped the troubled Marc. Duffy then got him a consulting gig at Mitsubishi until he landed financing from the Japanese apparel giant Onward Kashiyama. In doing so, Duffy cast himself as the Pierre Bergé—minus the sex—to Marc's Yves Saint Laurent: The indispensable keeper of gates, books, secrets, his life now in service to a drug-addled genius.

\*    \*    \*

Of his entire American cohort, only one other designer would come to rival Marc, to frustrate and obsess him, compounding his already raging inferiority complex: Tom Ford.

Tom Ford and Marc Jacobs had much in common. From tender ages, both knew they wanted to pursue careers in design. Growing up, both were closest to their grandmothers, who left deep impressions on their tastes and sensibilities. Ford studied at New York University and then Parsons, missing Jacobs's class by months. Both were incredibly attractive prodigies who partied at Studio 54 and gravitated toward older men; when Ford was fifteen, one of his first serious boyfriends was thirty-five.

Both, too, presented as remarkably self-possessed, geniuses at tamping down their insecurities and neuroses. After graduating from Parsons in 1986, Ford had a thin book to show, having majored in architecture before switching to fashion design. He spent months in search of work. "I called everybody," he said. "I interviewed with Calvin nine times . . . I interviewed with Grace Coddington." Ford was finally hired by designer Cathy Hardwick after calling her nearly every day for a month, from a pay phone in her lobby, politely asking for five minutes of her time.

"He was a gorgeous boy," Hardwick says. "We talked for half an hour, and at the end of the conversation, he convinced me to give him a job."

"I remember Cathy saying, 'You know, Tom is not like you and me,'" says Tova Narrett, who shared an office with Ford for a year. "She said, 'I've never seen anyone so . . .' I don't think she used the word *ambitious*. She said 'focused and directed.' She said, 'I think he has his future planned.' And I think Cathy was a little surprised by that."

In New York City in 1986, Tom Ford was on no one's radar: It was Marc Jacobs whom the fashion world had consecrated. By now, his clothes had made the cover of *Women's Wear Daily*; he'd been profiled by the *New York Times* and *Vogue*, the latter giving him big play as fashion's future. What Marc was doing was in line with the ideas of *Vogue*'s newly installed editor in chief, Anna Wintour, who jolted the industry in 1988 when she put a California-casual model wearing blue jeans and a couture Lacroix jacket on her inaugural cover, a strip of her belly proudly visible. "I remember the printers called us up because they thought we'd made a mistake," Wintour said. "It was so unlike the studied and elegant close-ups that were typical of *Vogue*'s covers back then, with tons of makeup and major jewelry." Wintour, like Marc, sensed what was coming: a stripping-away of artifice and a rejection of preciousness. Anything high fashion could be mixed with the low, and would probably be made better for it. Marc was bolder, though, in injecting joy and imperfection, and even a bit of humility, into this new kind of beauty.

"I'm appealing to people's sense of being happy," Marc said. "Which is always a lot easier than sort of, you know, shocking them with something that makes them scared or upset."

A widespread fascination with what was happening in downtown New York City was emerging. From punk and hip-hop and new wave to club kids and drag queens to the real-time novels of Jay McInerney and Tama Janowitz, American culture at large was increasingly fascinated with the fringes and freak shows of New York. It was the last days before Rudy Giuliani would impose order, when there was space in New York for broke bohemians. MTV, then only six years old, capitalized on this new infatuation, launching *Andy Warhol's 15 Minutes*, a half-hour series profiling the residents of a post-punk terrain that wasn't so much geographical as spiritual: If these were your people, you were downtown. The show introduced a revolutionary mix of high-low celebrity, one that Marc would later expertly manipulate: Jerry Hall, Debbie Harry, Stephen Sprouse, John Sex, William Burroughs, Robin Leach, Lady Bunny, Judd Nelson, and a then-unknown Courtney Love were interviewed. Pyramid, the Palladium, and Mudd Club were profiled.

This was Marc's world, and he, too, had his own segment, showing pieces from his latest collection. "Now I'm into like, T-shirts, and underwear, slips, stockings, et cetera," he says. It was the Madonna effect: Lingerie as outerwear, the upstreaming of club culture, the rejection of career gear. "I've got a lot of girlfriends who run around the city in nothing but their underwear; they throw a sweater over a slip or put on a pair of stockings and some sweater, or something like that."

It was a look that augured what was coming with grunge, the stripping-down of the shellacked '80s armored woman, with her aerodynamic hair and shoulder pads and power suits. Here was Marc's true genius on display: His ability to see what was coming, to predict what girls wanted to look like before even they knew, to transmute the lowly into the aspirational.

"The ideal girl will just sort of roll out of bed some night after taking a nap and put on a slip that looks like this and go out to some club or go out dancing or something," he says. "She'd be all dressed, but she'd still be kind of undressed . . . and she wouldn't have to do anything else."

It's hard to overstate what an extreme notion this was. Marc wasn't just positing this kind of girl as cool or different: To him, this way of being and looking was ideal. Imperfection was the new perfection.

"What I loved was seeing things that were imperfect to other people," he said, "and just finding the beauty in whatever it was, and not making a big deal of it."

While Marc was sitting for profiles with national publications, going from strength to strength with each new collection, and making the rounds at clubs and cocktail parties, he was quietly grieving. In 1987, his grandmother, who had run around New York telling everyone "My grandson is going to be the next Calvin Klein," had died.

"The most painful," Marc said of her loss. At the same time, his longtime boyfriend Robert Boykin was dying of AIDS. Boykin, seemingly so charmed, never announced his illness to friends; he just slowly faded from the scene, and people knew. It had been only two years since Rock Hudson, one of Hollywood's most rakish leading men, announced that he had AIDS, and President Ronald Reagan had only just publicly addressed the disease, which had previously been called "the gay cancer."

"Robert was one of the nicest guys around," says Anita Sarko, who deejayed regularly at Hurrah. Friends recall Boykin as completely devoted to Marc, insistent that his illness not slow down his boyfriend's progress. "Robert was not just anybody," says Merrill Aldighieri, another Hurrah compatriot. She recalls late-'80s New York as a purgatory of grief: "Once a month, you'd lose someone," she says. "It's like you were in continual shock, a constant, permanent dread. You weren't focused on who had just died—you were worried about who came next."

By the time Robert died, Hurrah had closed. The memorial was held at the Yellow Rose Café on the Upper West Side, Marc somehow managing to hold it together. "I don't remember anybody crying," Aldighieri says. "People looked kind of harrowed."

At twenty-five years old, Marc Jacobs had lost his grandmother, his parents and siblings, and his first serious boyfriend. He was the toast of New York and totally alone.

## CHAPTER 7

# WHY CAN'T I HAVE FUN
# ALL THE TIME?

THINGS WERE CHANGING SO fast that by 1992, Calvin Klein needed eighteen-year-old Kate Moss as much as she needed him. Klein was a master of minimalism who'd overextended his brand to the point of collapse. Like so many designers, Klein was both a hedonist and a control freak, and his problems with drugs, alcohol, and a cohesive, functional management style left his empire vulnerable.

"Calvin knew it was the young people who were going to get him out of this mess," says Madonna Badger, who with Fabien Baron, Neil Kraft, and Carolyn Bessette, was part of the new order. "It was a really amazing time to be at the company," Badger says, "because Calvin had just gone down to Hazelden. He was all, 'Peace, love, let's be friends.'"

Kate, with her elfin beauty and nonchalance, was the epitome of this loose, inclusive new philosophy. But for Kate, Melanie, and Corinne, every shoot they did, every seemingly lo-fi, carefree image, was in pursuit of one goal: Getting famous. Like Lee McQueen, they were determined to make the establishment come to them.

"They wanted to prove themselves," said London-based designer

Liza Bruce, who worked with the trio back then. "They wanted to get those ad campaigns; to get to New York was the pinnacle. Corinne was like, 'I'm getting us into *Vogue.*' "

Kate took the meeting with Calvin on her own, without Corinne or Melanie. She'd traveled to New York with Corinne's protégée Mario Sorrenti, who by now was her boyfriend, and they moved in with Mario's mother, Francesca. Mario was often traveling for work, and though Kate loved Francesca—and felt, as she would about so many older women, that here was a surrogate mother—she still felt very much alone. "I was always on my own," she said, "and I think that probably made me very vulnerable. There was nobody backing me up, really. But I just did it."

As she did in Galliano's studio, eighteen-year-old Kate Moss strode into her meeting at Calvin Klein with extraordinary self-possession. Baron had Kate put on a pair of Calvin Klein jeans before walking into the room, a string of hopeful models, including Cindy Crawford, waiting in reception.

In she came, with her jeans and little T-shirt, rumpled hair and no makeup. "Like, nothing," says Badger, who was in the room. "And back in those days, models *dressed* for go-sees. They did their hair and makeup."

Kate flopped down on the floor, and for a moment, the room was still: One didn't take such informal tack with Calvin Klein. But however nervous Kate was—and Badger sensed that Kate was quite nervous—her natural effervescence shone through, and when she plopped down on the floor, Klein took a beat, then sat right down next to her.

"She was a very sweet girl," Badger says. "She walked out of the room and Calvin was like, 'I love her. I love her.' "

Later, of course, he'd say that the moment he saw Kate he knew she was a star, just as Sarah Doukas would claim that she, too, saw

Kate Moss as her agency's next big thing. In the immediate, though, Klein had his doubts. Baron and Bessette remained strongly in the Moss camp, but when Klein consulted with stylist Paul Cavaco, who was working with Baron and editor in chief Liz Tilberis at the new *Harper's Bazaar*, Cavaco expressed reservations.

"I said, 'Well, I think she's gorgeous, but she's really little,'" he said. "I have a feeling that she may not work a lot.'" Cavaco was an industry veteran, but at forty-two, he was several generations removed from Klein's young team.

It was a risk, but Klein went with the kids. "For them, what is real is beautiful—looking plain is beautiful," Klein said. "What is less than perfect is sexy." Moss was their muse.

"Moss and only Moss," as Baron put it.

In less than two years, Kate Moss had gone from the cover of a cult UK magazine to fronting a campaign for one of the biggest designers in the world. She was becoming the star of her pack, yet her very few interpersonal relationships were disintegrating. Mario was always away. Her mother was distant and far from encouraging. Her younger brother, Nick, had decided he'd like to give modeling a try, too, and Kate's agent in London signed him, despite admitting that Nick was "not conventionally handsome." Nick, lacking his sister's looks, drive, and charm, had a short-lived career. Not surprisingly, he resented Kate.

"I hate talking about her," Nick said. "That's all I ever hear."

Her relationship with her father was a bit better, but this was before everyone was on e-mail or had cell phones, and keeping in regular contact was difficult. And then there was Corinne, who had been like an older sister to Kate. Kate was slowly distancing herself.

Corinne was developing a reputation for being hard to work with: She'd refuse to take direction; she threw fits; and whenever it looked like she was losing a battle, she locked herself in the bathroom until she got her way. She was growing exponentially resentful of Sims, Sorrenti, and Craig McDean, whose careers were all soaring while hers languished, convincing herself that of everyone, she had the most artistic integrity. Kate knew firsthand how intractable Corrine could be and wanted no part of it.

"Corinne would make me cry," Kate said.

That was the point.

"The more I piss you off," Corinne would say, "the better pictures I get."

Now Kate had to be topless for the Calvin Klein campaign, and she dreaded it. This obsession with her breasts was humiliating. Early in her career, she'd considered getting implants, but she changed her mind once she began getting work. It was another thing that set her apart.

She was teamed with Mark Wahlberg, then known as Marky Mark, a hip-hop manqué with a band called the Funky Bunch and a brother in New Kids on the Block. He had a bulging physique and a bad attitude. The idea came from David Geffen, the billionaire who'd just bailed out Calvin Klein and had recently seen Marky Mark, shirtless, on the cover of *Rolling Stone*.

It was not a happy set. Wahlberg spent some downtime tugging his dick while Kate rolled her eyes. Glenn O'Brien, who wrote the script for the TV spots, says Wahlberg would look at the pages and cross out things he didn't think sounded like him, "a sort of white South Boston version of Ebonics," O'Brien says.

Wahlberg also made it clear that Kate was, to him, nothing special. "I wasn't into the waif thing," he said later. "She kind of looked like my nephew."

"It didn't feel like me at all," Kate said. "I felt really bad about straddling this buff guy. I didn't like it. I couldn't get out of bed for two weeks." By now, Moss was drinking heavily. She saw a doctor and was prescribed Valium, but Mario's mother, Francesca, forbade Kate from taking it.

"Nobody takes care of you mentally," Kate said. "I thought I was going to die."

That campaign saved the house of Calvin Klein and launched Kate's career. Marky Mark may have been more recognizable, but Kate became the star, soon the sole face of Calvin Klein jeans, underwear, fragrance. She was always shot in black-and-white, set against a white seamless or flaking wall, sometimes nude, sometimes in a black tank and cotton underwear, her stark, fragile beauty amplified by lank hair and little makeup.

"For me, Kate's body represented closing the door on the excessiveness of the '80s," Klein said. "So many women models would come to me where they've distorted their bodies by implants in their breasts, changing their hips, changing their knees . . . I mean, you just cannot imagine what models were doing to themselves, what women have been doing to themselves. I think something changed dramatically in the '90s. And I was looking for someone who could represent something that's more natural."

The culture at large didn't see Kate that way: Up against the skyscraper supermodels of the '80s, their very perfection a comment on American supremacy, a small-boned, flat-chested model like Kate Moss was heresy. Someone her size hadn't been seen since Twiggy in the '60s; suddenly, Kate and Calvin Klein were accused of promoting anorexia, heroin use, child pornography, and the downfall of Western civilization.

She was on the sides of buses, kiosks, and pay phones, naked and draped across a velvet sofa in a ramshackle room, "FEED ME" often scrawled across the ad by protesters.

"I was thin," Kate said, "but that's because I was doing shows, working really hard . . . You'd get to work in the morning, there was no food. Nobody took you out for lunch when I started." Kate spent much of 1993 in tears. This was the same girl who'd once been told by her mother that life wasn't always fun and refused to believe it: "Why the fuck not? Why the fuck can't I have fun all the time?" Now she was beginning to see.

"If you were to say, 'What were the '90s like in America?' that has to be one of the great images," said feminist scholar Camille Paglia, calling the campaign proof that America was becoming a modern-day Babylon. "A dartboard for every point to be made about bad female body image," said James Wolcott in the *New Yorker*.

Klein created a similar controversy in 1981, casting a teenage Brooke Shields in a TV spot in which she squats on the floor, legs spread. "You want to know what comes between me and my Calvins?" she whispered. "Nothing." For all the backlash, that ad pushed denim from cheap leisurewear to luxury, and with the Kate campaign, Klein once again generated an unquantifiable amount of free press. That same year, he was not only able to buy out Geffen: He'd set the tone for fashion advertising for the rest of the decade, and Kate Moss, his star, was about to vanquish the supermodel as we knew her.

"Suddenly this little unknown fresh-faced, scruffy-haired, no-makeup boyish girl appears, with a new breed of photographer, who was taking much more natural light," said hairstylist Sam McKnight, who was also coming up at the time. "It was a new wave, and it . . . changed fashion forever."

After the Calvin Klein ads broke, Kate landed a spot in Dolce & Gabbana's 1992 fall campaign and was photographed by Steven Meisel, a star maker. She was getting booked for runway, which automatically put her in the same league as Cindy Crawford, Naomi Campbell, Christy Turlington, and Linda Evangelista.

The momentum was startling. Not all of Kate's fellow models were welcoming. Kate partly understood: She didn't think she was tall or beautiful enough either. She knew very little about fashion and clothes and had no real sense of style. But she worked hard and was, in the words of O'Brien, "like a duck"—you could shoot her from any angle; not one was bad. She was enthusiastic and candid and had a scrapper's mentality. She was not to be bullied and knew how to be a bitch.

"In photographs, it doesn't matter, but on runway, I think clothes look better on taller women," Kate said. "It must be a bit weird for them, everyone saying this is the new look when they've got the perfect face, the perfect body, the perfect everything. And somebody who's not at all perfect comes along and starts taking all their jobs . . ."

The Moss/Wahlberg pairing was so successful that Klein used the two again. These ads echoed Klein's campaign with Shields: Kate, topless, jeans slung low on her hips, walks around Marky Mark as he exclaims, "Wow! *That* could come between me and my Calvins." In a culture petrified of AIDS, this campaign's approach to sex was defiant.

The ads were shot by renowned photographers Herb Ritts and Patrick Demarchelier, who both favored luxuriant, sepia-toned glamour. But Kate's rawness undercut that, and Ward was putting Kate in jeans one size too big, then tugging them down and pinning them to create a silhouette that didn't yet exist: the low-slung jean, a cool-kid relation to McQueen's bumster. Creative director Fabien Baron, meanwhile, was funneling Corinne Day's aesthetic: louche and dishabille, a cultivated concoction of glamour and grime.

The ads were cool, Kate was cool, Mark Wahlberg was not. Klein dropped him. Kate was the future. She later inspired Klein to cast real people in his CK Be ads, an innovation that further pushed cultural standards of beauty. "She's very sensual and sexy," he said, "and she represented everything I was looking for."

"Heroin chic" became the appellation.

CHAPTER 8

# A CATALOG OF HORRORS

THE RUNWAY SPECTACLES CREATED by Lee McQueen and John Galliano rivaled the work of artists Damien Hirst and Tracey Emin: It was impossible to say which camp was more provocative and vulgar. "I'm about what goes through people's minds, the stuff that people don't want to admit or face up to," McQueen said. "The shows are about what's buried in people's psyches."

For his next collection, "Nihilism," McQueen pulped up his models, smearing them with crud and caked blood. He wrapped them in plastic, soaked the clothes to transparency, and sent the girls out in hip-hitting slashed tops, vulvas exposed.

"A catalogue of horrors," said Marion Hume in the *UK Independent*, which spread her outrage over three pages. "A horror show," she wrote, " . . . of battered women, of violent lives, of grinding daily existences offset by wild, drug-enhanced nocturnal dives into clubs where the dress code is semi-naked."

*New York Times* critic Amy Spindler spent much of London Fashion Week agonizing over McQueen. "A hard show to take," Spindler wrote. "[It] gave editors the aggressive British attitude they had been expecting. A little of it, of course, goes a long way, and Alexander McQueen provided a lot."

He had to. "He knew that if he could get press, he'd eventually get a backer," Andrew Groves says. McQueen was ignored by *Vogue* and *Women's Wear Daily*, yet sold two hundred pieces from that collection within months.

Isabella, meanwhile, was struggling at British *Vogue*. Her protégés, to the mainstream fashion world, seemed more like aggressive oddballs than viable talents, and she felt she didn't belong. "If you're beautiful, you don't need clothes," she told her *Vogue* colleague Hamish Bowles. "If you're ugly, like me, you're a house with no foundation; you need something to build you up."

Issie was relegated to styling people *Vogue* considered outré: the wild Irish rock star Sinead O'Connor, with her shapeless clothes and shaved head, and Hirst, who'd just sold a shark in formaldehyde for £50,000. She was disinterested in the idea that fashion was also a business, with budgets and deadlines and office hours. She was as much an artist as anyone she styled, an intimate of Jean-Michel Basquiat and Bryan Ferry, and comported herself accordingly. It was also another way of perfuming herself with glamour that she physically lacked.

"I would get to the office in Hanover Square at 9 A.M.," said Plum Sykes, then her assistant, "and I would get a phone call at nine thirty saying, 'I have had far too much gin to drink last night, darling, could you come over here and we'll just work from my bed.'" Sykes would go over to Elizabeth Street, where Issie would be lounging in her lingerie. "She didn't always go to the office," said Eve MacSweeney, now *Vogue*'s features editor, "but she was always genuinely busy doing things. It's just that she didn't do them in the conventional way, or in a way that necessarily made sense to a corporate entity like Condé Nast."

In the late summer of '93, Issie got her first and only big assignment for British *Vogue*: Alex Schulman, the editor in chief, had Issie cast a shoot for iconic photographer Meisel, his first for the magazine.

The idea was to find young aristocrats; what Issie brought was her radar for cool. She chose her cousin Honor Fraser, Sigmund Freud's great-granddaughter Bella, Lady Louise Campbell, her own assistant Plum Sykes, and Sykes's friend Stella Tennant. Of the group, Tennant was the most peculiar looking: She had a long, narrow face, short black hair, caterpillar eyebrows, and a large nose ring. Schulman wanted it out; Issie kept it in.

Meisel hired Joe McKenna, a young Scot who'd styled for *The Face*. He and Issie clashed right away: McKenna thought the clothes should be simple and clean; she thought the girls should look darker, rougher, sullen. She fought and won, slumming up her aristocrats with sludgy black eyeliner, leaving their hair undone. She pulled sharp little black dresses and thick-soled boots, threadbare sweaters and sumptuous furs.

She also worked in two chopped-up dresses by McQueen, causing a real fight with McKenna, even as McQueen himself showed up with his pieces in a plastic bag. The presentation unnerved McKenna. "I'd come from New York, where fashion was very slick," he said. "I was expecting a rack of clothes, or at least a garment bag." The dresses, at first, did nothing for him. "I just didn't get it," he said. "Until we put them on Stella Tennant. And then you could see that something was going on."

Meisel shot Issie's blue bloods in black-and-white, in empty pubs and narrow winding roads, dark sylphs with sad faces. In-house the spread was called "Anglo-Saxon Attitudes," but it became known as "London Babes." In that moment, it was a rare thing: a high-end fashion editorial with wit, suggesting downward mobility as the new aspiration, even among aristocrats.

Because it was 1993, of all the girls in that editorial, Stella was the breakout star. The next week, Meisel put her in a Versace campaign with Linda Evangelista, and then shot her, nose ring intact, for the cover of Italian *Vogue*. Karl Lagerfeld soon signed her to an estimated

$1 million contract as the face of Chanel. Not bad for someone who spent most of her time on a farm and, as Issie said, "smells disgusting but looks amazing."

By now, Issie had installed McQueen at her mother-in-law's house on Elizabeth Street, where he lived and worked with his boyfriend Andrew Groves, himself a designer who went by the name Jimmy Jumble. The two had met one night at a bar on Old Compton Street; kicked out for being too drunk, they went home together, and that was it. "I think what happened is he knew I could sew, and he said, 'I'm doing this show,'" Groves says. "I could never quite figure out if the relationship started first, or if I was making clothes for him."

The Elizabeth Street house was filthy and barely furnished. "Upstairs was just dirty, bare floorboards," Groves says. "Then on the ground floor was an old mattress that we were sleeping on, with old fabrics. The table was used for cutting. There was no proper water."

Installed next door was Issie's other find, a young milliner from Ireland called Philip Treacy. His approach to hats was like McQueen's approach to clothes: technical feats of irreverence. But Treacy was humble, whereas McQueen would bray to anyone nearby that he was the future.

"Alexander was quite hard-core then," Treacy says. McQueen didn't care that Issie had another protégé at Elizabeth Street, although Treacy did. "But I just had to get on with it," Treacy says. "Isabella made me work with him." Not long into their joint residency, Treacy's sister came by and met McQueen. She told Philip about their brief exchange: "She said, 'Detmar introduced me to Alexander and said he's the new Saint Laurent. Is he?' And I said, 'Possibly.'"

CHAPTER 9

# GRUNGE R.I.P.

NOT LONG AFTER ROBERT Boykin's death, Marc met a gorgeous young party boy named Scott Fritz. Men and women, movie stars and models all fell for Scott. He'd been shot by photographer Greg Gorman and later included in his book "In Their Youth," along with Leonardo DiCaprio, Viggo Mortensen, Brad Pitt, and Johnny Depp.

"Scott was an absolute beauty," says club promoter Chi Chi Valenti. "And a nihilist in a way."

Valenti befriended Scott at Jackie 60, a weekly party that she and her husband threw in the raunchy, blood-spattered Meatpacking District. Pansexual, druggy, with wings for female domination and live theater, Jackie 60 lasted from 1990 to 1999 and was a hedonistic response to a nightlife paralyzed by AIDS.

Marc considered Chi Chi "the Brooke Astor of New York nightlife" and had known her since their days at the Mudd Club. In a 1991 night-crawler diary for *WWD*, Marc called Jackie 60 "a must . . . Chi Chi is usually on the mike describing the theme, which can be anything from a tribute to Martha Graham to a Vivienne Westwood night. Jackie 60 is like going to a party in somebody's basement—don't go if you want disco effects and laser beams."

No one wanted to go to Pyramid or Area anymore. "By 1987, you would just notice the people that were gone," Valenti says. "That's why Jackie 60 was embraced. It was very much us saying that almost a whole generation of people have died, if not two, and now we move forward."

It was the twilight of the pre-Internet age, when those who most needed to could come to New York and dispatch with the past. No one would ask where you were from, how old you were, or how a party boy like you could afford living in New York City. At Jackie 60, you might have been caught on video having anonymous sex in the bathroom, and that video might have been screened for the entire club, but asking questions like these? Impolite.

"He was very secretive," Valenti says of Scott Fritz back then. "It was not unusual in our scene for people to come to New York and reinvent themselves."

"He just appeared," says Beauregard Houston-Montgomery. "He was very self-possessed, very beautiful. Stunning."

Scott worked as a waiter at Provence in Soho and was a heroin addict. Sometimes he'd just not show up, or show up high and say awful, cutting things to the patrons, as he often would to friends, but the owners loved him anyway. Houston-Montgomery felt that the drug use and the abrasiveness were scar tissue. "I think he was terribly abused in his past," Houston-Montgomery says. "When you look like that from the time you're a child, you're a target."

But Scott was also an enthusiast and a cultural omnivore. He loved Joan Didion and Tori Amos and dreamed of being a writer. He collaborated with Valenti and *Village Voice* columnist Michael Musto on plays for Jackie 60, including one of the club's biggest hits, *Coke-Whore!* He lived with Marc in the Dorilton apartment.

"Scott was a sweet guy with a beautiful face," Musto says. "Everyone was in love with him."

"Scott was a muse for Marc," Houston-Montgomery says. "They were a wonderful couple. Until the disease set in."

While everyone in the industry knew he was gay, Marc, who had the discipline to party less and work more, kept his relationships out of the press. As it was, he had begun attracting mainstream attention: He was pegged by *Vogue* as an emerging designer to watch in 1986 and received regular reviews in the *New York Times*. In 1988, he was profiled on CBS's prime-time newsmagazine *48 Hours*, positioned as the scrappy upstart to an establishment personified by the aging and logy Bill Blass.

"I find trousers are still not appropriate for business," said a guest at the Blass presentation. Ivana Trump, Pat Buckley, and Barbara Walters were all there, seated in gold-backed chairs at the Plaza Hotel. Carrie Donovan, the elder stateswoman of fashion critics, told Blass postshow that "those were some snazzy rags." By 1993, she'd be fired from the *New York Times*, replaced by the twenty-something Amy Spindler.

Blass showed taffetas and silks with silhouettes for battle, sleeves that looked like the jagged spine of a stegosaurus, all worn by young models aged with heavy makeup and immobile hair.

Marc, in his segment, was game to play the underdog. Here he was, the youngest designer to win the Perry Ellis Award for New Fashion Talent from the Council of Fashion Designers of America, roaming his threadbare offices in mismatched socks, guzzling coffee out of cheap paper cups, and chain-smoking, lighting one cigarette off the dying embers of another. He complained that he didn't have enough shoes for the models; those shoes were donated by Manolo Blahnik.

He stapled his own canvas to the runway and ran to the bathroom to throw up. When he finally pulled off his show—a collection filled with purple and houndstooth and knits, kind of youthful but not all the way there—he was charming and unashamed when asked what his dream was: "To be better. Bigger and better. To build an empire."

He was also carefully building his myth. He wore a ponytail, just as Perry Ellis had. Despite the image he crafted for *48 Hours*, he, too, circulated in Blass's world. At a lunch thrown by the heiress Veronica Hearst, he asked Blass, a heavy smoker himself, if they could light up. "He said, 'Go ahead, smoke," Marc said. "'Believe me, you won't be invited back if they don't want you back, but it won't be because smoking is the reason.'"

Marc went on record as a true artist, one who wasn't motivated by money: "I knew I would rather work in a supermarket and create clothes at night in my apartment than work for someone else," he said, failing to note that he came from a wealthy family and lived in a luxury apartment on the Upper West Side. He was working with a skeleton staff and a limited budget, true, but he had the world's top supermodels—Cindy Crawford, Veronica Webb, Christy Turlington—walking in his shows. He'd been covered by *WWD* and the *New York Times* since he was a student.

His ambition and addiction were concealed beneath the veneer of this sweet, soft-spoken, beautiful young man who radiated an intense desire to please but was most interested in pleasing himself. In much the same way, he made everyone who encountered him believe he was, in essence, a light, cheerful, and easygoing personality—not the survivor of a harrowing childhood, not a lonely soul who felt unlovable. Marc was a genius at presentation, at branding himself before people even knew that was a thing you could do. He was the most promising, most "together" prodigy the fashion world had seen since Karl Lagerfeld and Yves Saint Laurent emerged as rivals in the early '50s. He had Lagerfeld's sharklike determination and Saint Laurent's self-sabotaging nature, abusing himself with massive quantities of cigarettes, booze, drugs, and sex.

"Maybe everybody's insecure," Marc said, "but I find there are a lot of designers who seem so confident with what they say, what they do, their manner of dress. And I'm just not."

*     *     *

It would be easy to ascribe Marc's protestations to false modesty, given how successful he already was. But his personal life was a mess. His boyfriend, Scott Fritz, had been diagnosed with AIDS, and no one who knew Marc or Scott at this time recalls when Scott learned of his status, because both were so private. "I don't even know how long it was that he knew he was sick," says Chi Chi Valenti. "But it became so evident that nothing needed to be said."

Scott's depression exacerbated his drug use, and his failing immune system exacerbated the effects of heroin. Nodding off while smoking a cigarette, he started small fires in the apartment a couple of times a day. Marc, "put through every gate of hell and back," Houston-Montgomery says, could no longer take it. He moved Scott to a studio apartment in the East Village, paid his rent, and gave him pocket money. He couldn't tell if he was helping or hurting his boyfriend, now a professional and personal liability. "If you had AIDS, you couldn't afford the association," says Houston-Montgomery. "But Marc loved Scott."

Scott soon became feared in the East Village, a ravaged wraith. "I think his anger frightened Marc," Houston-Montgomery says. "If Scott didn't like you, it didn't matter who you were—he would lay you out." Scott was banned from every bar and restaurant in the neighborhood. "He was so enraged at his situation," Valenti says. "It seemed like he wanted to spread the sadness to other people." He was such a pariah that Valenti used to meet up with him on street corners, no one willing to have him in their home.

The last time anyone remembers seeing Scott was in Tompkins Square Park in the early '90s, during the Labor Day drag party Wigstock. Amid the twelve-inch platforms and beehives, Scott Fritz was the sight no one missed: filthy, covered in open sores, lying on the sidewalk and wrapped in rags. Houston-Montgomery had gone to meet him at the entrance on St. Mark's Place and Avenue A, and wasn't surprised to see that Scott had been kicked out of the park, too.

"He was yelling and screaming about the hypocrisy of everyone," Houston-Montgomery says. "Between the heroin and AIDS, he was wasting away."

The Tompkins Square Park incident became downtown legend. "He was like an old person with full-blown dementia," Valenti says. "The anger overtook all the normal impulses, the ability to adapt, the ability to not be a total burden. It was all gone."

Like Robert Boykin, Scott Fritz was remembered sometime after his death with a small memorial dinner. Scott's was at Provence, the downtown restaurant where he'd capriciously worked and insulted so many. In attendance was Scott's mother, whom Houston-Montgomery recalls as very thin, very beautiful, and very cold, sitting with an ever-present drink in her hand. Marc was there too, and Scott's mother was horrible to him. She blamed Marc for her son's demise, and he took it. "She *hated* Marc," Houston-Montgomery says. "*Hated* him. I understand why Marc did what he did. He didn't want to enable Scott, but at the same time he had to. What else was he going to do?"

Beset by calamity, Marc pushed forward. A profile in *WWD* in April 1988 mentioned only his professional crises—backers dropping out, a robbery, and a fire in his showroom—and lauded his stoicism. "I never stop; I live this stuff," Marc said. "It comes before everything in my life. Though it might sound cold, it's the very top priority in my life. If that ever stops, I'm in big trouble."

Marc was twenty-five years old and his greatest possibility yet was born of even more tragedy: He was one of the few, along with Isaac Mizrahi, being considered to take over at Perry Ellis, a house decimated by AIDS. Ellis, Marc's hero, had died of the disease in 1986. Control of the company had been left to Ellis's former boyfriend, Robert MacDonald, but he, too, was sick, and in 1990 died from AIDS-related complications. Designer Robert Forsythe, who had been hired around the same time as Marc to head up menswear, died in October 1991, also from complications related to HIV.

Marc's show that November was his audition.

"It was a make-or-break collection," says Tracy Reese, who helped Marc pull it together. Reese herself had just gone out of business, had no money, and, like Marc, was very depressed. They would work all day and go to dinner at ten thirty every night at Café Luxembourg on the Upper West Side, where a waitress named Patience would serve them chicken paillard and lemon tart and Marc would charge it. Then they'd go back to work till they fell asleep on the pattern cutting tables.

One morning Marc woke up crying. "We were stiff and cold, and he was nervous, and there was so much going on between his grandma and Robert," Reese says. "But that was an amazing show."

The *New York Times* called it "one of the season's most exuberant," a riot of "high-spirited, all-American styles." He showed stretchy gingham dresses, sequined madras jackets, and a filmy silk polka-dot jumpsuit, and won praise from New York's biggest buyers. "It made me happy," said Ellin Saltzman of Saks Fifth Avenue. Kal Ruttenstein, the senior VP at Bloomingdale's, raved about Marc: "He's getting better every season," he said.

Marc got the job at Perry Ellis, and as the most promising American designer of his generation, he was given a full page in *Newsweek* magazine, which called him "a relative child." He took Reese with him, along with his business partner Robert Duffy. To run the denim line, Marc hired Tom Ford, who was coming from Cathy Hardwick's small house.

It was not an obvious choice: Ford was a sophisticate. Years later, Marc would say his decision was deliberately counterintuitive. "Tom was a different person then," Jacobs said. "He was this WASPy, preppy, tasteful person—or at least that was the look he had at the time. I wanted him for Perry Ellis America, which was our jeans line, because I thought it would be interesting to bring a touch of sophistication to that. He used to make fun of the way I look, I remember."

It was the beginning of Marc's lifelong obsession with Ford: how much more handsome he was, how successful, how much more together. "Tom was definitely disciplined," Reese says. "Marc was not." Ford would come in early, freshly showered from the gym, toss his clothes in the washer, and get to work. He seemed secure and contained, while Marc was neurotic and jittery. Ford had no intention of working under Marc Jacobs for very long. "He's another person"—like Marc, Reese says—"who always had a big vision."

Reese lasted at Perry Ellis for one year; Ford, two, until he was poached by Dawn Mello for Gucci. As head of Perry Ellis, Marc himself didn't have much longer.

There was no more exciting place in early 1990s New York than the Lower East Side. The clubs and bars were tiny and ramshackle: Mercury Lounge, Save the Robots, and a few blocks north, Brownie's and the Green Door at Coney Island High. Over at Liquid Sky, which was both a shop and a clubhouse, Chloë Sevigny folded clothes for rave kids while they partied downstairs. Art school kids, indie rock boys and riot grrrls, skate rats and slumming trust funders congregated nightly on a desolate Lower East Side strip called Ludlow Street, where they drank at Max Fish and the Hat, saw art at the Alleged Gallery, shopped at TG170, grabbed coffee at the Pink Pony, midnight pastrami at Katz's Deli, and copped heroin at any nearby corner or bodega. The Lower East Side was Chan Marshall's first stop when she moved to New York. Jonathan Fire*Eater, the pulpy, Ivy League art-rock band that spawned the Walkmen, lived and played here. Spike Jonze, Mike Mills, and Tom Sachs showed their earliest work at Alleged. Sofia Coppola, Chloë, and Harmony Korine were regulars.

"That place was '90s New York to the death," said longtime fixture

Kid America. "It set off mad stupid fuckers trying their hands at making art or being creative . . . It was only ever a good thing."

It was not the downtown New York that Marc knew, but these were the kids he wanted to reach.

In 1992, Marc Jacobs was consumed by his newest collection. He'd pinned Corinne's photos of Kate Moss from *The Face* to his mood board and was obsessed with Nirvana and the entire grunge movement. His timing was precarious: on Seventh Avenue, a collection like this was progressive, but to the girls he was designing for, it was late, derivative, and unwanted. Grunge was already losing its appeal: It had rapidly gone mainstream, from the dominance of Nirvana and Pearl Jam to the popularity of thrift-store chic to Cameron Crowe's pallid Gen-X rom-com *Singles*. By September, Courtney Love was famous enough to earn a feature in *Vanity Fair*.

In November, the *New York Times* ran a piece called "Grunge: A Success Story," with a sidebar called "A Lexicon of Grunge: Breaking the Code." Megan Jasper, a receptionist at Sub Pop Records, happened to pick up the phone when the reporter called. She supplied the slang.

WACK SLACKS: Old, ripped jeans

FUZZ: Heavy wool sweaters

PLATS: Platform shoes

KICKERS: Heavy boots

SWINGIN' ON THE FLIPPITY-FLOP: Hanging out

BOUND-AND-HAGGED: Staying home on Friday or Saturday night

SCORE: Great

HARSH REALM: Bummer

COB NOBBLER: Loser

DISH: Desirable guy

BLOATED, BIG BAG OF BLOATATION: Drunk

LAMESTAIN: Uncool person

TOM-TOM CLUB: Uncool outsiders

ROCK ON: A happy goodbye

It was all made up, and that was the point: This had been for the misfits, and they weren't looking for anyone to understand. It was reverse snobbery, and it felt justified.

"Finally, Gen X got to say something, and we were finally in positions of power," says Erin Smith, who played in the proto-riot-grrrl group Bratmobile. "Gen X was about not wanting to grow up and not having to, and saying that it was not the baby boomers' culture anymore."

For Marc Jacobs, this was a defining moment, and with his next collection, he sought to distill it and destroy the '80s. "I didn't set out to be some hellion or heretic or rebel," he said. "It was one of the things I felt I did with such a kind of pure, divine integrity. Because it's just what I felt . . . [I] wanted to celebrate what I loved, and what I loved was seeing things that were imperfect to other people . . . I just did what I liked, and put it together in a way that felt contemporary." He took plaid flannel shirts he found for eight dollars on St. Mark's Place and had them shipped off to Italy to be remade in $1,000-a-yard silk. Itchy wool caps from the Salvation Army were remade in slouchy cashmere. Converse and Birkenstock did runs for him in duchesse satin.

He was inspired as well by the indie rock kids too shy to dance at shows, who stared at the floor. "There was also this idea of the shoegazer," he said, "this person who couldn't sort of look up, you know, that's sort of insecure. And I've just felt like I've always felt like that. I never felt like I fit in." Corinne Day's cover shot of Kate for *The Face* was Marc's lodestar. "It felt very empowering at that moment, because Kate was by no means frail and she was by no means fragile. She was a girl who had a lot of great energy and great spirit, and she's intelligent. So looks were deceiving. But I loved the feeling of knowing I wasn't alone."

So when, a few weeks before the collection was to debut, he got a call asking if Sonic Youth could shoot their new video in his show-room, featuring his yet-to-be-seen-collection, Marc said yes.

Sonic Youth was as unfamiliar with him. "We had no knowledge of Marc," says singer and guitarist Kim Gordon. "It was really coinciden-tal that he was doing the grunge collection." Their video concept was in line with Marc's feeling: For the model walking the runway naked, "we wanted a real girl," Gordon says. "We didn't want a model." Gordon, whose good friend Daisy von Furth was working with *Sassy* magazine, asked a couple of the fashion editors if they had any names, and one of them suggested an intern named Chloë Sevigny, who had sloe eyes, a large nose, and a bowl cut. She wore denim jumpsuits and button-up shirts from thrift shops. Marc loved her look.

"A lot of people who don't consider themselves 'fashion people' end up being so stylish, because they deliberately go out of their way to avoid what is fashionable at the moment," Marc said. "And in doing so, they create the next fashion. Someone like Chloë is so perfect as an example."

Marc showed the grunge collection in November 1992. Christy Turlington, Helena Christensen, and Carla Bruni walked in that show, but so did Kate Moss, and she was the only one who looked comfort-able in bedraggled hair and little makeup. Marc was frantic, all self-doubt and anticipation.

"He would just sit backstage and knock back drinks, he was so nervous," says his frequent DJ, Anita Sarko. "Champagne. I remem-ber him crawling on his belly, on his hands and knees, over the stage, going, 'Anna, was it okay?'"

Anna Wintour loved Marc, always had; she'd had Steven Meisel shoot Kristen McMenamy and Naomi Campbell in the clothes for a ten-page editorial, including a beatific portrait of Marc and an essay by Sub Pop founder Jonathan Poneman called "Grunge & Glory." But Wintour was the only member of the fashion press to back that collection.

Marc was castigated. The minute grunge showed up on Top 40 radio and in multiplexes and fashion magazines and Urban Outfitters, it was over, and even though Anna Sui and Christian Francis Roth had shown similar collections that season, the press accused Marc of killing the movement and lacking a true understanding of the industry. In essence, they were calling his work ugly and stupid.

"Grunge is anathema to fashion," said critic Cathy Horyn, "and for a major Seventh Avenue fashion house to put out that kind of statement at that kind of price point is ridiculous. Had there been more irony in the way he styled or designed the clothes . . . but it was done with such straightforward zeal to be hip and relevant, to be grunge. That was the turn-off for me."

"Punk was anti-fashion," said *Details* editor James Truman. "It made a statement. Grunge is about not making a statement, which is why it's crazy for it to become a fashion statement."

"Grunge: 1992–1993, R.I.P.," said *New York* magazine. "Grunge has run its course . . . For many, Marc Jacobs' grunge fashion collection was the final shove. Suddenly, Bergdorf Goodman was asking $275 for Jacobs' flannel-short prints on rayon shirts; his wool ski caps went for $175. Which makes it easy to understand why the rock-and-roll community that inspired the movement has turned its back."

"By the time you see [a trend] in Kmart, it can be three years [after the catwalk]," said Walter Thomas, then creative director at J.Crew. "The difference with grunge was that it was already for sale at Kmart."

Jacobs attempted a tribute but was accused of cannibalization. Within months he was very publicly fired from Perry Ellis. "You don't know what to do," said his business partner, Robert Duffy. "It made me feel very insecure, because I thought the grunge show was the best thing we'd ever done. When the press came out, the people at Perry Ellis were like, 'You people are idiots, you don't know what you're doing.'"

That year Kurt Cobain was photographed yawning, holding his baby daughter Frances Bean, and wearing a black T-shirt that read "Grunge Is Dead."

"Marc sent me and Kurt his Perry Ellis grunge collection," Courtney Love said. "Do you know what we did with it? We burned it."

## CHAPTER 10

# A NICE GIRL FROM CROYDON

DESPITE HER RAPID ASCENT, it took Kate quite some time to believe that she was beautiful.

She didn't have the elegance and sense of remove exemplified by Naomi, Christy, Linda, and Cindy. But that wasn't where the culture was going in 1992. Kate broke open the door for other girls who before would have been too odd or too ugly: Ève Salvail, with her shaved, tattooed head; Stella Tennant and her avian features; Kristin McMenamy, hard-looking, eyebrowless, more masculine than feminine; and Chloë Sevigny and Sofia Coppola, non-models with sleepy eyes and disproportionate features.

"I think Corinne actually helped Kate come to terms with the fact that she wasn't like those models, but it wasn't not beautiful," says Neil Moodie, who got his big break as a hairstylist with Corinne in the early '90s. "Corinne always seemed to find beauty in people that weren't obviously beautiful. She started taking the pictures she did to prove a point, really; to go, 'Well, there's beauty in lots of people. It's not just one type that should be in a fashion magazine."

Corinne was equally interested in derelict settings, what Kate called that Lou Reed thing, "that whole glamorizing the squat, white-and-black and sparse and thin, and girls with dark eyes." Corinne's bibles were Larry Clark's *Tulsa* and Nan Goldin's *The Ballad of Sexual Dependency*, two explicit chronicles of generational self-abuse. Here were young people in their own filth, pissing, masturbating, shooting up, and having sex. Corinne lifted these tableaux and administered the ultimate perversion: She made them fashionable. Her sets were barely furnished living rooms and bedrooms with flat light, exposed wiring, peeling wallpaper, and industrial carpet scraped with cigarette burns. Her models looked wan and weak, yet she refused to acknowledge the overtones of hard drug use. "I wanted the ordinary person to see real life in those pages," she said.

Corinne loved the outlaw, and liked to see herself as one, telling her friends that her dad was in jail and she rarely saw her mom. "She was very sad about it," says Ally Coker, Corinne's childhood best friend. "She always knew the truth."

By 1993, Corinne Day had been hired to shoot editorials for *Elle UK* and *i-D*, ads for Barneys, and the first Miu Miu campaign. She and Melanie Ward were profiled by *Interview* magazine that January, photographed with Kate. They expounded on their fashion philosophy.

"You have to take things from the past and make them into the present," Corrine said. She hated literal interpretations and fidelity to eras: "Just because you've got a 1960s top doesn't mean you have to put on a pair of platforms and false eyelashes," Corinne said. She and Melanie were among the first to jumble high and low.

Despite the attention, Corinne was bitter that Calvin Klein hadn't hired her for the Kate campaign. "It was that Kate looked like how Kate would look when Corinne photographed her," Neil Moodie says. She felt abandoned: Moodie, Melanie, James Brown, Mario Sorrenti—all had gone off to New York City, hired for major publications and campaigns, leaving her behind in London.

But Kate was still around, and the two had so much currency that when British *Vogue* commissioned a lingerie shoot, Corinne had creative control. She shot in Kate's London apartment, staged to look like Corinne's Brewer Street flat: modest and cold, with white walls and gray carpet, a mattress on the floor, a lank white top on a wire hanger near the windowsill.

"Under-exposure" ran as a seven-page editorial in the June 1993 issue, and it just about killed Corinne's career. Kate had been crying that day after a fight with her boyfriend, and Corinne exploited the juxtaposition of distress and seduction: She styled Kate in shrunken cotton tanks and silk underwear, some of it from a sex shop on Brewer Street. Kate appeared wrapped in a flat synthetic comforter; splayed on the floor, shot from above, looking like an overdose; silhouetted by a string of multicolored Christmas lights, wearing a thin pink tank and lace underwear, her frame particularly attenuated. "We thought, 'Let's do something showing how we all wear our underwear when we're hanging around the bedroom,'" said Cathy Kasterine, stylist on the shoot. "In the context of fashion at the time, and certainly at *Vogue*, it was unheard of."

In its wake, *People* magazine ran a feature called "How Thin Is Too Thin?" suggesting that Moss—"[who] looks as if a strong blast from a blow dryer could waft her away"—was responsible for the uptick in anorexic and bulimic teenage girls. Susan Faludi said Moss was undermining thirty years of feminism, that her body represented "a man's fantasy of shrinking a woman down to a manageable size." A counselor at an eating disorder facility in Connecticut said, "I wouldn't say Kate Moss causes anorexia, but I had an anorexic in here yesterday who said she wanted to look like Kate Moss."

"Hideous and tragic," said the editor of British *Cosmopolitan*. "I believe they can only appeal to the pedophile market. If I had a daughter who looked like that, I would take her to see a doctor." "Extremely close to perversion in their appeal," said the *Independent*, assailing Corinne for her "fascination with the freakish and the squalid."

"It wasn't very *Vogue*, I suppose," Kate said later. "It was very Corinne." Kate, Corinne, and Kasterine believed that the only subversive element was Kate's boyish figure.

"For a beautiful young girl like Kate to appear in such a raw way was: Who is this thin girl?" Kasterine said. "She has no boobs; she has no hips. I think that was the cherry on the cake of people's reaction against grunge as a movement."

Like Marc's grunge collection, Corinne's "Under-exposure" spread was rejected by the press, her peers, and popular culture. Today, both are considered among the most pivotal fashion moments of the 1990s. "It seemed strange to object to this kind of thing rather than the usual kind of photos with all the makeup, the padded bras, all the artifice," British *Vogue* editor in chief Alexandra Shulman later said. She called Corinne "a photographer of huge talent and integrity . . . she could capture raw beauty like few others."

Meanwhile, Anna Wintour asked to borrow shots Corinne had taken of model Rosemary Ferguson in the Brewer Street loft. Ferguson was another Corinne discovery: lithe, tall, cropped dark hair. She had an androgynous beauty that was more feminine than Salvail's or McMenamy's, and Corinne had a crush. "It was really strange, the way I felt about her," she said. These images of Rosemary were more overt than anything Corinne had done: She looked glassy-eyed and high.

"I thought, 'Oh man, maybe I'm going to change things at American *Vogue*,'" Corinne said. Her shots of Rosemary ran in an October 1993 story called "The Lost Youth," alongside documentary photos of strung-out teenagers taken by Larry Clark. The *New York Times* ran a spread condemning Corinne's work. She thought Rosemary would never talk to her again.

She didn't lose Rosemary, but she did lose Kate, who was advised by her agent, Sarah Doukas, to disassociate herself immediately.

Kate took that advice. Melanie Ward and James Brown also cut ties.

"James wanted to break away from that too, because he was involved in that shoot," says Neil Moodie. "He and Kate were such tight friends that he felt it would tarnish his career."

It wasn't just the controversy. Corinne's mood swings and her constant conflict with editors and art directors made her burdensome. "She would occasionally get quite angry about stuff without quite realizing it was happening," Moodie says. "She was a bit erratic in her thinking."

Meanwhile Ward, who had worked on the Calvin Klein campaign with Kate, was hired by Austrian designer Helmut Lang in 1992, and just a few years later was named an editor at *Harper's Bazaar*. While she and their friends were moving up, Corinne kept sabotaging herself, and Ward was disturbed by the darkness. "Corinne started to live a certain lifestyle," Ward says. "You really have to go deep into a certain world to document it, and that's the path that Corinne took."

Kate's loss was the most hurtful.

"It was very difficult for Corinne," says Mark Szaszy. He doesn't recall Kate and Corinne ever having a conversation about it. Corinne would just say, "You try to book her, and you can't."

Corinne told everyone she rejected Kate, not the other way around, and that things changed while working on "Under-exposure." "Halfway through the shoot," Corinne said, "I realized it wasn't fun for her anymore, and that she was no longer my best friend but had become a model. She hadn't realized how beautiful she was. And when she did, I found I didn't think her beautiful anymore."

Kate knew that breaking with Corinne was necessary, yet a part of her still wanted to be just a nice girl from Croydon. When she went home that Christmas and stopped by her local pub, the Blue Anchor, she realized that was impossible. Many of her old friends had other plans; some of the boys she'd gone to school with talked to the press, amazed that the plain Kate Moss was now a supermodel. Patrons at the Blue Anchor made snide remarks and turned their backs.

"She did feel kind of lonely," said Christy Turlington who, with Naomi Campbell, looked after Kate. "She went from being this little kid to being this creature."

It was what Kate wanted, but it was discombobulating. It was clear that she wasn't a novelty or a fad but, at twenty, might have longevity. She had been named the face of YSL Opium. She'd walked for Galliano and Marc Jacobs, and had appeared on the March 1993 cover of British *Vogue*, shot by Corinne Day; in 2010, she called it her favorite *Vogue* cover. She was about to be shot by Herb Ritts for the Pirelli calendar, a coronation. When Calvin Klein invited her to attend the thirteenth annual CFDA Awards with him, he was acknowledging that Kate's contribution helped save his house: In June, after buying out David Geffen, Klein reported double-digit growth in his jeans and CK divisions. And he took credit for shifting mainstream standards of beauty.

"People are saying now, 'The supermodel thing is over,'" Klein said. "I think I've brought a whole new crop of women to the runway. I was so bored seeing every one of the same supermodels come down the runway all the time, so I went out and found Amber [Valletta] and Kate and all of these new models. I mean, they weren't really doing anything, and I presented them as a whole new image. Then all of a sudden all of the magazines were latching on to them, and they became this waif thing."

After the CFDA Awards in 1994, Kate and a small group headed to Café Tabac, a chic celebrity hangout in the East Village. It was there she met Johnny Depp, who she'd been obsessing over for months. They had a drink, did some coke, and then went back to his hotel room, where they holed up the next day through a snowstorm.

"I knew from the first moment that we talked that we were going to be together," she said.

Kate and Johnny had eleven years between them but much in common. Both came from broken homes. Both had ravenous appetites for alcohol, drugs, cigarettes, sex. Both cultivated an arid cool: Kate was the accidental supermodel, Depp the punk-rock Beat poet who just happened to become a movie star. Both wore their staggering beauty with disinterest, even as their attempts to mar it with greasy hair and bad habits only underscored its imperviousness.

By the time Kate met Johnny, he had been divorced from his first wife and engaged three more times, to the actresses Jennifer Grey, Sherilyn Fenn, and Winona Ryder, and had just altered his famous "Winona Forever" tattoo to "Wino Forever." Depp was deep into booze and drugs, and his L.A. nightclub, the Viper Room, was his personal clubhouse, a space where celebrities could party with abandon, where it was rumored that Depp and his friends could watch knowing patrons having sex though a one-way mirror. The Viper Room's debauchery was a well-kept secret until Halloween night, 1993, when the actor River Phoenix collapsed outside the club and died on the sidewalk.

Phoenix was twenty-three, and his death, from an overdose of cocaine and heroin, felt inconceivable. He'd been a vocal vegetarian, pacifist, and social activist, one of the more seemingly gentle figures of his generation. In a pre-TMZ, pre-Twitter world, a young star like Phoenix could be well protected, his struggles with alcohol and drugs, bisexuality and suicidal impulses kept quiet. He'd say to his friends, "What would those twelve-year-old girls with a picture of me over their bed think if they knew?"

Depp could have said the same thing. When law enforcement and the media began looking into the Viper Room, Depp—who publicized his friendships with heroes Keith Richards and Hunter S. Thompson—expressed moral indignation. "When River passed away, it happened to be at my club," he said. "Now, that's very tragic, very sad, but they made it into a fiasco of lies to sell fucking magazines.

They said he was doing drugs in my club, that I allow people to do drugs in my club. What a ridiculous fucking thought!"

The headline-generating Depp-Moss romance continued apace, with Depp throwing Kate a private twenty-first-birthday party at the Viper Room a year later, interrupted by the cocaine overdose of another friend, actor Jason Donovan. After INXS frontman Michael Hutchence frisked him for contraband, Donovan was taken to the hospital.

Kate and Johnny were the chicest, druggiest couple since Keith Richards and Anita Pallenberg, the epitome of cool in a *Trainspotting* culture. But Kate was often on edge with Johnny, afraid of his moods yet more afraid he'd leave her. She overlooked a lot, including one night in the presidential suite at New York City's Mark Hotel. The cops were called and found Kate sitting amid the wreckage; Depp was arrested for causing nearly $10,000 in damage to a $2,200-a-night room, but even his perp walk was the height of grunge chic: There he was in low-slung blue jeans, a grubby white T-shirt, a brown jacket, and a green knit cap pulled over long, lanky hair, sunglasses on. "Johnny invented grunge," director John Waters said. "He looked good under arrest."

Depp was held in three different jail cells and attended to by a string of female cops in all of them. Woody Allen later memorialized the incident in 1998's *Celebrity*, with Leonardo DiCaprio and Charlize Theron standing in for Johnny and Kate.

Not everyone got the appeal. Anna Sui recalls going over to Kate's apartment in the Village for a small after-party, Johnny ignoring Kate. "He was always in the corner, with his guy friends," Sui says. "I think we were just, like, the fashion people or something."

Just as she didn't feel equal to her fellow supermodels, Kate didn't feel worthy of Depp. She did everything he told her to; suddenly, the girl who'd last read *The Celestine Prophecy* was reading the Beats and trying to pronounce "Kerouac" to reporters. "It must make you feel secure if you know what you really want to do," she said. "I want to find something I really love, because I don't love modeling. I've got all these people around who are so passionate about what they do. I envy them . . . Fashion's not satisfying to me at all. You can't change the world through fashion because the average person doesn't look at fashion pictures."

She had no idea how revolutionary she already was.

CHAPTER 11

# FASHION PEOPLE
# HAVEN'T GOT ANY BRAINS

ALEXANDER MCQUEEN SAW THE fashion establishment the same way Corinne Day did: They both thought it was ridiculous; they wanted not to be accepted, but to be recognized as geniuses; they both wanted things done their way; and they both got a giant charge out of tossing off versions of one sentiment: Fuck off.

"It was about protecting himself," says McQueen's ex-boyfriend Andrew Groves. The tension between elegance and vulgarity in McQueen's clothes reflected his binary nature. "He could be incredibly generous on one hand and absolutely brutal on another," says Chris Bird, a friend through much of the 1990s. To Bird, McQueen reminded him of the artist Francis Bacon: the chronic deformation of beauty, the chain-smoking and substance abuse, the tug toward rough trade, the meanness balanced by tenderness. "That's what was so difficult about him as a character," Bird says. "These contradictions."

There was the Algerian woman, an illegal immigrant, who early on worked for McQueen as a pattern cutter. He paid her a pittance, yet she was so devoted she worked overtime, staying round the clock as a show approached. "As soon as he had to start filing for tax and could take the cling wrap off his face because he wasn't claiming dole money anymore, he got rid of her," Bird says. "He'd invite her to shows and give her standing room, the lowest in the pecking order. She sent him Christmas cards, and he ripped them up."

With Isabella Blow, McQueen veered from devotion to disdain. They'd bond over their childhood traumas; then he'd turn around and complain about her dependence on him for love, dresses, money, credit. He took cash from actor Rupert Everett to make a suit and never did it. He'd see a rival in the pub and, as one friend says, "it was ashtrays at dawn."

"He got away with a lot," Bird says. "He could be really nasty, really rude to people, and he got away with it because of who he was. And he could be gregarious and loud and boisterous and good fun. But it was like walking on eggshells."

In the fall of 1994, McQueen was living with Andrew Groves at the flat on London's Elizabeth Street loaned to him by Blow. She was at a low point. Her disapproving father, who considered *Tatler*, where she once worked, "a magazine for drug dealers," had died the year before. He left Issie with only £5,000, the same amount her grandmother had left the help. Whenever Issie was upset, she'd run right over to McQueen. She was drawn to him as to no one else, not even her husband.

"It was an odd relationship," Groves says. "I remember at Elizabeth Street, she'd come by and say, 'Oh, I found out I can't have children, I'm infertile.' She came round when she found out she'd been disinherited. She didn't know how to cope with these things."

As long as she was in a position to help McQueen, she knew she could control the relationship. Issie channeled her maternal longings through her protégés, but for McQueen, who already had a close relationship with his mother, Issie's attention could be smothering.

She knew it: "As my therapist says, the umbilical cord has a price tag on it."

\*       \*       \*

By now, McQueen had conscripted his friend and former classmate Simon Ungless to design prints for his next collection. Ungless promptly stole fabric from the cupboards at Central Saint Martins. McQueen also hired Katy England, a stylist who was working at the new fashion and culture magazine *Dazed & Confused*. She, too, was informed by the youth culture of London, by the raves and shoegazers, the squats and loft parties. She was younger than Issie in every way.

As a student, McQueen had written a fan letter to the set designer Simon Costin, and in turn, Costin asked if McQueen would let him build sets for his next collection. McQueen had no budget and Costin was happy to work for free, so that was that. This collection was inspired by McQueen's amateur ornithology and fascination with Hitchcock heroines: He called it "The Birds." It was shown in an old warehouse in King's Cross that was used mostly for raves, and the set was sparse: Costin slashed the black runway with white stripes, creating the illusion of road. At the last minute, McQueen decided to adorn his models with painted-on tire tracks: fashion roadkill. He thought it was hilarious.

"We literally took the tire off my car and rolled it in the grease that was on the floor and then rolled it on their bodies," said Trino Verkade, his longtime assistant. "It was very raw. It was something that you do when you're young and open."

McQueen was growing. He did a new version of the bumster, this one in second-skin black with a plunging backline—the eveningwear of butt cleavage. He showed tight skirts and jackets with nipped-in waists. He hired Mr. Pearl, a young, stunning, expert corset maker, to walk in the show, two decades before gender-bending became commonplace. Mr. Pearl's philosophy of grotesquerie was in line with McQueen's: "In its discipline, corsetry is empowering," said Mr. Pearl, who'd whittled his waist down to eighteen inches. "It is about displacement, moving, arranging, and elongating the vitals."

McQueen also sent out one model in an open silver lamé jacket and lace underwear, another wrapped in cling film and bound with string.

Among those in attendance at McQueen that London Fashion Week was Barbara Weiser, Marc Jacobs's old champion at Charivari. "It lacks the kind of inspiration and burning creative spirit I would associate not only with English fashion, but with young people," she said. "It is strange to see so talented a designer committed to the unwearable," said the *New York Times*, while acknowledging that McQueen was "easily the most talked-about designer to be showing this year."

To Simon Ungless, "The Birds" was McQueen finding his voice. "It hit the moment when people were ready for tailoring and modernity, with the sportswear references in the fabrics that predated Prada's nylon range," he said. "The strength of the collection was phenomenal, the slickness of it. It felt like it could have been staged anywhere."

Yet McQueen and Groves were so poor they had to borrow £20 for cab fare to get to the show. When it was over, they packed up the clothes and went to Burger King, where they ordered fries and Cokes and promptly dropped the tray, picking their dinner up off the floor.

Then they went to a café on the corner of Old Compton Street and met with Eo Bocci, the Italian fashion manufacturer. He had just seen the show and told McQueen he wanted to buy 51 percent of his business for £10,000.

"Lee said, 'Fuck off,'" Groves recalls. "It was his usual reaction of: 'You dragged me all the way here to insult me by saying that?' I don't even think it was the money—it was the 51 percent control."

"Alexander knew his worth, and he was right," Philip Treacy says. "He was quite hard-core then. He thought major designers were shit, just useless."

Eventually, they struck a deal: Bocci would license the McQueen name for a few years, and McQueen would finally have some cash flow. He felt that his next show, whatever it might be, would be the last where he could go full-on.

\*     \*     \*

That next collection, 1995's "Highland Rape," was the breakout. It was the apotheosis of every theme McQueen had been working through: cruelty, vulnerability, transgression, sex.

"He was focused on the street," says friend and fellow designer Miguel Adrover. "He had this anger to express himself, to stand up to the industry." McQueen had recently approached Central Saint Martins about teaching a class, and they'd said no. He couldn't understand it. There was such hysteria over this upcoming collection, with McQueen showing for the first time in a tent at London Fashion Week, that students were color-Xeroxing the invitations. On the day of the show, kids were trying to crawl in under the canvas and editors were getting shut out, yet he was living and working in a dismal, low-ceilinged basement flat on Hoxton Square. He had the same conflicted feelings about himself that the fashion world did: He was the future and he was unworthy.

"There's all these things I never knew; he kept things sort of away," says Andrew Groves. "One evening we're in the flat. It's a squat—no TV, no electric key.* And suddenly he says, 'Oh, I've got to go out now. I've got to go meet Princess Diana at the British Fashion Council.' And he wore a dirty shirt that had been on the floor for a week. He was probably embarrassed by it, and that was his way of dealing with it."

McQueen described "Highland Rape" as "the way I'm feeling about my life."

His women were bound in breast-bearing jackets with regal lapels, dresses torn open at the crotch, tartan pieces joined with exaggerated pins. He'd had their thighs smeared with makeup to look as though they were dripping menstrual blood.

Much of the British press accused McQueen of misogyny. "McQueen's new collection . . . [is] a must for every discerning girl's

---

* Tenants prepaid on the key, which would then switch on the electricity.

wardrobe, along with a can of Mace," said the *London Evening Standard*. McQueen professed indignation, saying he was inspired by the English massacre of Scots in the eighteenth century. He also hinted that he was impacted by violence he witnessed as a child. "I saw my own sisters being beaten to a pulp," he said. Even his intimates weren't sure what to believe.

"He always used to go on about that in the press," says Andrew Groves. "But he'd never talk about it. I couldn't tell you how many brothers and sisters he had."

"The charges of misogyny with 'Highland Rape'—there was certainly an amount of backpedaling to say, 'I'm not,'" says longtime friend Chris Bird. "Because he wasn't. He *loved* strong women. He wanted his models to be strong."

Isabella also contributed to "Highland Rape." She believed part of her job was to educate McQueen, and she plied him with fine food and wine and books, schooling him in history and art. She called him "a wild bird with a good silhouette." Designer Julien Macdonald, another Issie protégé, believes "Highland Rape" would not have been as highly realized without her. "Isabella was much more intelligent than he was, and she would always be trying to shove books down his neck," Macdonald says. "Once he decided on a theme, Lee would use his twisted mind and twist it."

"My role is to pass intellectual information on to the designer," Isabella said. But McQueen didn't need her as much as she thought.

Issie wasn't ready to admit it to herself yet, but she was being replaced by Katy England. The more successful McQueen became, the more she feared she would lose him, and so she acted out, demanding free clothes and unlimited attention.

"Everyone gets frustrated and annoyed with me in the office," she said. "I'm sure they find me a complete pain." But she couldn't stop herself.

"Issie feared that all these people she introduced to McQueen would take his love away from her," says Detmar Blow. She was already dealing with an avalanche of loss: Her forty-two-year-old cousin Andrew was mauled to death in Tanzania. Andrew's older brother Simon dropped dead from a heart attack one week after, and within the year, her uncle died from the stress. She'd undergone three rounds of IVF, blaming long-ago abortions for her infertility. She and Detmar had no money, and with Elizabeth Street unfit for living, they were suddenly homeless in London.

The Blows moved in with Philip Treacy, who'd since upgraded to his own flat in Chelsea, for six months. Then they decamped to Detmar's uncle's for two years. Still, says Julien Macdonald, "she'd give Lee everything. They'd be having coffee and sandwiches in the café—there were no fancy restaurants. And she'd just be penniless."

McQueen wasn't much interested in hearing about it, because he was poor too, and if Isabella couldn't manage life, what fault of it was his? Here he was, not far out of Elizabeth Street himself, little old ladies in Texas willing to spend thousands of dollars for one-off pieces that would never go into production while he was living on canned beans.

And then, a few days after "Highland Rape," he got a call from American *Vogue*, wanting one particular piece for editorial.

"That dress cost us seven pounds," Andrew Groves says. "We paid £3 a meter for the fabric and then we paid £1 for the spray paint." Anna Wintour hadn't been to any of McQueen's shows, and McQueen didn't like it. McQueen said American *Vogue* could borrow the dress only if they flew it to New York and back, in its own seat, with an escort. It was a fuck-you and they took it, and the dress was shot by Richard Avedon. "Fashion people haven't got any brains," McQueen said.

## CHAPTER 12

# A HANDBAG THAT COSTS AS MUCH AS A MONTH'S RENT

IT HAD NOTHING TO do with the grunge collection, according to the public line by Perry Ellis International; the women's-wear line hadn't been profitable enough, and Marc was let go. He said he was happy to move on. "It's come at the right time," Marc said. "I think it's time for me to build a company like the company I've been working for in size and scope."

In truth, he was devastated. It was the first time in his career that he'd been rejected. It was his greatest childhood trauma, and it never left him. He'd been anointed as a star from the time he was a teenage boy at Charivari, and in January 1993, one month before his firing, he'd been named Fashion Designer of the Year by the CFDA. Now, approaching thirty, he found his career in crisis. He couldn't cope. "Marc's way of dealing with these problems was to get high," Robert Duffy said. "He wasn't sitting in the negotiations with the Perry Ellis lawyers. He never even met the Perry Ellis lawyers."

"He couldn't find a job," says Diane von Furstenberg, who tried to get him on QVC. "Even they wouldn't pick him up. I was so humiliated for him, so upset. He ate a lot of humble pie."

Marc was worried other designers might eclipse him. Isaac Mizrahi, his superstar classmate at Parsons, had made the cover of *New York* magazine a few years earlier, in October 1990. Dubbed "the great hip hope," he'd not only worked for Perry Ellis but had once been the great man's favorite protégé. Mizrahi pounced.

"If it's so chic to look grungy, then why isn't it chic to eat rotten chicken?" he said. "Now, excuse me, I am offended by people who look ugly. Offended! And some designers are jumping on this bandwagon, trying to make people look ugly. And I think that is *wrong*." During the fall collections in Milan that year, influential fashion critic Suzy Menkes handed out badges stamped "Grunge Is Ghastly."

The *New York Times*, which had recently devoted many column inches to this exciting new trend, joined the backlash and assailed Marc. "His final runway show for Perry Ellis last November was a mess," said writer Rick Marin. "The music—by the alternative bands Sonic Youth, Nirvana, and L7—was loud, aggressive, and to some, overbearing . . . One model even wore a nose ring."

Jacobs sat in his favorite restaurant, Café Luxembourg, and chain-smoked Marlboro Lights while telling Marin that history would prove his grunge collection, with its rejection of '80s contrivance, unassailably right: "Twenty years from now, when people look back at that decade, they're going to remember Joan Collins in *Dynasty* and Vanna White and Nancy Reagan and tell me how beautiful that whole thing is?"

He went on to predict that the '80s would be remembered as "aesthetically appalling," then mocked the number of designers, such as Mizrahi, who were still referencing Jackie O and Audrey Hepburn. "When you ask designers who their icons of style are," he said, "very few give references to a girl who exists today. If you look at Hollywood now, if you look at Julia Roberts or Juliette Lewis or Winona Ryder, maybe they look like they don't wash their hair and wear dresses from thrift shops, so all these purists think they should be wearing couture dresses and feather boas and diamonds from Harry Winston. They don't understand there's a glamour there, too."

There were other designers who felt the same way: Anna Sui, Todd Oldham, downtown New York's Daryl K. Sui, whose company was privately held, emerged unscathed from her own foray into grunge; it helped that she was becoming part of a young Hollywood circle that included the Beastie Boys, Sonic Youth, Spike Jonze, Ione Skye, Vincent Gallo, and Sofia Coppola. Marc wasn't there yet.

Oldham, too, was real competition: A young designer from Texas, he'd moved to the East Village in 1989 and quickly won backing from the Japanese conglomerate Onward Kashiyama, which at various points invested in Sui, Daryl K, and Marc. By 1993, Oldham was a frequent style contributor to *Sassy* magazine and MTV's four-year-old *House of Style*. He was as informed by grunge and indie rock as Marc was, but he had a gentler, more media-friendly presence: You didn't have to be the coolest girl in the room to wear Todd Oldham's stuff.

Still, it was those Lower East Side girls who inspired Oldham too. "That's where my friends were, and that's where they hung out," Oldham says. "It really was the best . . . The world was hungry for new ideas; you could actually have success. I remember so many amazing East Village nuts that would have beautiful moments of big, international success that wouldn't be the same now, because there was an incredible thirst for a new idea."

Wendy Mullin, a Kansan by way of Chicago, was one. She moved to SoHo in 1992 and got a job at Rocks in Your Head, one of the best independent record stores in the city. Mullin began selling her customized guitar straps out of the store to Courtney Love, Sonic Youth's Thurston Moore, and Bikini Kill's Kathleen Hanna. It was a time when a struggling designer who knew enough of the right scenesters could loop into the Lower East Side nexus: Chloë Sevigny and her boyfriend, Harmony Korine, who was working on a screenplay with Larry Clark; Mary Frey, who ran Liquid Sky and married Kate's ex, Mario Sorrenti; Aaron Rose, founder of the Alleged Gallery; Chan Marshall, working on an album under the name Cat Power; graphic artist Mike Mills; Spike Jonze, a photographer who'd worked on Sonic

Youth's "100%" video and started his own skateboarding company, Girl; Jackie Farry, who worked at the International Bar in the East Village by night and was Kurt and Courtney's nanny by day. "It was this organic movement," Mullin says. "It was literally kids hanging out." Twenty years on, fans would tweet to their idols, looking for virtual intimacy; in 1993, a girl like Mullin could walk up to a star like Kim Gordon at a show and say, 'Hey, I hear you're doing a clothing line—do you need help?' " Which Mullin did, and Gordon took.

Not since the 1970s had fashion been so informed by rock 'n' roll: specifically, hip-hop and indie rock. Russell Simmons, who spent the early '90s watching everyone from Karl Lagerfeld at Chanel to Isaac Mizrahi to Tommy Hilfiger to Marky Mark for Calvin Klein pander to the hip-hop crowd, launched his own label, Phat Farm, in 1992. "The clothes were patronizing," Simmons says. He knew there was an underserved market from his earliest days in hip-hop, when he negotiated a million-dollar product-placement deal for Run-D.M.C. The result: 1986's Top 40 crossover smash "My Adidas."

"That changed everything," Simmons says. "We were built out of a rebellion for things that other companies would not deliver. There was a hole in the market you could drive a truck through."

Marc felt the same.

The Beastie Boys were second only to Nirvana at this moment. *Check Your Head*, released in 1992, collapsed the boundaries between indie rock and hip-hop, white and black hipsters, and the Beastie Boys began monetizing their cultural currency. They launched their own record label, Grand Royal, and signed Luscious Jackson, Ben Lee, and Sean Lennon. The founded a magazine by the same name, running stories on the history of the mullet and interviews with Ted Nugent and Kid Rock.

"The magazine and record label was a way to celebrate and name-check fringe culture, to capture the mystique as a place to go," says

Mark Lewman, who edited two issues. "We had this simple ambition of a newsletter, but then we saw a couple of other bands' fanzines and they were just like, 'This is what the band's up to now and this is what they'll be doing,'" said the Beastie Boys' Mike D. "So we made it into a proper magazine." The first issue had a print run of 7,500 and circulation quickly doubled.

Next, the Beastie Boys formed two clothing lines: X-Large for boys, followed by X-Girl. In 1993, they approached Kim Gordon to design for X-Girl, and she asked Daisy von Furth for help.

X-Girl was meant for the Marc Jacobs girl: She was cool but gawky, wanted to look pretty instead of sexy. She aspired to the minimal chic of such nouvelle vague stars as Jean Seberg and Françoise Hardy. She loved prep, skate, indie rock and hip-hop culture in equal measure. She wanted to buy rock tees at her favorite shows but didn't because the cuts were large and boxy, the fabric thick and unyielding: for boys only.

"We were pretty organic about our whole evolution," Gordon says. "X-Girl was a reaction to baggy men's streetwear. We were trying to make clothes that were flattering. For me, the '60s were really strong; my sensibility was more Godard, filmic. Daisy went to prep schools in DC—she brought the whole prep sensibility. That's her."

"I think X-Large and X-Girl were part of this idea in the air, that 'do it yourself' thing," said Mike Mills, who designed the X-Girl logo. "The idea that you could start your own fashion line and you didn't have to go to fashion school . . . There was no shame in that, and you weren't ruining your punk credentials." Both Sonic Youth and the Beastie Boys had headlined Lollapalooza, and "it was this moment where a lot of those bands and a lot of those cultural figures had the power to play on the really big stage and not sell out in any way," Mills said.

Chloë Sevigny was working as the X-Girl fit model, a refugee from the Liquid Sky scene. She had just been the subject of an eight-page profile by Jay McInerney in the *New Yorker*: "Chloë's Scene" was a portrait of the It Girl on the verge, holding forth on Karl Lagerfeld—who "ruined the house of Chanel"—and the supremacy of *The Face* and *i-D*: "The British magazines are much further ahead in terms of what's happening on the street." Chloë was about to star in *Kids*, Larry Clark's contemporaneous feature film about ravers and skate rats on the Lower East Side. McInerney wrote that she'd blown off the chance to shoot with Steven Meisel, preferring to stick with her tribe.

"X-Girl was a little more snobby," Chloë later said. "The Liquid Sky thing was a hippie, kind of raver, free-love whatever, whereas X-Girl was more retro, a little more 'too cool for school.' At Liquid Sky, I had to listen to jungle music all the time and have all these kids bum cigarettes off me. And I really wanted to be across the street listening to Bikini Kill."

For X-Girl, "it was all about being cool and having stuff that other people didn't have," Daisy says. They were inspired by the small French labels A.P.C. and agnés b, which make simple, chic, fitted clothes in high-quality fabrics: the epitome of stealth street luxury.

"At the time, everything was Lycra, and everyone was dressing very '70s—lots of grunge, vests, floppy hats, and corduroy," Daisy said. "And the initial thing was sort of rejecting that. We were just like, 'Oh my God, can we get a stiff dress with a zipper up the back?' We wanted things to be fresh and new and clean again."

While Kim Gordon and Chloë Sevigny were embraced as fashion stars for the downtown set, Marc Jacobs was packing up his offices at Perry Ellis, nearly six months after his firing. Duffy, who wrangled partial backing from Perry Ellis in exit negotiations, took out a second mortgage to finance their new venture, Marc Jacobs International Company, L.P.—a gamble given Marc's volatility. They moved where they belonged: downtown, to Spring Street, both still reeling. Duffy couldn't believe what his job had become: He'd spent most of his time at Perry Ellis covering up Marc's drug habit. "I thought it would be the worst thing for our careers if people knew," Duffy said. "If people knew! People in this industry were doing it with him!" Marc's humiliation and self-pity aggravated his drug use.

He decided to skip a season and gather his thoughts. He partied hard, had late dinners at Café Luxembourg, plotted his next move. His depression turned to anger, and it fueled him. A friend remembers going to dinner with Marc during that time and Marc plotting his revenge: "I'm going to make a handbag that costs as much as one month's rent," he said, "and girls won't care. They're going to buy it."

## CHAPTER 13

# COOL BRITANNIA

FOR EVERY YOUNG GIRL who felt freed by Kate Moss, there were those who felt Kate set an equally impossible standard: How many girls could become as thin as her without developing a drug habit, or by starving themselves? She was considered the true poster child of ectomorphs.

Kate, usually such a sphinx, stood up for herself: She didn't have an eating disorder. "I always used to get teased for being so thin," she said. "They pressurize girls so much into being something that they're not, that society thinks or that the media thinks they should be. If they're pretending to be somebody else, they're not going to be their best."

She was as insecure as anyone, not such a fan of her face. "I never liked it," she later said. "I wasn't the prettiest girl in class. No breasts, short legs, gangly teeth." She asked Fabien Baron if she should get veneers. "She never fixed anything," he said. "She's not perfect at all physically. You have to deal with the little teeth, the crooked legs. She has the mental power to put it forward."

Ever in search of a surrogate family, most especially a mother, Kate leaned most on her hairstylist James Brown, who'd lived with her at

Corinne and Mark's place on Brewer Street; casting director Jess Hallett; Jen Ramey, one of her agents; Fran Cutler, the social-climbing party planner; Oasis's Noel Gallagher and his wife Meg Mathews; rock 'n' roll fairy godmother Marianne Faithfull; socialite Lucie de la Falaise and her husband, Marlon Richards, son of Johnny Depp's good friend Keith.

She felt most drawn to Marlon. "When I met Marlon, we had this weird thing, because he was so uncomfortable in his skin, and so was I," Kate said. "We were very uncomfortable. We bonded immediately."

She trusted Johnny above all. She still felt like an imposter, everyone "so fashion-y, and I was from Croydon." She was still a child in many ways, with her love of disco, Big Macs, and trips to amusement parks. Kate wanted to be with Depp all the time, but he had to work, and when she complained of being lonely and bored in L.A. he'd say, "Well, go shopping then." He advised her not to speak to the press—"never complain, never explain"—but she was also advised to keep her mouth shut by her New York–based publicist, who thought Kate's Croydon accent was as incongruous to her beauty as Mike Tyson's voice was to his strength.

At the same time, Kate was absorbing her new power. She was becoming the face of her generation, the embodiment of what the '90s were shaping up to be: shambolic, adolescent, druggy. A homemade approach to art, photography, fashion, and beauty was on the rise, this generation insisting on authenticity and democracy. Kate was the first true rock 'n' roll supermodel, and her greatest asset was her innate sense of cool.

It was evident from the beginning. Other models on go-sees were dressed head-to-toe in Chanel or Versace or Max Mara, but Kate would be in her drainpipe jeans and Adidas, or a floor-dusting black cotton dress with a denim jacket.

"Kate's look really reflects what has gone on in the music world, and that has influenced fashion," said Anna Sui. "The spirit is less 'look at me, look at me.' The same has happened with clothes."

Kate's personal style was unprecedented, an exhilarating mix of backstage glamour and postmodern minimalism, seemingly within reach for any girl on the street. Her favorite pieces were vintage slips, Mary Jane pumps, little black cocktail dresses, Adidas and Converse, skinny jeans with plain tanks. Her hair was always simple, hanging straight or scraped back in a messy bun; her makeup and jewelry minimal; her nails short and bare. One fashion editor saw Kate around this time in the garden at the Ritz in Paris, after she'd walked in the Yves Saint Laurent show, and in these lush surroundings, here was the fashion world's most privileged urchin, smoking a cigarette in full show makeup, wearing a slouchy black sweater, a long black skirt, and sneakers. She looked chicer than anyone else.

Kate's lo-fi attitude was shrewder than she knew. By 1995, just as Marc had predicted a few years earlier, "supermodel backlash" was in, cited by *Entertainment Weekly* as a larger national obsession than the O. J. verdict. "The pendulum has swung," said Michael Gross, who had just published *Model: The Ugly Business of Beautiful Women*. "Supermodels just got too big for their Manolo Blahnik[s]."

Aaron Spelling's *Models Inc.*, a nighttime soap meant to capitalize on the supermodel craze, premiered to dismal reviews and lasted just one season. Robert Altman's *Pret-a-Portér*, his 1994 spoof of the fashion world, was a commercial flop, grossing less than $6 million in the US. Ford Models' 1995 airing of their Supermodel of the Year competition was such a bomb they didn't try it again.

Actresses and rock stars were replacing models on the covers of fashion magazines. Julia Roberts, Courtney Love, Winona Ryder, Gwen Stefani, Drew Barrymore, Björk, Gwyneth Paltrow—these were all younger, cooler, more relatable and interesting figures than supermodels. That year, when Uma Thurman wore a spare, pale lilac gown to the Academy Awards, "all of a sudden, middle America knows what Prada is," said stylist Elizabeth Saltzman. It was a significant moment for fashion: Before that night, Prada was known only for its plain black nylon backpacks. "When supermodels became part of Hollywood, sneakily, Hollywood became an important part of fashion," Saltzman said. "Supermodels are over—dead, passé perhaps. But movie stars never are going to be."

The supermodels tried valiantly to reinvent themselves, some succeeding better than others. Cindy Crawford, already the singsongy host of MTV's *House of Style*, made a disastrous acting debut in the $30 million action film *Fair Game*, which tanked. "It's not like I was dying to be an actress," she said. Christy Turlington retired from runway work and enrolled at NYU. Naomi Campbell released her first and only album, *Babywoman*, a critical and commercial disaster (except in Japan, where it sold close to one million copies); in her liner notes, she thanked Robert De Niro. Campbell also published *Swan*, a ghostwritten thriller about a supermodel. It received awful reviews, the acclaimed critic Gilbert Adair calling it the realization of Roland Barthes's predicted "death of the author." Campbell shrugged it off, admitting it wasn't her work. "I just did not have time to sit down and write a book," she said.

The concept of "expanding the brand" was erupting, especially among models, with their short shelf lives. Campbell and Turlington, along with Elle Macpherson and Claudia Schiffer, launched the Fashion Café in New York's Rockefeller Center. It was meant to be a franchise in the Planet Hollywood mold, but it hadn't occurred to the investors that most people didn't associate models with food. The Fashion Café was a flop.

Kate kept her head down. She was less inclined to try any of that, despite the scripts that flooded her agent's office, despite her dream of being a rock star. In mid-1994 she had to be convinced to publish a book. Initially, she was approached about doing an autobiography, which was ridiculous: She'd had such a short life, what was there to say? *Kate: The Kate Moss Book* succeeded because Kate sold herself as she was: A model. "It's easy to do other things once you've got a name, but it's hard to get people to . . . take it for what it is, instead of a model doing something else," she said. She contributed a brief forward, opaque as ever. "I don't know why any of this has happened," Kate wrote. "The chain of events that followed has led me to where I am now, and I wouldn't attempt to question any of it, or ask why. It's none of my business."

She was similarly unwilling to explain herself while promoting the book, a task she'd dreaded. "I'm uncomfortable with publicizing myself as a model," she said. "I can only say, over and over again: 'That's what I do,' and let people make fun of me."

Her self-effacement served her well. Just one year later, Kate Moss was an icon in her native England, a Gen-X Marianne for the Brits. The political, economic, and pop-cultural renaissance in London was at its apex in 1996: The election of Tony Blair, the dominance of Britpop and the Young British Artists and the impact Kate's cohort was having in magazines and on the runway all gave rise to a wellspring of national pride known as "Cool Britannia."

There was a through-line from the early work of Corinne Day to what was now happening in British art, literature, music, and film. *Trainspotting*, a propulsive, filthy, real-time chronicle of heroin culture, was the biggest movie in Britain that year. Like *Kids*, *Trainspotting* was that rare thing: a fictional depiction of subterranean youth culture as it really was; unlike *Kids*, it was a critical and commercial success, on par with *Pulp Fiction* as the most revolutionary film of the decade.

Oasis, Blur, Pulp, Suede, and Elastica were sleek and literate, arch and stylish. Collectively slotted as Britpop, these bands were all angles, a stark counterpoint to the sloppiness and waning relevance of grunge. The movement, said Elastica's Justine Frischmann, was "a manifesto for the return of Britishness." And no single was an unlikelier hit than Pulp's "Common People," which savaged the culture's current fascination with the poor, epitomized by Marc Jacobs's grunge collection: "Laugh along with the common people / Laugh along even though they're laughing at you / and the stupid things that you do / because you think that poor is cool." That the song referenced Central Saint Martins College says it all: The machinery behind fashion was becoming mainstream.

*Newsweek* ran a cover story called "London Rules," in 1996, followed by a "Cool Britannia" insert in *Vanity Fair* in 1997. Oasis's Liam Gallagher and his then wife, Patsy Kensit, made the UK edition's cover; also profiled were Blur's Graham Coxon, Damien Hirst, emerging designer Stella McCartney, and Sophie Dahl, granddaughter of Roald and the latest Issie discovery. Dahl was an unlikely model for the moment, blond, blue-eyed, and voluptuous. "A great big blow-up doll," Issie said, and as ever, her instincts proved right: Dahl modeled for McQueen and Versace and was chosen by Tom Ford as the face of YSL Opium. "We all just thought she was a fat teenager," said Plum Sykes.

Issie and McQueen got over their latest rupture to pose for this issue of *Vanity Fair* and were shot on the grounds of Hedingham Castle by David LaChapelle. McQueen was in a corset and red leather gloves, wielding a torch and looking like a madman. Issie was behind him, hoisting his floor-length skirt, and the message was clear: She was in service to him.

And, of course, shot in a knee-length navy blue skirt, black Mary Janes, and a Union Jack sweater, there was Kate Moss. In retrospect, it's clear who should've been on the cover of the UK issue: Kate led the Brit Pack. She was the first supermodel who was coming of age with the Internet, the first one girls looked to off the runway: What Kate wore, whether on the street or the red carpet, was much cooler

# IN THE BEGINNING THERE
# WERE THREE MISFIT GENIUSES . . .

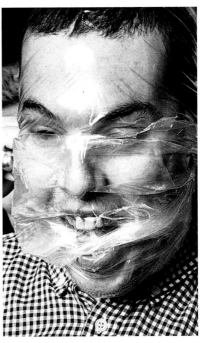

A jubilant Marc Jacobs celebrates his second runway show for Sketchbook in April 1985. The *New York Times* lauds his designs as "whimsical" and infused with a "childlike grace"; by October, Sketchbook is shuttered and Marc is out of a job. © *George Chinsee/Condé Nast*

Lee Alexander McQueen stayed on the dole as long as he could, and was often photographed with his face wrapped in cling film so the government wouldn't catch on—but he also hated the way he looked, and eventually got plastic surgery. © *Stephen Callaghan/Rex USA*

The unlikeliest supermodel since Twiggy: in October 1993, a nonchalant nineteen-year-old Kate Moss makes the rounds during Fashion Week in Milan, drinking, chain-smoking, and casually dispensing her idiosyncratic glamour. © *Gamblin /Paris Match/Getty Images*

ABOVE: Before he ever knew Kate Moss, and before Kate ever knew Johnny Depp, Marc Jacobs lounges and smokes at the April 1990 after-party for Depp's film *Cry-Baby*. © *Ron Galella/Getty Images*

TOP RIGHT: In 1990, two years in as the head designer at legendary American sportswear label Perry Ellis—and the youngest ever honored with the Council of Fashion Designers of America's award for New Fashion Talent— Marc Jacobs poses with a dotty friend at home. © *George Chinsee/Condé Nast*

Just two years away from creating the collection that revolutionized fashion, Marc, here with a Perry Ellis model in 1990, struggles to inject youth and verve into an ailing house. © *Thomas Iannaccone/Condé Nast*

Kate and Marc, seen here in 1998, began the decade as two fashion-world misfits, bound by deep insecurity, troubled child-hoods, and a hard-core love of the party.
© *Steve Wood/Rex USA*

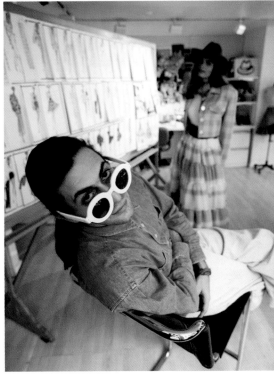

Cool, casual, and thoroughly unpretentious: Marc, here in his Perry Ellis studio in 1991, presented himself as a new kind of American designer in stark counterpoint to Bill Blass, Donna Karan, and the aging establishment.
© *David Turner/Condé Nast Publications*

Marc, with his muse and sometime-model Sofia Coppola, herself a standard-bearer of a new kind of beauty, at a Louis Vuitton event in 1999. © *Rex USA*

Marc backstage with models at his infamous 1992 grunge collection, which he's called his favorite of all time. It was a critical and commercial disaster and got him fired from Perry Ellis; today, it's considered the most influential American collection of the 1990s. © *Kyle Ericksen /Condé Nast*

Marc decides to yield to commercialism and in 1996 presents the counterpoint to grunge: his so-called glam collection, which intrigued execs at Louis Vuitton. Kate Moss loved this gold gown so much she ran around town in it after the show. © *Robert Mitra/Condé Nast*

Humbled by his first-ever critical drubbing and unsure of his future, a somber Marc refuses to capitulate, his white sneakers a small note of rebellion. © *Stephen Sullivan/Condé Nast*

Frustrated with Vuitton execs, Marc decides to follow his own impulses and hires Stephen Sprouse, a longtime hero, to design a graffiti-inspired logo for handbags. The Sprouse collaboration was an unprecedented success for Vuitton, and the embrace of street culture by luxury conglomerates was complete. © *Dimitrios Kambouris/Getty Images*

Hired to reinvent the French luxury house Louis Vuitton in 1997, Marc spent nearly a year fighting with executives over the direction of the brand. When he finally showed in 1998, he knew his first collection had failed to impress. © *Pierre Verdy/Getty Images*

Wrung out from struggles with drugs and alcohol, a post-rehab Marc Jacobs stops caring: he gains weight, lets his hair go greasy and long, and starts smoking up to two packs a day. © *George Chinsee /Condé Nast*

# THE FACE

## THE 3RD SUMMER OF LOVE

Stone Roses on
Spike Island,
an A-Z of the
new bands, Daisy
Age fashion,
Hendrix and
psychedelia

'Kiss my butt!'
Sandra on
Madonna

Prince in
Minneapolis:
tour preview

JOHN WATERS / MICKEY ROURKE / MARSHALL JEFFERSON / TIM ROTH

The shot that changed fashion forever: a teenage Kate Moss on the cover of the 1990 issue of UK style bible *The Face*, shot by her mentor Corinne Day. This image wound up on the walls at Marc Jacobs and Calvin Klein, and went on to demolish prevailing standards of beauty.

A coquettish Kate backstage with boyfriend and photographer Mario Sorrenti at Paris Fashion Week in 1991. © *David Turnley/Corbis*

Quickly adopted by the supermodels she would soon displace: Kate with Linda Evangelista and a partied-out Naomi Campbell in 1993. © *David Mcgough/Time Life Pictures/Getty Images*

A supermodel for the street: Kate, in a shapeless black skirt, denim jacket, and her beloved Adidas, shot in Paris in 1993. © *Geoff Wilkinson/Rex USA*

By 1992, Kate was the new face of Calvin Klein. Her look was in such opposition to the supermodels of the '80s that Kate was accused of promoting heroin use and anorexia. © *Paul Harris/Hulton Archive/Getty Images*

With Naomi Campbell, turning a sheer silver dress into something youthful and modern at a party in London in 1993. © *Richard Young/Rex USA*

The fashion world's most privileged urchin lounges in a luxury hotel in Paris in 1993. © *Geoff Wilkinson/RexUSA*

Kate met Johnny Depp in February 1994, and they became the chicest, druggiest couple since Keith Richards and Anita Pallenberg. When Depp dumped Kate in 1998, she spun out of control. © *Catherine McGann/Getty Images*

Kate quickly became one of the UK's most debauched libertines, often partying with Jude Law's wife, Sadie Frost, and Ron Wood's daughter, Leah. The tabloids dubbed them "The Primrose Hill Set." © *Dave Benett/Getty Images*

Kate, who long harbored dreams of rock stardom, with idols and fairy godparents Jo and Ronnie Wood, Marianne Faithfull, and Anita Pallenberg in London in 1999. © *Dave Benett/Getty Images*

A genius of counterintuitive couture: Kate's simple gray Cerruti shift dress—a piece any young woman could have worn to the office—was a revolutionary choice for the red carpet at Cannes. *Vogue* deemed it "unforgettable." © *Pool APESTEGUY/Benainous /Duclos/Gamma-Rapho/Getty Images*

While supermodels Christy Turlington, Naomi Campbell, and Shalom Harlow walked in Marc's grunge collection, it was only Kate Moss—slouchy, slight, imperfect—who inhabited its spirit. © *Kyle Ericksen /Condé Nast*

By 1995, Kate Moss was becoming the face of Gen X, and her affect throughout Isaac Mizrahi's behind-the-scenes documentary *Unzipped*—quiet, watchful, a little bit ironic, and a little bit over it—further distinguished her from the diva supermodels in her orbit. © *Everett Collection/Rex USA*

After a near decade-long estrangement, Kate reunites with photographer Corinne Day, who discovered and mentored the young model, at the Face of Fashion private view at the National Portrait Gallery in London in 2007. Corinne, who was suffering from a brain tumor, had only three years to live. © *Dafydd Jones*

Two odd-looking, working-class kids turned arbiters of beauty: Kate—in a sheer dress that recalls her silver sheath from 1993—and McQueen at a charity bash in London in 2004. © *Richard Young/Rex USA*

A typically insouciant Kate at the premiere of *Titanic* in 1997. © *Richard Young/Rex USA*

A tense, wired McQueen poses with his mentor and muse Isabella Blow at a party at Annabel's in 2004. Devoted to each other, yet by then deeply estranged, both were battling depression. © *Retna/Photoshot*

"I don't know if I can survive in fashion without murdering someone": The ever-beleaguered Alexander McQueen in 1999. By then he had been at Givenchy for three years, and was breaking under the stress. © *Michael Birt/Contour by Getty Images*

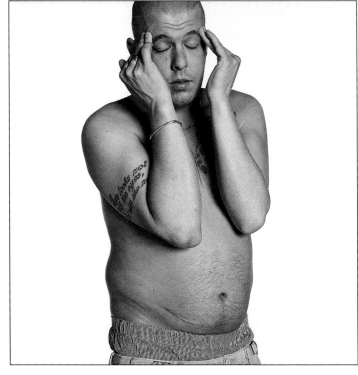

For his London Fashion Week debut in 1993, McQueen sent pantsless models down the runway, sending the fashion press into paroxysms of outrage. It was famously described by the *Independent* as "a catalogue of horrors." © *Brendan Beirne/Rex USA*

When McQueen debuted his "bumsters" in 1994—super low-slung pants that showed the ass crack—he scandalized the industry and sparked the invention of the low-rise jean. Here we have his refined version—the evening wear of butt cleavage. © *Guy Marineau/Condé Nast*

For 1997's "La Poupée," McQueen, ever the provocateur, sent a black model in gold shackles down the runway. He then professed outrage that anyone would interpret it as a reference to slavery—he was inspired, he said, by Hans Bellmer's disfigured dolls. © *Steve Wood/Rex USA*

His breakout show, "Highland Rape," was McQueen working through his favorite themes: oppression, transgression, violence, rage, and lust. He fought back when the press accused him of misogyny, maintaining that the show was only "about England's rape of Scotland." © *Charles Knight/Rex USA*

With 2000's "Voss," McQueen elevated the fashion show to performance art: His models were contained in a box, unable to see out, keening against the glass. Kate Moss opened the show, and it closed with the re-creation of a morbid tableau featuring a masked, overweight model surrounded by moths. © *Giovanni Giannoni /Condé Nast*

Though their friendship was long since destroyed, McQueen was devastated by Isabella Blow's suicide. He attended her funeral on May 15, 2007, and was soon treated by Isabella's psychiatrist for his own depression. © David Hartley/Rex USA

McQueen's suicide in February 2010 stunned the fashion industry, and he was the first designer whose death felt like a larger cultural loss. Kate Moss was among the mourners at St. Paul's Church in London. © Jeremy Selwyn/Evening Standard/Rex USA

Alexander McQueen, here on the runway in October 2009 after "Plato's Atlantis," taking the last curtain call of his life. © *Giovanni Giannoni /Condé Nast*

Marc Jacobs, now the global leader of luxury, was so very happy to be there. © *Martin Scholler/August*

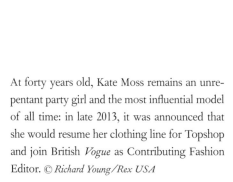

At forty years old, Kate Moss remains an unrepentant party girl and the most influential model of all time: in late 2013, it was announced that she would resume her clothing line for Topshop and join British *Vogue* as Contributing Fashion Editor. © *Richard Young/Rex USA*

to them than what she modeled. Her paparazzi photos were becoming indistinguishable from her editorials.

After Kate ordered twenty-two pieces from Clements Ribeiro—who had done the Union Jack sweater she wore for *VF*—buyers switched their orders to match hers. And after walking for new designer Matthew Williamson in 1997, Kate made the front page of nearly every British tabloid in his pink dress.

Williamson hadn't grasped her power just days before, when they were sitting in his drab apartment, empty McDonald's wrappers strewn all over the floor. If she had a sense of her influence, Kate never let on. Her involvement led to supermodel Helena Christensen also walking in his show, which won him coverage in British *Vogue*, and launched his career. "I realized the importance and impact for an unknown designer of having Kate involved," Williamson said. "I owe a lot to her."

CHAPTER 14

# THOSE SKINNY FASHION
# BITCHES IN THE FRONT ROW

LEE MCQUEEN WAS LOSING himself. Now he wanted to fit in with the fashion people he had once ridiculed: He got his teeth fixed, had liposuction on his stomach, and got the wattle under his chin removed. He took to life at Hilles, Issie and Detmar's country pile, and Issie made sure falcons were on hand for her bird-obsessed protégé. His friends found it all so pretentious: Lee McQueen, the cabdriver's son, pretending to be landed gentry.

They tried to keep him grounded. Andrew Groves got someone to leave a message on McQueen's cell phone, pretending to be an executive at the High Street chain, Topshop, and asking McQueen to do a collection. "I forgot about it, and then two weeks later we're sitting on a bus and Lee says, 'Guess what? Topshop phoned last week and they want to do something,'" Groves says. "It was so mean, so mean."

Groves knew McQueen would soon be gone. "I remember him telling me that someone at British *Vogue* said that we should split up, because he needs to be out with someone else," Groves says. "That it would be better for his career. There were all these hangers-on and people who just wanted to be friends with him because of who he was, and people who just wanted to be friends with me because I was going out with him. It starts overtaking you, and it's like an express train—you can't stop it."

McQueen tried. He was happiest in Soho's gay bars, hanging out with prostitutes, going on and on about the crabs he caught. He'd begun spending time in New York, crashing with his friend Miguel Adrover instead of staying in his usual suite at the Mercer Hotel. McQueen and Adrover would take ecstasy and cruise sex clubs in the Meatpacking District, or go to Bowery Bar, where they'd sometimes see Marc Jacobs—"always more fucked up than Lee," Adrover says—then collapse in Adrover's basement apartment. McQueen was becoming high fashion now, but when Anna Wintour pulled up outside Adrover's one morning to see McQueen, he wouldn't come out. McQueen insisted Wintour come to him and was told by her driver that "Anna don't do pavement." Neither blinked, and Wintour went on her way.

At Hilles, Issie was becoming alarmed. One weekend McQueen came with two women, a couple; the next day he told Issie they'd all just had sex. McQueen also told Detmar and Issie how he liked to be degraded, how one partner made him have sex with another man while he watched—that he didn't like it, but that it played into his sense of victimization. "He was very attracted to people being abused," says Detmar Blow. "He was about victims. That was his love." McQueen had always been interested in darkness and perversion, but it had never defined him: When he was younger, there was much about Lee McQueen that was buoyant and light, sensitive and caring. Those aspects were receding.

Issie was afraid of losing McQueen too. She was increasingly deferential to him, like everyone else in his circle, even as she worried for his sanity. "She was terrified," says Detmar Blow. "She was very concerned about the people he was hanging out with. She'd say to me,

'I can't understand how he can do all this work on so much coke.' He was doing kilos of it."

One weekend, McQueen was sitting around with Detmar and Issie and a few others at Hilles when he suddenly lit into her, saying enough with taking credit for his career. *He* was the designer, not her. "*I* fucking discovered Alexander McQueen," he said.

He could be so cruel. After Issie confided in him her inability to conceive, McQueen later turned to her husband and said, "So, I hear you're shooting blanks, Detmar." He'd see her coming his way in tears, undone by her latest crisis, and say, "Here comes mad old Issie."

"Lee wasn't the nicest person to her, but she loved his genius," says Julien Macdonald. "He was so crazy. One minute he'd be a wonderful person, and the next he'd be somebody else, telling people to piss off."

By now, most of McQueen's friends suspected he was bipolar; in eight years' time, Issie would be diagnosed with the disorder.

"The signs were there all along," Groves says, but the highs and lows were easily blamed on the mad rush to complete and stage collections. Alice Smith also thought McQueen might be bipolar. "He was extremely happy and vivacious sometimes, and others he could hardly speak." She recalls seeing him and Issie sitting together at a Central Saint Martins show right after "Highland Rape." They were in the front row, Lee with his capped teeth and his suntan, Issie by his side, both staring into space. Smith went over to say hi, and McQueen ignored her, not even removing his sunglasses. Humiliated, she walked away. Halfway through the show, she saw McQueen and Isabella get up and walk out, and though Smith had seen McQueen's bad side before, this was disturbing. He knew what his presence meant to these students. "I think he was either doped up, or he had just reached his maximum stress level and couldn't take anything else on board," Smith says. "I remember thinking, 'My God, what's happened to him?'"

\*　　\*　　\*

After "Highland Rape," everything Lee McQueen had been working toward became real. He was named Designer of the Year by the British Fashion Council. He had the most prestigious slot at London Fashion Week, showing last. He had serious backing by Onward Kashiyama. Louis Vuitton Moët Hennessy was circling.

LVMH was formed in 1987 when the fashion and champagne conglomerates merged. Bernard Arnault, the CEO, was most interested in expanding the new company's fashion holdings and reviving its mustiest houses. In July of 1995, Arnault appointed John Galliano as the head designer of Givenchy, making him the first British designer to take over a French house since Charles Frederick Worth in the nineteenth century. Galliano's appointment was a critical and commercial success, and Arnault wanted to move him to Dior. He was considering Alexander McQueen for Givenchy.

McQueen was breaking a little under the stress. His next show, "The Hunger," inspired by the Tony Scott film of the same name, was underwhelming, and he knew it. He and Andrew Groves had broken up, and it had gotten nasty at the end, McQueen flying into terrifying rages. He was seeking relief in hard drugs and anonymous sex and had lost nearly all his old friends. He had this fancy new circle—the socialite Annabelle Rothschild, drum 'n' bass star Goldie, Naomi Campbell, Kate Moss—but the party was the bond. Hardly anyone came backstage after that show, and he was overheard saying to himself, "That was the end of the old, reckless McQueen."

After her last encounter with McQueen, Alice Smith was surprised when he invited her to a gathering. "Come to my party, loads of Charlie," the invite read. Smith showed up, and Katy England was there, but no Isabella and hardly anyone else, maybe fifteen people in Annabelle's cavernous Notting Hill town house. McQueen spent most of the night doing coke in the bathroom with Goldie, and when he was out in the living room, the few friends who'd shown up were dancing strenuously, trying way too hard to have fun. He couldn't hide his disgust.

"I remember going up to him and saying, 'Are you all right?' And he said, 'I'm fine, I'm fine,' and he made it clear he was not going to be talking to me about whatever was going on," Smith says. "He just got black moods, and he couldn't shake them off."

The same was true of Isabella. She'd been at loose ends since fall of 1994, when British *Vogue* sidelined her before sacking her: She was far too mercurial and extravagant and had run up the budget on the now-famous "London Babes" shoot to nearly £80,000. She felt useless. "She would say, 'I'm so unhappy, I'm so unhappy,'" said Plum Sykes. "And I'd say, 'But what about Detmar? What about this fabulous thousand-acre estate? What about your gorgeous flat in town?' And she'd say, 'But Plum, I haven't got a child.'" She'd go by Philip Treacy's studio and sing her lament: "She would come to visit me and say, 'You can make hats, and I can't do anything.'"

Isabella kept throwing herself at McQueen, and bullied the esteemed fashion director Michael Roberts, hired by the *New Yorker* in 1996, to see a show. "I have to admit, I didn't get it," said Roberts, who found the entire production "chaotic, damp, and smelly" and the designer himself deeply un-chic, "tongue-tied and chubby." She found another young protégé, a charming, good-looking Welsh boy nimble with knits. As with Philip Treacy, she promptly brought Julien Macdonald around to McQueen and insisted he be hired. McQueen told Macdonald he had a bag of dog hair underneath his desk, and could he knit a sweater out of that? Macdonald said absolutely not, that was disgusting. He was hired. He received no salary but was paid in clothes.

He might have been young and inexperienced, but Macdonald was perceptive. Isabella, he thought, "was living her life through Philip Treacy." She loved Lee most of all, and he often treated her like shit, "and she would take it." Isabella got her revenge, barging backstage right before a show, demanding hair and makeup, calling McQueen's headquarters over and over and over until they loaned her pieces that she never returned.

"We used to say that the press office at McQueen deserves a medal," Treacy says.

To the fashion press, Issie and McQueen still presented themselves as inseparable, the muse and the mastermind. And McQueen did love her. She was his most articulate ambassador, explaining his point of view as he never could. "What attracted me to Alexander," she said in 1996, "is the way he takes ideas from the past and sabotages them with his cut to make them thoroughly new and in the context of today. It is the complexity and severity of his approach to cut that makes him so modern. He is like a Peeping Tom in the way he slits and stabs at fabric to explore all the erogenous zones of the body."

Lovers without the sex. "Dante," his next show, would be dedicated to her.

After revisiting his core themes in the lackluster "Hunger" collection, McQueen needed to show true artistry. The UK press had gone from outrage to boredom. "His ideas appear too wrapped up in his angry young man pose," said the London *Times*. "If McQueen could only bring himself to curb some of his more childish tantrums," said the *Guardian*, " . . . we might see the stuff of greatness." He wanted the job at Givenchy, and declared himself a convert to luxury. "I think people want that now," he said. "They don't want to look as though they bought all their clothes in a thrift shop."

"Dante" was his most ominous, seductive show yet. His woman could no longer be interpreted as a victim; she was a predator, lascivious and lethal. McQueen referenced the tintype porn and religious iconography of Joel-Peter Witkin, sheathing his models in military coats and corsetry, their pallid faces slashed with crimson lipstick. He sent Stella Tennant down the runway with a hooded falcon on her arm. He crowned one model with a pair of Philip Treacy's antlers and wrapped another's head in lace, a skeleton claw covering her mouth.

Writing in the *New York Times*, Amy Spindler described "Dante" as a combination of "blueblood and hot blood." McQueen, she said, "brought the excitement, edge, and theatrics he is known for, but added a wonderful fourth element for the first time: maturity."

To a point: McQueen had seated a skeleton front row, and while the press wondered what McQueen was trying to say about beauty, superficiality, and the existential point of fashion itself, they missed the obvious, says Simon Costin: "His words were: 'Those skinny fashion bitches in the front row.'"

CHAPTER 15

# THE DECADE OF
# THE DILETTANTE

MARC JACOBS WASN'T WORRIED about Alexander McQueen: They trafficked in different terrain. As far as he was concerned, he had two major rivals: Isaac Mizrahi and Tom Ford.

Mizrahi was so much like Marc, a witty, hyper-verbal, chain-smoking New York Jew, as much a frustrated performer as a gifted designer. Yet while Jacobs floundered, Mizrahi had become a mainstream star.

The 1995 documentary *Unzipped* followed Mizrahi as he designed his fall/winter 1994 collection, cawing neurotically all the way. Its critical and commercial success proved that the general public was increasingly curious about the inner workings of fashion. "I thought that, at the time, there was such an incredible glamour, such a wonderful backstory that no one was telling about the supermodels, what it was like in fittings, backstage, et cetera," Mizrahi said. "Frankly, I was more intrigued by that than [by] what was on the runways."

Tom Ford, meanwhile, had been poached by Gucci way back in 1990, while Jacobs had been toiling away at Perry Ellis. Ford's mandate with Gucci was not just to revive the brand, but to turn it into the juggernaut it once was, and where Jacobs had failed, Ford was succeeding: He was so secure that he turned down an offer from Valentino in 1993 because he wouldn't have creative control.

Yet, as with McQueen, the mainstream fashion press was slow to notice Ford. His first mentions in *Vogue* and the *New York Times* didn't come until 1995, the same year he won the CFDA's International Award. "Everyone is tired of restraint," Ford said in January of that year. Kate Moss, he said, was our Twiggy, Stella Tennant the new Grace Kelly. But he was interested in overt sexual glamour, and called for an end to bohemian, grunge-inflected chic. "We need quality items back in our lives," he said. "People can be too ready to trade comfort for quality of life. But there can be excitement in making the effort, taking time to look beautiful and sexy."

Ford was a gentle provocateur, working with a languid, androgynous sexuality that hearkened to the 1970s: low-slung pants, plunging necklines, and body-conscious silhouettes in silk, satin, and velvet. He was inspired by the same Gen-X figures as Marc Jacobs was, but he infused them with old-Hollywood glamour. "Movie stars were beating down Gucci's doors in the '60s and '70s," he said. "Fast-forward to 1995, and who are today's movie stars? Brad Pitt, Uma Thurman, Winona Ryder, Johnny Depp. It's the same Gucci—just a modern version." He understood the resistance to status dressing, and minimized the Gucci logo: This generation's rejection of conspicuous consumerism had stuck.

By the end of the year, Madonna wore Gucci to the MTV Video Music Awards: a pair of black hip-hugger pants and black bra under a plunging aqua silk top. It was the exact look worn by Amber Valletta in the print campaign, down to the long blond hair and smoky eye. "Madonna looked like a replica of a Gucci ad," said *W*.

"That really put us on the map," Ford said. One year later, Gwyneth Paltrow wore Ford's slinky red velvet suit to the VMAs, and Gucci was suddenly a Gen-X brand.

Marc's work was the opposite of sex: His girl, like Corinne Day's, was unpolished, but a bit more urbane, bookish, and twee. She listened to Pavement, wore very little makeup, and was interested in the fringe. The celebrities who later exemplified his brand, Sofia Coppola and Kim Gordon, were starting their own fashion lines. Marc's generation of designers rejected Seventh Avenue, and this generation of girls was rejecting designers.

While quietly designing for Iceberg in Milan and consulting with Mitsubishi in Japan, Marc tried to rebound in America with a younger, cheaper line. Before he ever debuted Marc by Marc he launched Look, and hired Mike Mills to shoot the catalog and Daisy von Furth as the stylist. "It wasn't like Marc by Marc Jacobs, which was for cooler girls," Daisy says. "Look was made for the department store. It was like Garanimals, candy-colored, mix-and-match." They shot on top of the World Trade Center, without permits.

"One of the shared aesthetics we had was that UN, Pan Am sensibility," says Daisy. The space-age fonts, the blue-and-white color palette, the casual jet-set chic were all elements of X-Girl's branding, mainly conceived by Mike.

Then there was Sofia, known mainly as the dilettante daughter of Francis Ford Coppola. At twenty-three, she'd already attempted several careers, most famously as an actress. In 1990, her father cast her in *The Godfather Part III* after Winona Ryder, distraught over her breakup with Johnny Depp, dropped out. Sofia had never acted before. "I had connections," she'd say. Sofia had trouble pronouncing the name Corleone and couldn't shake her Valley girl drawl, but thought she'd be fine because "when my father was writing the script, he based a lot of the character on me." She won the Razzie that year for Worst Supporting Actress and Worst New Star.

After that, she moved on to designing costumes for *Spirit of '76*, directed by her brother Roman. Then she and her best friend Zoe Cassavetes, another Hollywood legacy, did a show for Comedy Central called *Hi Octane*, which profiled stars in the Coppola orbit. It lasted only four episodes, but its greatest segment is a sit-down with Thurston Moore and Anna Wintour, who'd just asked Kim Deal of the Breeders to write something for *Vogue*. They talk about how kids in the mid '90s want to look.

THURSTON: [Kim] has some interesting styling concepts, I noticed. I've done some shows with her and she likes to sort of keep her hair, um, very dark and greasy. And it's a special look she has, and I always wondered how she did it, and one time I noticed in the dressing room before she went on, she was looking for something to grease her hair with, and she went to the deli tray and she took the sandwiches and she opened 'em up and she took the mayonnaise and started like, wiping her hair in it, and it looked great! And she went out and totally rock 'n' rolled.

ANNA: I see.

Then Thurston realizes he's failed to charm and that Anna Wintour doesn't care if he thinks she's cool.

THURSTON: Do you remember your first fashion show that you went to?

ANNA: I was working for a British magazine at the time called *Harpers & Queen*, and it was before there were the tents and the sort of huge production, and Robert Altman making movies and everybody being so famous. I was the *junior* of junior junior assistants at the time, and I was sitting way in the back row, and the woman that I was working for, to show how important she was, she would have a hat and gloves. In those days, if you were an editor, a senior editor, you showed yourself being a senior editor by the white gloves that you wore. The shows were in the evening, and the men would wear black tie. There would be lots of empty seats, lots of people wouldn't come, the shows would take two *hours*, just for the girls to go backwards and forwards, and they looked so haughty. And to see how it's gone from a sort of black-tie experience with ladies in white gloves to the zoo that it now is . . . is amazing.

Fashion wasn't just in the throes of a generational coup d'état: What was happening now would change everything, and would—along with technology—democratize the industry, turning real people into models, reality show contestants and pop stars into designers, teenage bloggers into front-row eminences. At the moment, though, it all seemed so transient, a kind of subcultural prank that would eventually cease to amuse.

That same episode of *Hi Octane* included a piece on the X-Girl fashion show, a guerilla happening staged on Lafayette Street, right across from Marc Jacobs's show and timed to begin when his ended. That way, they caught such high-fashion spillover as the *New York Times*'s Bill Cunningham; supermodel Linda Evangelista and her boyfriend, *Twin Peaks* star Kyle MacLachlan; Steven Meisel; and Anna Sui. Kim and Thurston were there, of course, as were Francis Ford Coppola, the Beastie Boys' Adam Horovitz, Dinosaur Jr.'s J Mascis, and brother-sister celebutants Donovan Leitch and Ione Skye. Cindy Crawford ran a segment on *House of Style*.

Kurt Cobain had killed himself two days before, and the mood was unsettled.

"It was horrible," Kim Gordon says. She had been at Daisy's apartment when she got the call. Sofia arrived to find Kim in tears.

They went ahead with the show on April 7, 1994. It was staged mainly by Sofia and Spike, not yet a couple. This presentation was a first: regular girls as models—Chloë closed the show as a bride in a white A-line minidress and pink hair—staged on a sidewalk, attendance generated by word of mouth. Kim doesn't recall clearing the idea with Marc or his people: "Marc had a lot on his mind."

It was a scene founded on authenticity, yet so many were copying each other. Sofia launched her own X-Girl-like line called Milk Fed, mainly T-shirts with silk screens of Che Guevara and slogans such as "I Love Booze" and "Wasted." She asked Chloë to model for her debut show at Bloomingdale's; Chloë turned her down flat. Undaunted, Sofia enlisted her friends Zoe, Amanda de Cadenet, and Stephen Dorff to model in a three-page spread in *W* magazine. "I always wanted to be a designer, but I didn't think I knew enough," Coppola said. "When I helped Kim Gordon and Daisy von Furth put on the X-Girl show in SoHo, I discovered they didn't know how to sew, either. I realized I admire people who just jump into things and do it."

Daryl K, the designer Kim and Daisy had befriended, was shocked to see pieces reminiscent of her clothes in the X-Girl collection. "It actually all came from me," she says. "Kim never, ever mentions me. Ever. I really don't want to be a woman who has to say that, but . . . I have to say it. Because I wasn't . . . I didn't have money. I didn't have connections. And I never had the publicity machine behind me."

"I think I vaguely remember her thinking we copied her pants, which wasn't true," says Daisy. "I mean we 'altered' a lot of other people's clothes—APC, agnés—but not hers specifically."

The upside of this revolution was that even amateurs, albeit rich, well-connected ones, could become fashion designers. The downside was that a gargantuan talent like Marc Jacobs and a struggling one like Daryl K were overshadowed by rock stars and hobbyists. "Perhaps the '90s will be remembered as the decade of the dilettante," Christina Kelly wrote in *Spin*'s July 1995 issue. "While stars take their secondary interests out of the realm of hobbies and make money off them, the obscure and dedicated perfect their crafts and fume on the sideline."

She went on to note Coppola in particular: "At the outset of each new venture, [she] always states proudly that she has no training whatsoever in her new line of work. Really? No way!"

Marc first met Sofia before he'd done the grunge collection, around the time she was interning at Chanel. "I was about seventeen or eighteen," she said. "I had seen pictures of his clothes and I asked my mom to take me to meet him." The two became fashion-world friends, much the same way Sofia and Zoe and Donovan were sure to socialize with Anna Sui whenever she came to L.A. "I would always stay at the Chateau Marmont, and so every afternoon they would come over to the Chateau and have lunch and hang out by the pool," Sui says. "I saw them all every day. It was just people to hang out with."

Marc understood the odd currency these celebutants had, but he had no time for them. He was at a crucial point in his career, launching his own house one year after his disastrous grunge collection. Marc resurfaced in April 1994, also showing just days after Kurt Cobain's suicide. So much was changing: Kate Moss was transforming herself into a sex bomb, posing as a pinup girl for Pirelli and YSL. Lollapalooza, an alternative music festival founded in 1991, was by now a mainstream phenomenon, as were piercings and tattoos. The optimism of Britpop was now far more appealing than mope rock, and was epitomized by Oasis's 1994 hit single "Live Forever." That song "was written in the middle of grunge," said Noel Gallagher. "I remember Nirvana had a song called 'I Hate Myself and I Want to Die,' and I was like . . . 'Well, I'm not fucking having that.' "

Marc was still defending his grunge collection, still agitating against an industry that not only refused to accept how the modern girl wanted to look but blamed him for it. "People still complain about editorial—I hear about 'the girls in magazines with sloppy hair who look all strung out, like poor, little ugly things,' " he said. "Any woman I would like to sit down and have a conversation with will not dress up to look like a photo in a fashion magazine . . . I can't really have an intelligent conversation about this woman who will say, 'I can't go out of the house looking like a junkie.' Nobody is *telling* you to go out of the house looking like a junkie. It's a *fashion* magazine. In the '50s or '60s in Diana Vreeland's day nobody in *Vogue* looked exactly normal, they were all painted up with big hairdos."

Marc's next show was a small triumph, attended by supporters like Anna Sui and *Harper's Bazaar* editor in chief Liz Tilberis, who called the show "unbelievable." He didn't abandon his rock 'n' roll girl, but now she bent toward mod and glam; for all his bitterness, he acquiesced to commercialism and cleaned her up. There were coats in plastic and leather, lots of animal prints and skins, and a Skittles-inspired color palette, along with modest hemlines and suits appropriate for work. "The collection represents a balance between reasonable, sober, and familiar design and rather raucous, way-out styling," said the *New York Times*, calling the show "a resounding success." Marc was still adored by fashion editors and insiders, but he had yet to succeed where it most counted: sales. "Maybe five girls own his stuff in New York, and three in Texas," said *Vogue*'s Candy Pratts Price.

The association between Marc and Sofia would intensify over time, as Sofia began to establish herself as a legitimate working artist. But in the mid-'90s there was no shortage of cool girls available for transactional relationships. Enter Courtney Love.

Not long after Kurt Cobain committed suicide, Love flew to New York, and one afternoon, Anna Sui got a call from her SoHo shop: "[The manager] says, 'Anna, you can't believe what the store looks like.'" Love was tearing through the clothes, throwing them all over the floor, saying over and over that "Anna should have called me before she designed this; I could've told her." Then Love asked for a Magic Marker so she could make a list of all the drugs she was on. It was a long list, and included her contraceptive sponge. Sui invited Love to dinner that same night with Marc Jacobs.

Back then, designers weren't equal to actors and rock stars, so that night, Anna and Marc waited hours for Love. In she stumbled, with her entourage and her baby, Frances Bean. Courtney babbled all night long. "With Courtney, there's no dialogue," Sui says. "It's a monologue. A lot of detours and unfinished thoughts." Also at that dinner was Kal Ruttenstein, fashion director of Bloomingdale's, and Love passed Frances Bean over to him. "He was not a baby person," Sui says. "And while Courtney's like, 'Blah, blah, blah,' the baby kept throwing up on him.'"

It was the perfect metaphor for the mid-'90s fashion world: an incoherent junkie rock star passing her vomiting baby off to industry royalty, so eager for her endorsement they took whatever degradations came their way. Marc, especially, was great at striking up friendships with celebrities, and he had an affinity with Love that Sui did not: He, too, was a drug addict, just a more functional one. For now.

## CHAPTER 16

# THE QUEEN OF
# PRIMROSE HILL

THREE YEARS ON, CORINNE Day still missed Kate. "I felt hurt that our relationship, I knew, was over," she said. "It's always like that when you lose someone you love and you're going in separate directions."

The entire fashion industry had pulled away from Corinne by now. Writing in the *New Yorker* in 1996, Hilton Als noted her absence as Juergen Teller, Mario Sorrenti, David Sims, and Craig McDean "have all benefited . . . by imitating aspects of Day's groundbreaking work." Als called her early images of Kate "a first testament to the fashion industry's now pervasive flirtation with death." The aesthetic went beyond heroin chic: It was fashion as mortification, on display everywhere, from ads for Jil Sander and Prada to the runways at McQueen and Westwood. But it was Teller's unvarnished image of Kristen McMenamy, naked but for "Versace" scrawled between her breasts, inside a lipstick heart, that most echoed Corinne's early work. So, too, did his stated philosophy.

"I couldn't identify with the images in *Elle* or *Vogue* or *Harper's Bazaar*," he told the *New York Times*. "Nobody in the world we're walking around in actually looks like that. And these photos I took of Kristen are actually pathetic in a way—but I think it's a lot worse, what they put on the cover of fashion magazines. What they're trying to sell—the lipstick, the breast implants, all that stuff—is a lot more offensive to me as a human being."

Corinne was more offended by such blatant co-optation and her forced exile. "Fashion's become an all-boy world," she told Als.

Corinne's first love was rock 'n' roll, and she began shooting for *Spin*, *Rolling Stone*, and *Raygun*. She became obsessed with a band called Pusherman, which no one could figure out: Corinne had impeccable taste, and Pusherman wasn't very good. Their sound was a mélange of neo-hippie-inflected grunge in its death throes. But it quickly became clear that Corinne was fixated on Andy Frank, the lead singer, and she followed him everywhere. Corinne's boyfriend, Mark, never said a word, just pretended it wasn't happening. "Mark was so in love with Corinne, he would almost let her get away with murder," says Neil Moodie.

Andy, aside from going out with Corinne's best friend, was deep into heroin. "Every time Pusherman gigged, there'd be a party," Corinne said. "Everybody took drugs. Every single kind of drug. And when you're surrounded by people who take drugs every day, all the time, you think it's normal, and you think everybody does it, and you end up spaced out all the time and it was great. It was great, great fun."

Corinne had replaced Kate with a teenage girl named Tara St. Hill. She, too, was from a difficult home, had lived in squats and gypsy sites, and moved in with Corinne and Mark for a while. Tara offered to be Corinne's new stylist, and her boyfriend, George, tall and lean, with hollowed-out cheeks and long black hair, quickly became one of Corinne's favorite subjects. Corinne didn't pay either one of them, but they didn't mind.

In the summer of '96, Corinne finagled a shoot for Pusherman with *Interview* magazine. They shot at New York City's Gramercy Park Hotel, then a dilapidated rock 'n' roll hangout, and the band was a mess, "off their heads on heroin," says stylist Karl Plewka. "They're all doing pints of gin and tonic—pints. One of them was exposing himself to my assistant . . . They were sending people out to buy drugs on St. Mark's Place."

During that trip to New York, Corinne suffered a major seizure. She was rushed to Beth Israel Hospital and diagnosed with a brain tumor. Doctors told her it had been growing for at least seven years and had to come out immediately.

As soon as she was able, Corinne snuck out of Beth Israel and flew home. She'd deal with it there.

Kate, too, was coming apart, her drug use out of control. Depp, who was beginning to slow it down, couldn't take it. In one sitting she could snort three grams of coke and drink a bottle of vodka, which a doctor said was the best liquor for preserving her looks; she put stuff away so hard and fast that her nickname was "the Tank." A friend says she suspected Depp was cheating on her. "She'd phone him all the time, on sets, in hotels," says the friend. "She never expressed concern about his drug use. She expressed concern about being separated from him on jobs."

In public, she looked more together and stylish than ever. Her life was mainly a game of dress-up, and she reinvented herself as a new kind of Hollywood consort. As actresses were aspiring to be models, wearing Prada, Chanel, and Versace on the red carpet, Kate, as always, went the other way, doing vintage. She began working a Zelda Fitzgerald vibe, a flapper thing in line with Depp's literary tastes. Magpie and grunge felt very old to her now, and she began a serious grooming regimen: red nails and lipstick, glossy hair and cat eyes. To the premiere of Depp's film *Ed Wood*, she wore a vintage white silk slip dress with a tinsel overlay, once allegedly owned by Errol Flynn's wife. In London, she began shopping at Steinberg & Tolkien vintage, where she snapped up dozens of little black cocktail dresses from the '40s, '50s, and '60s.

"It's more fun getting dressed up in high heels and jewels and a gorgeous dress that makes you feel sexy than having to, like, work a pair of jeans and make that sexy," she said. But when she did stray from her vintage finds, she tried to find designers who weren't as available or exposed. In 1996, that was Marc Jacobs. When she wore a simple gold floor-length dress of his to an event, she earned Marc's undying devotion. It wasn't traditional red-carpet fare, but on Kate it was transformational. "I cannot think of a better testament to Kate's chic, glamour, and beauty," he said, "than the proof of her ability to turn a simple slip—unadorned, not overly accessorized—into a gown fit for a goddess."

Kate's penchant for clean lines, few accessories, and a well-scrubbed face with a strong red lip mirrored the style of her old Calvin Klein colleague Carolyn Bessette, now married to John F. Kennedy Jr. People who knew both women through the '90s say neither influenced the other, though they both lived in the same small apartment building in the Village for years. Rather, they were similar creatures, both wild party girls underneath their cool blond facades. Both stood apart in any room by counterintuitively under-dressing. Carolyn's wardrobe was made up of a few key designer pieces, mainly Prada and Yamamoto, but for day she wore Levi's jeans and Petit Bateau tops. When she married JFK Jr. in a Narciso Rodriguez slip dress, Bessette launched his career and single-handedly upended the bridal industry. Gone were the traditional princess silhouette and elaborate headpieces; now, brides wanted to look like her: sleek, austere, and modern.

Kate created a similar inversion at the 1997 premiere of Depp's directorial debut, *The Brave*, walking the red carpet at Cannes in a gray, sleeveless, to-the-knee Cerruti shift dress. It was such a simple piece, easily appropriate for the office, and it worked precisely because Kate got the juxtaposition. *Vogue* called her choice "unforgettable."

The next year at Cannes, she did it again, wearing a vintage white column gown by Madame Grès, hair tugged into a bun, well-scrubbed face. She was photographed with Claudia Schiffer, who was in full makeup and a lacy black tea-length dress. By '80s standards, Schiffer, the Bardotesque blond bombshell, would've been considered the more beautiful, but Kate, swerving once again, outshone her. "She was going in the complete opposite direction by choosing something so plain," said Tracy Tolkien, who called the Madame Grès "a great example of Kate thinking, 'What will other people be wearing . . . how can I stand out?'"

Not long after this appearance at Cannes, Kate and Johnny, unraveling for months, broke up for good. They had a massive blowup at his house in L.A.; she thought they'd been living there together, but he thought she was crashing. He'd tried living with her in New York, but that lasted less than six months; as wild as Johnny may have been, even he couldn't take the partying and the clinginess. According to a friend, he told Kate she was "a crazy bitch," that they were done. Kate couldn't believe it.

"Johnny broke her heart," says the friend. "She went mad."

Kate and Corinne were so estranged that neither one knew how badly the other was doing. Corinne checked into the hospital as soon as she got back to London, and her prognosis was grim: Surgeons were able to remove 80 percent of the tumor, but the rest would keep growing. They told her she had eight years to live. As soon as she heard the news, she turned to Mark and said, "Take my picture." It was her way of coping: Here she was, just another subject.

"Looking through the camera, everything felt like it was in a movie," she said. "Or that I was in the camera. Nothing felt real. And I didn't digest how I felt, or what I thought. You just go with it."

"That was Corinne feeling out of control, trying to get some control in that situation," says Tara St. Hill. "It limited her involvement in life, because she was always behind the camera. So when everyone was getting fucked out in a field or partying, there's always the camera blocking you from the people, the moment. That moment in particular, she felt really out of control."

Corinne spent Christmas in the hospital, and when she was released a week later, she went right to a New Year's Eve party thrown by Pusherman "as if nothing had happened," Corinne said. Like Kate, she fell back on drugs: She was already dying, so what did it matter?

"I don't think she sought out darkness," Tara says. "I think it just happened along the way."

Heroin had been part of the fashion scene for most of the decade. But the February 1997 death of Mario Sorrenti's brother Davide— also a fashion photographer, only twenty years old when he OD'd on heroin—ended all that. The industry-wide denial of heroin, its use and glamorization, was over.

"It's been used as an accessory in every shoot," said photographer Dewey Nicks. "It's the Manolo Blahniks of this particular period." Bill Mullen, the creative director of *Details*, said models were often shot glistening because they were having "junkie sweats." "The people in charge of things encourage the models to destroy themselves," said Davide's girlfriend, model Jaime King. "If a girl becomes a star and she starts to do drugs, no one does anything to stop it. As long as she keeps making money, it's fine."

Davide's mother, Francesca—who watched over Kate Moss when she came to New York at nineteen, back when she was dating Mario— went public with everything she knew: the agents who doubled as dealers, the gift bags of coke, the makeup artists who covered track marks. "Our business has become heroin chic," said Francesca, herself a fashion photographer. "Someone taking pictures of that magnitude has to have experienced hard drugs."

Editors from *Vogue*'s Anna Wintour to *i-D*'s Terry Jones declared a moratorium on heroin chic.

"They literally said, 'We are not looking for any heroin pictures,'" said photographer Michael Williams. "We want everything positive and healthy." The actress Juliette Lewis wrote a scathing letter to *Detour* magazine after yet another heroin-inspired layout ran in its May 1997 issue: "This," she wrote, "was the most deliberate junkie layout I have ever seen, and I don't know why this is being allowed."

Even President Bill Clinton weighed in: "Many of our fashion leaders are now admitting—and I honor them for doing this—they're admitting flat-out that images projected in fashion photos in the last few years have made heroin addiction seems glamorous and sexy and cool," he said. "And as some of those people in those images start to die now, it has become obvious that this is not true."

Kate said nothing. She knew she was the face of heroin chic, but she'd rarely explained herself publicly and wasn't going to join an increasingly confessional culture and start now. She was still the industry's hottest model, her $2 million contract with Calvin Klein the biggest one going. Besides, what would she say? She was out of control on drugs and booze, reeling after her split with Johnny.

"Sleeping around, doing more drugs," a friend says of that time. "It gets back to him that she's out of control, and he's not surprised. He did drugs, but he knew how much to take and how much not to, and she just wouldn't stop with the drugs and the drinking."

Kate threw herself into partying with the Primrose Hill set. The British tabloids began reporting Kate's hookups with several of her best female friends, including, most notably, Sadie Frost, who, says this friend, began to fall in love with Kate. When Frost told her husband, Jude Law, that she'd been hooking up with Kate, he was excited by it; the three became entangled. Normally, Sadie was wildly possessive of Jude. When he went off to film *I Love You, I Love You Not* with Claire Danes, Sadie lost it: "I'm gonna kill her," she raged. "I've sent her little death threats." At the time, Danes was sixteen.

But Kate was the queen of the Primrose Hill set, so Sadie kept her mouth shut. "They all partied together, slept together," says a colleague, who found none of them capable of true connection. "There were no real repercussions," she says. "It was a very soulless life that they led." Kate often slept with her friends' boyfriends, and actress Patsy Kensit forbade then-husband Liam Gallagher from being alone with Kate after learning they'd spent the night together.

Minor pop star Pearl Lowe and her boyfriend, Danny Goffey of Supergrass, were also involved with Sadie and Jude: As Jude denied and Pearl did not, Sadie slept with Danny and Pearl with Jude, until Jude fell in love with Pearl. The swapping stopped. All of it, Pearl later admitted, was fueled by booze and drugs. Whenever she'd try to get clean, Kate and the Primrose Hill set would disappear.

"It wasn't so much the friendships, because a lot of them weren't friendships at all," Pearl said. "Put down the drugs and you don't have much in common." Kate had the highest tolerance of them all, says her colleague, capable of doing "cocaine, champagne in piles, an eight-ball by herself . . . and not even be fazed by it."

"She can drink anyone under the table," says a friend. "She can drink a liter of vodka in one sitting; she'll go out on a Thursday and come back on a Sunday. There's not much she doesn't like." Anyone who tries to quit or dial back is a traitor to the cause; Kate's friends are expected to party at all hours, whether it's 7 P.M. or 5 A.M. "She doesn't like her own company," said the friend of that time. "She's addled by the drugs and doesn't like to think."

Corinne, too, was harder and harder to reach.

"After having the tumor removed, she remained in that dark side of life for about a year afterward," Neil Moodie says. "I think a lot of that was a 'fuck life' kind of thing, like, 'Somebody's not watching over me, so fuck everybody.'" All of her friends, he says, were alarmed by her drug use.

In 1997 Corinne got an assignment to shoot a fashion editorial for UK *Penthouse*, which was relaunching; in need of work and money, she took it. Rosemary Ferguson, one of her early discoveries, agreed to model; Moodie did the hair; Tara was the stylist; and Pusherman's Andy Frank tagged along. They went up to Wales for the shoot, where Andy stayed in a cottage the whole time, shooting up, and when Corinne wasn't working on the editorial for *Penthouse*, she was taking pictures of Andy. "It was a bizarre obsession," Moodie says.

After the shoot, they all piled back in the van, Andy at the wheel. He was high on heroin, and only Corinne knew it. After he lost control of the van, driving it into a ditch, Corinne insisted they get back on the road so Andy wouldn't get arrested. "We're lucky we're alive," Moodie says. "Rosemary was furious straightaway. She was like, 'We could have fucking died. This is ridiculous.'" Corinne and Andy drove home on their own.

Not long after the accident, Andy moved to L.A., and Corinne lasered in on Tara, herself lost to drugs, high all the time on heroin or ketamine or whatever was around. Corinne would go over to Tara's and snap away, and when Corinne asked to shoot Tara's boyfriend George in the nude, Tara convinced him.

"When we first started doing stuff, going to raves and warehouses and parties and stuff, it was all quite upbeat and positive and E in fields and sunshine and chatting to people and feeling like you loved everyone 'cause you were off your head," Tara says. "[Corinne] absolutely loved life. Unfortunately that scene, the more you get involved in it . . . she met other people that were into other things, and even the people she already knew became more entrenched in it. As time went on, the drugs became different, the places we went became different, and it became darker."

Despite her tolerance for drugs and alcohol, Kate was on her way to becoming another casualty. In New York City, Kate would often hang out at the downtown French bistro Les Deux Gamins, where waitstaff noticed she "always looks so tired—she'll say she doesn't know what time zone it is."

Yet things seemed to be going her way: In 1998, Kate Moss was registered as a trademark by her agency, Storm. She was worth almost $30 million. She had a chance at reconciling with Depp.

That summer, she and Depp went to a Rolling Stones show in New York, and she accompanied him to the Cannes premiere of *Fear and Loathing in Las Vegas*. The next day, he blew off all his interviews, and when he did finally sit down with the press, Depp made an un-characteristically blunt statement about his private life: He and Kate Moss were done. "We both know there's no going back," he said. This was news to Kate, who reportedly then threw such a savage party at the five-star Hotel du Cap-Eden-Roc she was banned from the hotel. (Kate denied this report.)

Just a few weeks later, in June, Depp met Vanessa Paradis, the French singer and actress who so resembled Kate she'd been ap-proached as the new face of Calvin Klein. Within weeks, Vanessa was pregnant, and Kate completely spun out, spending a wild two weeks in Ibiza. Jason Lake, her island hookup, promptly spilled all to the press, expressing his amazement that this "kinda rough" girl who knocked back vodka and tequila every night was the world's most famous model. "We'd both get really pissed, but she could get really loud," Lake said. "That voice—it fucking carried."

She dyed her hair pink, walked the runway for Versace, and was shot by Juergen Teller for *Dazed & Confused*. She partied with McQueen and had a fling with Lemonheads front man Evan Dando, who had his own issues with heroin. She felt propelled by a momen-tum she no longer controlled: "I was living fast," she said. "It was, 'Sleep? Why? Why not go on? There's too much to do. There are too many places to go.' "

In November, she broke down at a dinner with Meg Mathews and Noel Gallagher, who'd recently had his own come-to-Jesus moment. "I was a big, fat rock star with a big, fat bank account and a huge fuck-ing house in the country, with a year off and nothing to do," he said. "So I done what comes naturally—drink and take drugs. From March till June it was intense. It was all day, every day." He'd been watching the World Cup in bed, his wife Meg passed out, when suddenly he couldn't breathe. In the middle of the night, he called a doctor.

"He looked at me and he said, 'I'm not even going to ask you if you take drugs. There's nothing we can give you. Stop doing it.' I just thought, 'I'm not going to end up . . . a sad miserable cunt who is either getting high or coming down and always moaning about something. I just thought, 'This is it.'" He stopped.

Kate showed up two hours late to that dinner with Noel and Meg, ordered nothing, and spent thirty minutes in tears. Then she went to another party, stayed out till 3 A.M., and checked into the Priory later that morning.

Kate claimed "exhaustion," but she seemed on the verge of a nervous breakdown, her system overloaded on substances. There was no one in her life with any leverage; even her agent, Sarah Doukas, admitted as much. "There are some things I know I can never discuss with her," Doukas said. "We're close, but when you're an agent, there's a line."

The Priory is both a rehab center and a mental health clinic; patients admitted for depression typically stay two weeks, while those in for substance abuse tend to stay for six. Kate was in for five, and her admission was international news. "This is not a sad story," said author Michael Gross, an expert on the industry. "So many models end up anywhere from desperately unhappy to dead. But Kate pulled up short."

Upon her release, Kate's stepfather wasn't so sure about her prognosis. "I [had] been talking to Kate for thirty minutes, and she explained she had gone to this place, the clinic, for two weeks for a rest, but promised it had nothing to do with heroin," he said. "Maybe I'm a bit naïve and maybe I am wrong. I don't know, but she told me, 'It's not heroin, I am taking no drugs at all.'"

CHAPTER 17

# PARIS DOES
# NOTHING FOR ME

MCQUEEN, AT TWENTY-SEVEN YEARS old, was rumored to be the first choice for Givenchy, taking over for John Galliano, now at Dior. For all the debate over whether he was more shock than substance, these rumors lent him indisputable credibility.

He wanted it, but he was smart enough to know there were reasons why he shouldn't. In September 1996, he told *Women's Wear Daily* that the pressures of doing his own line—four collections a year, top priority—were taxing enough, and the responsibility of creating six additional lines per year for a French haute couture house seemed inhuman. "I can't imagine anyone doing that," he said. "My first concern has to be McQueen. Givenchy would be a lot of money, but I'm not really into that. Plus, Paris does nothing for me . . . Basically, all these big companies don't care about you as a person. You're only a commodity and a product to them and only as good as your last collection."

It was a remarkable insight. The takeover of these French houses by multibillion-dollar global conglomerates was a new phenomenon, as was installing young designers to reinvigorate these houses, first with Tom Ford at Gucci, then Galliano at Givenchy. As early as 1996, Ford was critical of the demands placed on designers. "I don't agree with these mini-collections that come out every six weeks," he said. "First of all, fashion doesn't need to change, even every six months—that's already a lot. Honestly, I wish we all had one fashion show every year for fall, and spring clothes would be a lighter-weight version of that. That's what I want."

Still, there was a part of McQueen that very much wanted the appointment and all it would confer. He wanted to be the anointed one, the one to beat out all the other designers rumored to be under consideration: Vivienne Westwood, whom he loathed, Gaultier and Alaïa, whom he respected enough, and Marc Jacobs, whom he didn't respect at all. Then again, McQueen had never even been to a Givenchy show. For all his bravado, he didn't know that he could do couture.

Not long after his success with "Highland Rape," McQueen told his friend Chris Bird that he didn't want to be a fashion designer anymore: "He said to me one night, 'All I want is a house, and I'm going to give up fashion and go into photojournalism.' But he'd become a brand."

McQueen asked his oldest friends for advice. Alice Smith, Chris Bird, Miguel Adrover—all thought Givenchy would be a mistake and told him so. It was still a moment when you could tell Lee McQueen the truth.

Smith saw a fidgety McQueen at her offices in Shoreditch. "I said, 'Why would you want to go work for another company, whether it's Givenchy or whatever? Your name is on its way.' I thought he was going to be enormous. Perhaps he didn't."

Adrover thought McQueen was nothing more than another showy acquisition for LVMH, and that taking the appointment was the ultimate sellout. "Lee was much more powerful than Givenchy," Adrover says. "Lee was representing the days he was living. Givenchy was already dead. I understand the money side, but the big houses trick you—flying first class, five-star hotels, money for your own line. And most people buy it."

*Vogue*'s André Leon Talley was equally cynical: Of LVMH's Bernard Arnault, he said, "The man is most concerned about the media attention." It wasn't about the couture, which made no money; it was about branding, and these young designers were key to pushing the ancillary products that drove revenue. "It's the perfume bottle and the handbag, and how to keep attention there," Talley said. "It's about a marketing strategy, making young people who are so radical the couture choices. It's all about media hype. [Arnault] could have taken the Princess of Wales as the designer, and he would have been very happy."

When formally offered the job, McQueen told LVMH execs that he needed a moment: "I have to go take a shit," he said—allegedly. Some friends say this happened during a phone call, others say it happened in a meeting, but really, it's just another part of the myth. Just as the lowly apprentice Lee never sewed "I am a cunt" into the lining of Prince Charles's jacket, just as Isabella Blow never paid £5,000 for his thesis collection, this too likely never took place, but as Andrew Groves says, "it kind of doesn't matter, because it just sounds right."

To the press, McQueen professed to know little about Galliano, his lifelong obsession. "He's a really nice guy," McQueen said. "But he comes from a time when fashion was about elitism. In the 1980s, designers were seen as kings. But the 1990s is no longer about elitism; it's about the general public, and not putting yourself on a plane higher than anybody else."

Even after accepting the job, McQueen agonized. The two most important women in his life—his mother and Isabella—both thought he should absolutely take it. Issie offered to accompany McQueen to Paris for his first meeting with LVMH, and he was grateful: He'd have someone who knew the industry's practices, whom he trusted implicitly. But he'd miscalculated. Issie was not well. He wasn't at LVMH headquarters for an hour when frantic phone calls kept coming from Issie; she'd locked herself out of her apartment and needed McQueen to come get her immediately.

"She's doing my fucking head in," he said. "She's doing my fucking head in."

On October 14, 1996, LVMH announced that Alexander McQueen was taking over at Givenchy. Initially, Arnault wanted the McQueen name too, but, like Marc, Lee knew that was career suicide. "I didn't like the way LVMH ran Givenchy," he said. "So I wasn't going to let them into my own company." In the end, he got £1 million for a two-year-contract—not a lot of money for the workload—and used some of it to fund his own line. He told the press that when it came to the world of French couture, "they don't scare me, and I'll just tell them to fuck off."

McQueen's appointment left founder Hubert de Givenchy disconsolate. "I find it a total disaster, and I suffer," he said. "But what can I do?"

"I don't know whether I can survive in fashion without murdering someone," McQueen replied. "There are so many people who expect you to do the obvious thing. All they say is, 'Do a good coat.' If people want a boring coat, they can go to DKNY."

The British press reveled: Now running a legendary French fashion house was a self-described "yob" who luxuriated in vulgarity. McQueen, ever the showman, was happy to oblige, sitting with journalist after journalist and playing up his piggishness. "I was prepared for what Alexander McQueen looked like, because I'd seen him at the end of the last fashion show, paddling around with rolled-up trousers like Mr. Prufrock," said Lynn Barber in the London *Observer*. "But I wasn't prepared for how he speaks. Put it like this: If a Spud-U-Like could speak, it would speak like Alexander McQueen. It takes a while to sort out the words from all the adenoidal snuffles and snorts, and half the time they're only space fillers like, 'know what I mean.'"

Weeks before LVMH formally announced his appointment, McQueen presented "La Poupée." If Bernard Arnault had any hopes of cultivating a gentler Alexander McQueen, this show disabused him. It was inspired by the work of German artist Hans Bellmer, most famous for his life-size dolls, deformed through the repeated detaching and reattaching of limbs. The models' heads were caged behind spikes, their eyes splattered with glitter, and they seemed to be walking on water. His hustler's showpiece: the black model Debra Shaw, barefoot and breasts exposed, arms and legs locked in a steel manacle. McQueen commissioned the piece from his close friend Shaun Leane, a genius jewelry designer who was initially flummoxed. McQueen didn't even know what he wanted: shackles? A full body cast? Leane was at a loss, but McQueen didn't care.

"Lee was constantly pushing," says Chris Bird. "There used to be conversations like, 'Lee, it can't be done.' And Lee would be like, 'Just find a way. Just fucking find a way.'" Anyone who couldn't was off the team.

Issie was next—she knew it. When McQueen took the job at Givenchy, she assumed she'd be the house muse, that McQueen would put her on salary. That was how things were done.

He gave her nothing. She was heartbroken.

"She gave Lee everything," says Julien Macdonald. "All her money, all her time, all her energy. She introduced him to everybody. And then, when he went to Givenchy and he had money, he told her to piss off. He had millions, she was penniless, and he gave her *nothing*. He just shut the door."

Issie was frantic. She'd been fired from her latest job at the *Sunday Times* and was petrified that people thought she was crazy. What if people thought even Alexander McQueen couldn't take her anymore? And how ironic was that, given that he was out of control on coke?

Still, she kept her mouth shut. "I think she felt that if she talked out of turn that she would lose that opportunity," Michael Roberts said. "She always held on to the possibility that it would be made right in the end." But just a few months later, while being profiled for the *Daily Telegraph*, Issie got drunk on champagne and the truth came out.

"The role of a muse is changing," she said. "Traditionally, we haven't been paid, but as Bryan Ferry once said to me, one should be paid for ideas as well as the physical manifestation of them. If Alexander uses some of my ideas in his show, and he has, I don't get paid. He does . . . I've decided I'm going to be paid from now on too. Before this, my only reward was seeing the people I've discovered taking off, and that drives me nuts, because they leave me behind."

It made McQueen furious. His great baseline fear was that everyone he knew, except his mother, was using him. Issie would ask, "Do you remember the good old days? You knocked me up"—the most poignant metaphor a childless fashionista could conjure. And McQueen would say, "That world is gone, Issie."

LVMH had little interest in controlling McQueen as a designer. As a person, however, the company had a say. Right after his appointment, he was brought in for a talk: No more gay pubs and sex clubs in Soho, no more prostitutes or drag queens, no more friends from the old days. It was devastating; McQueen always felt most at home in Soho. "You'd never see him anywhere fancy," Julien Macdonald says. "He was always like a slapper on a back street, always at a seedy gay club. That's where he probably related to the people—not glamorous, not at all. Just normal people." McQueen met with his old friends to say goodbye.

"We got dropped," Chris Bird says. "He's not hanging out in Soho anymore. He's hanging out with Madonna at Nobu." Bird hadn't had a direct conversation about it with McQueen, but he realized things had changed on those rare occasions when they'd bump into each other. Bird would suggest they meet up for a drink, and McQueen would say, "Oh yeah, yeah, sweetheart—call the office and we'll see what we can arrange."

"You never saw him," Macdonald says. "He became more insular. He threw himself into his work."

For someone who'd just sat down with Charlie Rose and reiterated his opinion that "fashion people are not that intelligent," McQueen had no problem adapting. He was running around with Kate Moss and Naomi Campbell, Bella Freud and Elton John. He hated taking the Eurostar, so LVMH flew him and his team back and forth, from London to Paris, as much as he wanted, albeit commercial. They also gave him a driver and a flat in Paris. He was surprised by the size of his office—at eight by twelve feet, it was the size of a walk-in closet— but he really didn't mind. In London, he still lived in the basement flat at Hoxton Square.

"We were so excited to be there," says Simon Costin, his set designer. "It was so sort of glamorous. The first few months were a real romp."

McQueen brought along Costin, Katy England, and his trusted designer Catherine Brickhill. He didn't want to live alone in Paris—he didn't speak the language and felt the French looked down on him— so he had Catherine and Katy share his flat on the rue de Berne. It was small, and there was lots of street noise, and they were all surprised that LVMH thought this was suitable. LVMH regarded them "as street urchins," said Catherine Brickhill, so they acted that way, leaving the apartment strewn with beer bottles and cigarette butts.

"Brits in Paris, just taking over a huge fashion house," said Jodie Kidd, one of his favorite models.

They set to work immediately; they had three months till McQueen's first collection.

McQueen's debut at Givenchy was a fashion-world fixation. Was this lunatic capable of going commercial? "A major question in Paris will be whether the designers continue with exaggerated, unwearable show clothes, or reverse the trend and design clothes that women can easily wear," Bill Cunningham said in the *New York Times*.

McQueen showed his sketches to Simon Ungless, who found them underwhelming; McQueen scrapped the whole thing and started over. He made excessive demands on the house's seamstresses, and when they protested that something couldn't be done, McQueen wouldn't hear it. "This is couture, darling," he'd say. "You've got to be able to do it." His trademark wit was intact, and he sent his first model down the runway to Sparks' "This Town Ain't Big Enough for the Both of Us"—a message to John Galliano.

McQueen's debut won mixed reviews. "A baffling array of unwearable garments," said Sue Carroll in the London *Mirror*. Heath Brown in the *Times* was far more laudatory: "The gamble has paid off," he wrote. "McQueen pushed the boundaries of fashion to its limits."

His collection was Grecian-inspired, done in white and gold, a nod to the house's label. His models wore armature, exaggerated nose rings, dead birds, and gold-plated rams' horns. The latter were from Isabella, who slaughtered a ram at Hilles on McQueen's request. She sat front row, even as her cousin Honor Fraser—whom Issie had launched with the "London Babes" shoot—walked the runway as house muse. And after the show, amid the mixed reviews and the snipes about a cabdriver's son at Givenchy, Isabella defended him. "Alexander is dealing with an old albatross," she said. "McQueen and Givenchy are like a love affair, and we've got to give them a chance."

It was more than LVMH was willing to do. McQueen had no idea what to expect, no instruction in running a couture house, and he felt set up to fail. Julien Macdonald, who later took over from McQueen, had the same experience.

"They never helped us," Macdonald says. "They never did anything, never gave us any advice. You were on your own." Macdonald says his first day "was a nightmare. The first thing they asked me to do was a pre-fall collection. I didn't even know what a pre-collection *was*. I'd never done one in my life. I just remember going into Lee's old office and just *screaming*: 'Oh my God!' I called up a friend and said, 'What's a pre-collection?'"

Macdonald found the schedule inhuman—and unlike McQueen, he wasn't designing for two houses. For eight shows a year, he had a design staff of four. "I had to be there all day, every day," he says. As shows approached, Macdonald got four hours of sleep a night, and barely had time to recover before doing it all over again. "Nobody can prepare you for the amount of work and pressure it takes," Macdonald says. "It makes you mad. It was a torturous three years of having zero life; you constantly have to look for inspiration. You need to be an experienced designer to pull it off. Myself and Lee, we were too young and inexperienced."

After that first show for Givenchy, Lee McQueen was gone. He was Alexander now, the imperial genius, and those friends he kept were on his payroll: There was no room for talking back or truth telling. He was under too much pressure and on too many drugs. His next collection, for his own line, was to be shown on February 28, little more than a month away. In the wake of his lackluster debut, he could not fail.

"Givenchy was the point where Lee started to change, on many levels," Simon Costin says. "The stress involved in doing prêt-à-porter, couture, and his own label was pretty horrendous." Costin, like others before him, began to suspect McQueen was bipolar; the swift mood swings couldn't be just the drugs. "He was up and down a lot more, harder to work with," Costin says. "You never knew what mood he was going to be in when you got to the office." Each morning, McQueen's staff would whisper to each other about his mental state, whether it was okay to approach or better to wait. The wrong guess could get you fired.

"The fashion bubble does very strange things to people," Costin says. "Their sense of what's real and what isn't goes out the window. They're leading what seems to be quite an artificial existence, surrounded by people who just say yes to everything. And the people who perhaps answered back or said, 'Don't be ridiculous,' would disappear."

Rumors abounded that Bernard Arnault thought McQueen was a disaster. When American *Vogue*'s Kate Betts asked McQueen about the mixed response to his debut collection, he lit into her. The *Vogue* headline subsequently asked, "Does Alexander McQueen have enough talent to keep Givenchy going?" Betts wrote that the collection he was working on was "almost revolting." He developed a persecution complex.

"It's like Hitler's Holocaust," McQueen said. "He destroyed millions of people because he didn't understand. That's what a lot of people have done to me, because they don't understand what I do." He told Charlie Rose that any criticism was mere jealousy. "All of a sudden . . . you're on the same level as all these designers, and you realize all the people you looked up to wasn't as great as you thought they were. They have claws and they have knives and they're throwing everything into your back."

McQueen's second collection for Givenchy, his fourth show in three months, was shown in mid-March, to much greater effect. "As much as Mr. McQueen maligned the classics of Hubert de Givenchy in the past, a historic core can give a young designer some much-needed stability," Amy Spindler wrote in the *New York Times*. "And someone as brash as Mr. McQueen is smart enough to eat a little crow." But only so much: This show was presented in a slaughterhouse, and for each tidy, sheathlike look there was a model dressed as a wench, his favorite, Kate Moss, in "the prettiest camisole, puckered and falling from the shoulders for a Beaux Arts barmaid look," said Spindler.

It was also a gesture to Bernard Arnault and LVMH: They were getting what they paid for. "I don't think they wanted to push what they were doing and what they were about," says Simon Costin. "I think they needed someone who would toe the line a little bit more, would work on their heritage and their history, not try to take it in a completely different direction. He was too extreme for them, probably."

McQueen's next Givenchy collection was slated for July. He was motivated by coke and conceit; he never lost the feeling, growing up as he did, that the bottom could drop out at any time: "I've never seen my life as 'stable' as a fashion designer," he said. "You can't count on it for years. You can be as quickly dropped as you're quickly picked up." But creatively, he never panicked, even though every four weeks he had to produce a new collection.

"I never saw him without an idea," says Simon Costin. "There was always something brewing. I never saw him sitting blankly, going, 'Oh shit, what am I going to do?'"

For this couture collection, McQueen and Costin came up with an "Island of Dr. Moreau" theme: These Givenchy women were the victims of a mad doctor who slayed and flayed women and beasts, then sewed them together. McQueen loved using real skin and bones, and someone, most likely McQueen himself, started a rumor that he'd be using real human limbs this time. He'd also used blood and semen before, which he'd collect from friends and lovers. The fashion world was horrified, and they loved it: After the show, prominent French retailer Maria Luisa Pomaillou described McQueen as the future.

"I was against it in the beginning," she told the *Times*, "but it is the only way, the only solution, for couture now. It's no longer a private joke for a few people."

Issie had a new protégé, American designer Jeremy Scott. It was like taunting an old lover with a new one, and Scott implied that McQueen was threatened: "Isabella told me he threw an ashtray at her and wanted to kill me," Scott said. He was twenty-four years old, as brash as McQueen, his top row of teeth encased in a gold grill that spelled *J-E-R-E-M-Y*. The fashion press loved him.

In 1997, the *Independent* ran a profile of Scott called "Move Over McQueen—Here Comes the Kansas Ranger." Like McQueen before him, Scott claimed that there was no designer "who really inspires me," that "London is too closed" to be a fashion capital, and called Galliano's work "garbage." He was the perfect protégé for Issie at the moment, and her artful feints, the idea she'd love another designer as much, if not more, kept McQueen coming around.

It was also her way of getting back at McQueen for replacing her with beer heiress Daphne Guinness. Issie had insisted her new friend Daphne meet McQueen, and Daphne, who loved fashion, kept putting it off; she admired McQueen too much. "I didn't want to be a groupie," she said.

And then, one day, crossing the street, Daphne literally ran into McQueen, who said, "Oi! I'm the person you don't want to meet!" They became close, and Daphne, emboldened by her wealth and stature, would challenge him. "Daphne was the only one to stand up for Issie in front of McQueen," says Detmar Blow. "She told him, 'Everyone gets a contract, Issie gets clothes. Issie can't live on clothes alone—she needs to eat.' That takes courage."

Still, McQueen would come to Hilles for weekends away, more insufferable with each visit. Having come from celebrating Tony Blair's election, the man who once snuck out to meet Princess Di was feeling autocratic. "I am the tycoon now, Detmar," he said.

It was doubly cruel because he knew how insecure the Blows were about money: Issie could barely earn it and never keep it, and Detmar, as a lawyer-cum-gallerist, wasn't bringing much in either. "She had a childlike perception of money," said Philip Treacy. "She would say, 'I'm going to be a bag lady, I just know it.'"

"Nobody could control her spending," says Macdonald. "She and

Detmar never had any money, but then they'd go up to Hilles and there's loads of meat, and servants running around."

McQueen still loaned her some pieces, which she found a pathetic metaphor for their relationship. "He likes to use the clothes as power over me," she said, but from McQueen's perspective, Issie had become a bottomless pit of need: There was no satisfying her, and she was self-destructing. She wanted to be the Amanda Harlech to his John Galliano; McQueen thought Issie was delusional.

"She'd made some pretty rash and not great decisions about her own career," says McQueen's friend Chris Bird. "She'd gone on holidays and not returned. She wasn't turning up for work and getting fired and she puts her hope on Lee . . . His instinct was, 'I want to be my own person. I don't fucking want her here. I don't want her in fucking Paris—I get enough of her in fucking London, you know?' " There was no escape: When Issie came to the shows in Paris that year, she rented the apartment McQueen used when he first went to Givenchy.

Philip Treacy was worried too: Issie only wanted hats that really covered her face. She was never a beauty, but she had style and joie de vivre; now, depression was molding her features. She was suddenly looking very old and tired, with huge bags sagging under her eyes, lids half-closed, mouth downcast. McQueen suggested Issie get plastic surgery; instead, she went to Philip for hats, and when asked about her new look, she gave a tortured explanation.

"Fashion is a vampiric thing," she said. "It's the hoover on your brain. That's why I wear the hats, to keep everyone away from me. They say, 'Oh, can I kiss you?' I say, 'No, thank you very much. That's why I've worn the hat. Goodbye.' I don't want to be kissed by all and sundry. I want to be kissed by the people I love."

Issie and McQueen, and Marc Jacobs as well: Here were the fashion industry's most influential, beset by so much self-loathing amid so much beauty that they were carving themselves up, abusing themselves with drugs and booze, cigarettes and degrading sex. McQueen told Detmar that he needed to be humiliated sexually in order to work: "He'd say, 'That's the way I want it.' "

"Lee was very sexual," says Macdonald, and back when he was in business only for himself, "he'd go to a lot of leather gay sex clubs, underground clubs." But increasingly, the dark, anonymous sex became a form of self-punishment: "I think the way he tried to metabolize [his pain] was by having sex," says Chris Bird. "His personal relationships were very volatile."

For all their dysfunction, Issie always kept the door open for him at Hilles. There, he could do what he liked with whomever he liked, and it would stay behind those walls. When it came to that, Issie would never judge.

LVMH may have been underwhelmed, but for the second time in two years, the British Fashion Council honored McQueen as Designer of the Year. In so many ways, his installation at a couture house was perfect for his singular vision, and his work was becoming bolder. He kept pushing the house toward the future: wiring his models in rainbow LED lights; sheathing them in PVC, plastic, metal, and leather; bleaching their eyebrows and masking their faces with war paint. His creations approached art, yet they were unwearable. Hubert de Givenchy remained unimpressed.

"Making dresses which are unsellable or at least unwearable, what good is that?" he said. "It is the road to destruction. To want to make things which are simply fantasy is disastrous, because it is not representative of good taste in France."

McQueen still hated France. He could barely speak the language and couldn't understand why the onus was on him, the genius, to win the approval of the French. The old ladies who came in for fittings looked down on him. He was getting slaughtered in the press, and no one at LVMH stood up for him.

"The couture collections were amazing," Macdonald says. "The ready-to-wear—nobody bought the clothes. If you looked at the figures, it was a disaster. The brand never made any money, and there was all this hype around Lee."

At least he still had his own line. Ever shrewd, he'd lined up American Express to sponsor his spring/summer '98 presentation. McQueen told them the show's theme was "Golden Showers," and when they protested, he claimed to have no idea why: This was a sexual reference? Really? What did it mean?

He laughed, and left the show untitled.

Again, McQueen worked closely with Simon Costin on the set; this time, *Jaws* was the inspiration. They got sixteen sheets of donated Plexiglas, which Costin used to build a runway filled with water. It was lit from below, and black ink snaked through the tank as rain fell from the rafters. There were dresses in white muslin, turned sheer in the showers; snakeskin and slashed torsos; a metal jawbone and an aluminum rib cage. It was his sexiest, most accomplished show yet.

"Mr. Arnault can take back his Givenchy job, but he can't take back the wealth of experience Mr. McQueen has gained from his time spent in the couture ateliers," said the *New York Times*. "Every minute of it was visible on the runway, where he proved he has built a solid, bankable, grown-up house of his own." The reviewer went on to add that "the age of churlishness, it seems, is over."

Behind closed doors, that wasn't the case with McQueen. Despite the constant rumors of his imminent dismissal, editors and critics loved him, and when his press was good, he believed it. He began feeling only as strong as his team: Costin, Ungless, Leane, Brickhill. They were known as the Family, a reference to the Manson cult. But after the London *Observer* ran a group profile, McQueen was done sharing credit.

"As Lee became more well known and the brand expanded, we

weren't allowed to give press interviews," says Costin. "Everything came under the name of McQueen—we weren't allowed to have individual voices within that. Which I didn't think was right. Everyone needed recognition for the work they were doing; it was for the greater good."

McQueen's crudeness was calcifying. A boyfriend had recently tried to commit suicide, and his reaction, says Chris Bird, was alarming: "Lee said, 'How dare he try to kill himself in my fucking house?'"

That relationship didn't last much longer, and McQueen began seeing escorts and porn stars. In Paris, he'd go to the Queen nightclub on the Champs-Élysées and be escorted into the roped-off VIP section. "I think he quite liked it," Costin says. "It separated him from people that he really didn't want to engage with."

"I think people have to understand—because I was in a similar situation at Givenchy—basically, you believe in your own importance," Macdonald says. "Everybody saw him as this superstar, the next big thing, and he believed it. And actually, the people who really helped him, he kind of cut them off."

McQueen was now constantly on coke, even asking Eric Lanuit, the head of PR at Givenchy, for help staying awake for his shows. "He would call to ask for certain 'vitamin substances,'" Lanuit said in the documentary *McQueen and I*. "I'm not talking about vitamin C, I am talking about cocaine."

McQueen also felt he needed it to cope with the constant rumors of his imminent firing: "Sometimes he would just break down because he was so sensitive," one colleague said. His staff would literally tiptoe into the studio in the mornings.

After the success of "Untitled," Simon Costin gave an interview to *i-D*, and when McQueen saw it he went ballistic. Costin wrote him a letter, expressing disappointment in his old friend Lee.

McQueen was enraged. He took the letter and called his top

people, Katy England and show producer Sam Gainsbury, into his tiny office. He read Costin's note aloud, incredulous, saying over and over, "He can't talk to me like that!' "

Costin was fired.

"That, to me, was an example of how removed he was from how he used to be," Costin says. "It had all shifted to this point where he felt people couldn't speak to him in an honest, heartfelt way . . . The people who answered him back would disappear or go or not be working anymore. It was interesting to see how these celebrities become what they become. I can't imagine anything worse."

CHAPTER 18

# IT'S THE GIRL,
# NOT THE CLOTHES

AS SHOCKING AS MCQUEEN at Givenchy was the appointment
of Marc Jacobs at Louis Vuitton that same year. Vuitton was stagnat-
ing, a 143-year-old French luxury house that produced monogrammed
bags and suitcases. Bernard Arnault wanted to expand into ready-to-
wear and had been watching Marc's evolution. He was maturing, and
his last three collections earned high praise. "Mr. Jacobs's mission,
where he set his sights three seasons ago, is refinement," said the *New
York Times*. "Each season he has peeled away themes and adornments,
leaving behind bare luxury in fabric and discreet touches like raised
seams and beading so fine it appears pressed into the fabric."

Marc was a risk. He'd been fired from Perry Ellis; his own company had gone bankrupt several times; there were plenty of designers who were far more famous. Arnault consulted with Marc's
great champion, Anna Wintour. "She pointed us toward unexpected
choices," Arnault said. "I speak very openly to her, and this was quite
audacious—it was not about picking the big names of the moment."

Vuitton conducted a public audition, commissioning one-off
bags from Vivienne Westwood, Helmut Lang, Romeo Gigli, Manolo

Blahnik, Azzedine Alaïa, and Isaac Mizrahi. None impressed. Arnault's first choice, menswear designer Paul Smith, passed.

In the way athletes study game film, Arnault watched reel after reel of fashion shows for months. He sent trusted adviser Concetta Lanciaux to New York, where she interviewed nearly every designer in town, including Michael Kors, whom Arnault would install at Céline, and Anna Sui.

In May 1996, Lanciaux went to see Marc at his offices on Spring Street. When she walked in, he tried to seem nonchalant: He was on the phone, chain-smoking and chatting away, as if he were dealing with a delivery boy bringing in lunch. His counterintuitive approach had the desired effect; luxury, after all, needed to be cooler and less affected now.

"I knew he was the one," Lanciaux said later. "It was the way his office looked and felt . . . his long hair in the ponytail. I had a feeling. I . . . there was a connection. Marc is always elegant, no? Even in his sneakers." He took her on a walk through SoHo, pointing out the girls he found most chic. "Suddenly, he would stop in the street—not listening to what I was saying—because he had seen a girl who in some way epitomized the style of his own designs," she said. But he was careful not to point out girls who were scruffier, edgier, odd looking; this afternoon, he went for the Carolyn Bessette Kennedys, "these skinny, tall, elegant blond women," Lanciaux said. "It was amazing—the absoluteness of his vision."

The hire was motivated, in large part, by what Tom Ford had done for Gucci, which "had a terrible image," Wintour said. "All those '70s playboys in Gucci loafers! And now, you can't get into the Gucci store in Milan."

For Arnault, these appointments—Galliano, Marc, McQueen—were as much about shock value as art and commerce, their wild reputations as valuable as the clothes they made. Marc's contract was 500 pages long.

"It's the girl you identify, not the clothes," said Candy Pratts

Price. "But he also lives the life of those clothes. We go out and stay out till three. We drink and smoke cigarettes and do everything naughty . . . We know where we want to take those clothes."

By now, much of alternative culture was mainstream. In March 1997, a cleaned-up Courtney Love wore white Versace to the Oscars; within a year, she was shot by Avedon as the new face of the label. Chloë Sevigny, she of the bowl cut and the disastrous freakshow film *Gummo*, was hired by Miuccia Prada to star in the spring/summer Miu Miu campaign. In one shot, she was styled in rust-colored trousers, clunky blue sandals, and a buttoned-up shirt: This was the new chic.

Sofia Coppola, too, was becoming an unlikely aspirational figure. Her beauty was in no way conventional—better yet, it was interesting. Her nose was large, her figure boyish, her expression flat, her style subtle. She'd already been shot by Steven Meisel for the cover of Italian *Vogue*, starred in a Black Crowes video, and was shot by then-boyfriend Dewey Nicks for British *Vogue* in 1994. "I like to be comfortable because I am Californian," she said. "Nothing too severe or feeling like I am wearing a costume." Her favorite fashion moment was Marc's grunge collection, which was "exactly what I wanted."

Yet she wasn't his first choice for his inaugural campaign, shot by Juergen Teller in early 1998. He asked Kim Gordon, and that she said yes was another marker of how fast things were changing. Kim Gordon wasn't selling out, nor was she buying in: She and Marc were equally bloodless and cool.

Marc was hired as head designer at Vuitton in January 1997, in a deal brokered by Duffy. He insisted that Arnault buy the third of Marc Jacobs International that, till now, had been bankrolled by Perry Ellis. "I knew it was crucial," Duffy said. "If they went ahead and put money into us, it would be their first major American investment, and for that reason alone they would not let our company fail."

When Marc got the job, his first calls weren't to friends but to professional contacts: Candy Pratts Price at *Vogue*, Kal Ruttenstein at Bloomingdale's. He thought he'd be treated as a boy king, as Tom Ford was at Gucci, and was shocked to discover "all this palace intrigue, French backstabbing" when he went to Vuitton headquarters in Paris, where he'd be working for half the year. Marc, like McQueen, was a true believer in his own talent, but he was given no guidance. Nor did he speak French, and the honeymoon periods he'd had in Paris were swiftly undercut. As they had with McQueen, LVMH gave Marc a budget apartment, one on a low floor with noise, streetlight, and neighbors who complained his music was too loud. The Vuitton staff mocked him.

"Tell us," one Vuitton executive asked, "'ow are the clothes that Meester Jacobs is making? Is he still doing the 'grunge'?"

Marc was told he had free rein, and he was panic-stricken. "It's like having the liberty to do whatever you want," he said. "But it's too much freedom, in a weird way."

Yet it had a salutary effect on his own line. Marc used much of the LVMH money to hire the best public relations firm in fashion, KCD, and to hire more people; he now had time just to design. The Marc Jacobs collection he showed in New York that spring won raves for its effortless sophistication. He showed henley tops made of cashmere—proof that he'd been onto something with his grunge collection—and was lauded for his rare internal compass, one that could not be replicated because, as the *New York Times* noted, "that emotion comes from within, from a life, from a circle of friends and from an awareness of contemporary culture that is entirely too intuitive to be stolen."

"Hip . . . savvy . . . very beautiful," said *Women's Wear Daily*.

But while Marc's own line was hitting a creative peak, his work for Vuitton was causing him agony. He was beginning to suspect he'd made the biggest mistake of his career, and that any missteps he made at Vuitton would hurt his own line. He freaked when LVMH execs told him they wanted to open a Vuitton boutique on the Champs-Élysées; it was "touristy," Marc said, the kind of street where "people don't buy fashion." He found himself in discussions that would have been comical were there not so many billions at stake. They wanted him to be edgy but traditional, and he had no idea what that meant. Did they want his first Vuitton fashion show to be a spectacle, like something McQueen would do? Or did they want something more old-world and sedate? Could he introduce irony, reappropriate the logo, fuck with it? Or did he have to show respect?

No one gave him an answer.

"I have to assume that Vuitton hired me on the basis of my audition project," he said. "And that certainly wasn't very . . . I mean, it was creative in a basic way. I think you have to give them nice things—not extreme or avant-garde or weird. I mean, I don't have very wacky instincts anyway. But that's part of my personal torment in all of this—I'm starting to think that that's maybe what people want, or maybe what people expect."

"It was like he wanted the whole thing to disappear," said Anna Sui, "because it was just too much."

Between February and March, Marc calmed down. He focused on the warm reception his eponymous line had received in New York. Meanwhile, he and Duffy were proceeding with plans to open the first Marc Jacobs store, on Mercer Street in SoHo, later that year—a necessary expense, given that barely any department stores in New York, let alone the country, carried his designs. He'd cut off his hair and hired new people, not without resistance from LVMH.

Everything was a fight, including the ad campaigns, which Duffy insisted reflect Marc's vision. "I don't like the idea of an advertising company thinking up what looks young and cool as opposed to a real young person just feeling what they think looks contemporary and right," Marc said. "I mean, I don't sit down and think, 'Okay, I'm going to create a cool sweater.' I sit down and think about a sweater and it's not, you know, this great effort to be 'with it.' "

Since he was getting no feedback, Marc decided that his debut collection for Vuitton should be logo-free, a bold move for a brand built entirely on that logo. "I thought I would be very clever," he said years later.

He began talking about how he wanted to produce things that were a little bit "fucked up"—scarves that would pill, bags that would scuff. He was so in love with the idea of imperfect beauty, of the casual way that rich people treated their most expensive items, just using and loving the shit out of something.

Now Vuitton execs got involved. "I prefer not to put a product on the market if I cannot guarantee its quality," said Yves Carcelle, then president of Louis Vuitton. "This is something we have to discuss deeply with Marc, because it is a constraint. I will not sacrifice the reputation of quality for the sake of looking for the most trendy thing."

As Marc's debut approached, LVMH considered canceling, and publicly humiliated their latest acquisition. "We are together now for life," Carcelle told the *New Yorker* at the time. "The deal we have made—we are, in a way, married. It's frightening."

Marc's next formal presentation to Arnault was on June 23, and he and Duffy were in a panic, up till 3 A.M. the night before. Once again, Arnault was underwhelmed. "The feeling was that it wasn't strong enough," Marc said. He was beyond frustrated: "Depending on what day of the week it is, the stuff I make has to preserve the tradition of Vuitton or it has to rock the world." All Marc wanted was Arnault's approval.

"In so many ways," Marc said, "I've felt like this little boy trying to please a father." Once again, he found solace in drugs and alcohol, using heroin and cocaine and drinking every day and night.

"It's such a cliché," Marc said, "but when I drank I was taller, funnier, smarter, cooler." Or so he thought. He was getting thrown off planes, once carried off on a stretcher and forcibly hospitalized. He wouldn't come to the office for days on end, causing his staff to work weekends, and when he did show up, he was a monster. "He could be so mean to people," Duffy said. "It started affecting the people who were working around us [and] it had to be addressed. I never felt it was part of his creative process. He was just trying to escape."

Duffy was in an impossible situation: As concerned as he was, he couldn't go to Arnault—what if he fired Marc? The company they'd worked so hard to build might never recover. Carcelle, unaware of Marc's addictions, broached the idea of canceling the collection altogether, and Marc didn't show until 1998. With LVMH's financial resources, Duffy hired a team that he hoped could compensate for Marc's free fall: Juergen Teller's stylist wife Venetia Scott; Katie Grand, who'd worked extensively with Kate Moss and Melanie Ward for *The Face*, *i-D*, and *Dazed & Confused*; and Camille Miceli, who'd been Chanel's PR director.

At best, Duffy knew he was enabling; at worst, he was placing the company over Marc's chances for survival. "It was so hard," Duffy said, "because I know that Marc is someone who is in a lot of pain. And I was just letting him destroy himself."

CHAPTER 19

# WHEN THE LITTLE GLOW
# IN YOUR FACE GOES

KATE HADN'T WALKED DOWN a runway sober in over a decade, or done a shoot where she wasn't on something. As she said about shooting in Europe, pot was a constant presence on sets, and "after the first picture, it's 'Skin up!'" When she checked into the Priory, she did the whole supermodel thing, rolling up in big black sunglasses, everyone looking at her like she was ridiculous. She took them off.

In therapy, she realized that the old truism about addicts applied to her: The minute you start using is the minute you stop growing, and she'd been using since she was fifteen. She told a friend that she'd realized no matter how much she loved Johnny Depp, they "were toxic together," and being in the Priory was helping her to accept that. She wanted to be more than a face, a model, a hologram.

"I was in denial for a long time, I think," she said. "I don't think I was being overdramatic when I went in for treatment, that's for sure."

The icon of heroin chic going to rehab just as heroin chic was being abandoned by the industry—it wasn't nearly as cynical as all that, but Kate was becoming passé. She'd helped save Calvin Klein's house, and now Calvin dumped her, saying that he'd "never meant to create a monster." Gisele Bündchen had only been on the scene for a year, and she was becoming a superstar, a bronzed, athletic goddess reminiscent of the '80s Amazons. Maybe the pendulum had swung.

Once so enigmatic, Kate now granted several interviews to well-chosen publications: *The Face*, *Interview*, British *Vogue*. It was time to change the narrative. Her generation was becoming the establishment—McQueen at Givenchy, Marc at Vuitton—and she would not be left behind. "I always said I was never going to go for it in a major way because I never wanted to go into rehab," Kate said. "I never, ever wanted to end up in the position [where] I couldn't have a drink. Which is probably the first sign of it: 'No, I never want to not be able to have a drink.' You moderate things so you don't have to get to that point. But I couldn't keep myself in check anymore. Couldn't do it. I kind of lost the plot really there a little bit."

In truth, she was only out of the Priory a couple of days before she got back on drugs. "She doesn't think she's got a problem," says a friend of that time. "It's everyone else who doesn't understand."

She spent December partying in Thailand with Ronnie Wood's son Jesse, and February off in Barbados. She was rushed to the hospital in March, Sarah Doukas telling the press that "Kate is living a very quiet life" and that "her hospital treatment has nothing to do with drink and drugs." But Kate didn't think rehab meant quitting. "I don't think you have to not like sex, drugs, and rock 'n' roll just because you stop," Kate said. "I'm changing, but I don't feel like I'm turning into a person who doesn't like that kind of lifestyle." She saw a psychiatrist once a week and attended Alcoholics Anonymous and Narcotics Anonymous meetings. "What did I learn in rehab?" she said to one friend. "A lot about alcohol!"

She now kept the bacchanalias behind closed doors. She spent nights ensconced with the Primrose Hill set, still close to Sadie Frost. She'd had a falling-out with Anna Friel, who was thankful: "I'd [otherwise] be dead from all the drugs I was doing with Kate."

Sexually, Kate appeared more out of control than ever: one account has her as the supermodel who'd attend a party and station herself outside the bathroom door, yelling, "Anyone want a fuck?"

Then there was Naomi Campbell, who, another friend said, frightened Kate, even though the two were very close. They had much in common: Both were middle-class girls from London discovered as teenagers, and both had difficult relationships with their mothers. But mainly, both were fond of cocaine. They liked to snort it using rolled up hundred-dollar bills, and had members of their entourage to procure the drugs, then act as mules on international flights. It was pre-9/11, and these were supermodels flying first class; they didn't go through security like everyone else. When they were really fucked up, they'd fly private.

Naomi had gone into rehab in 1999, and later said she'd been using since '94. "I was living this life of traveling the world and having people just give you anything," she said. "[But] the little glow in your face goes . . . it's a very nasty drug."

"When I first started working with Naomi, she said she was sober," says a former assistant. "Two weeks in, our first trip, we went to Paris and she pulls out a bag of cocaine and did it in the open. It started a new chapter." Part of the assistant's job was clearing out Naomi's minibar and stashing all the bottles in her own room "so it would look like she wasn't drinking. Then we'd be drinking and doing coke till 7 A.M." Kate was far more casual about her drug use. "I'd get really scared if Kate was drinking or doing coke in the open," says the assistant. "But Kate would say, 'Stop worrying—they already think that I do this, so why not let them?'"

When Kate and Naomi joined socialite Annabelle Rothschild and Alexander McQueen for an event in Spain, the designer almost didn't make it out alive. Later that night, after the event, all four returned to the hotel with another friend and began doing piles of coke. "Lee took me into the bathroom and did a line with me," says the assistant. "He looked really sad and said, 'I'm really tired of this shit.' And the more coke he did, the more worked up he got." At seven the next morning, the assistant got a frantic call from Kate, who had discovered McQueen passed out on the bathroom floor. "Kate was off her rocker," says the assistant, "manic and chain-smoking and drinking champagne." Over and over, she said, 'Oh Jesus Christ! I just want him to get up! He's got to get up and go to work in London tomorrow!'"

McQueen did wake up, and the girls put him right to bed. "He asked for a cigarette," says the assistant. "He looked so sad and depressed." As usual with Kate and Naomi, there was about $6,000 in cash strewn all over the floor, in hundreds, dusted with coke residue. After rousing McQueen, the assistant checked on Naomi back in her room. "She was half woken up and had a pile of coke next to her, and she was doing lines and the color of her skin was gray."

And so Kate resumed the life and times of a supermodel.

Corinne Day had a new project. The working title was *Diary*, and it was going to be *the* document of her generation, a 1990s version of Nan Goldin's *The Ballad of Sexual Dependency*. She was spending most of her time with Tara St. Hill, getting some of her greatest stuff: Tara in her seedy apartment, high on ketamine; Tara crying, a wreck over a fight with her boyfriend; Tara with her tights down, squatting over a toilet.

"She'd bide her time," Tara says. Corinne's approach was to shoot everything always, in the way that people on reality TV say they forget the cameras are there, Corinne's subjects did too. "And then," says Tara, "that moment would happen."

Corinne got her moment one night at Tara's flat, right after her dealer arrived. Tara and the guy got high, then went off to her bedroom to have sex, Corinne in tow, snapping away at the edge of the bed. Tara later said she was so high that she had no idea Corinne was doing that; Corinne said Tara was a drug addict with no boundaries.

"She was quite comfortable being naked and having sex in front of me," Corinne said.

For Tara that was it. She cut Corinne out of her life and went to rehab. When she emerged, she and her ex-boyfriend George saw an advance copy of *Diary*. It included the nude of George that Corinne had promised never to publish and the coital image of Tara. They ran over to Brewer Street and begged Corinne to remove those images: just those two, leave in whatever else. Corinne repeatedly refused, her calmness infuriating. Tara's drug counselor asked Corinne to take out that one image of Tara, so precarious in her recovery. Corinne said no.

When the book was published, Corinne had a huge launch at the posh Gimpel Fils gallery in Mayfair, images of Tara on the wall, signed copies stacked neatly on tables for sale at £60 per. Tara was on the cover, a shot of her face in close-up, eyes closed, a ball of blue powder wedged in her right nostril. Corinne, so long in exile, was finally getting media attention again: The UK *Times* devoted a spread to Corinne's latest work, but it wasn't what she hoped. "She turned Kate Moss into a modeling sensation," the article read. "But Corinne Day's latest photographs show her friends in varying states of intoxication. Why does she seem so addicted to the seedier side of life?"

Even Corinne didn't know.

Tara showed up and began rifling through as many copies of *Diary* as she could, tearing out the pages of her and George. Scandalized partygoers approached and asked her to autograph the copies she'd defaced: Here they were, meeting a real-life drug addict, Corinne's new star. Tara walked up to Corinne, said, "Congratulations on all your new art-world fame," and walked out the door.

CHAPTER 20

# CAN EVERYBODY NOT GIVE LEE ANY DRUGS?

MCQUEEN MAY HAVE BEEN of the establishment, but he was still fighting it. If the old guard found his work at Givenchy disappointing, that was their fault: "All of a sudden, we had these wallies saying, 'This is not couture, this is a lot of bollocks,'" he said. "But being about couture is trying to find new clients for couture, and it's hard to do that when you have the press saying that this is not for [the socialite] Anne Bass. I mean, I don't want to bloody dress Anne Bass anyway, you know what I mean? Why interview someone I don't want as a client anyway? Interview Courtney Love or someone. The Courtney Loves, the Madonnas—these are the new customers. The reason I am doing this is because I am twenty-seven, not fifty-seven."

It was unlike McQueen to complain, but nothing about him was recognizable anymore. He had a bottomless capacity for cocaine. A lifelong asthmatic, McQueen took up cigarettes, which shocked even him. "I never smoked in my life until I started at Givenchy," he said. He smoked as much as Kate Moss and Marc Jacobs, two packs a day.

"Every six months you do a show and get publicity and sell perfume," McQueen said. "But it's between those six months when there [aren't] those shows that it deteriorates. No one in the fashion press or the buyers actually sees the trauma you go through to get things done."

But the more he abused himself, the better his work became. His fall/winter 1998–99 "Joan" show, inspired by Joan of Arc and reflective of his ongoing martyr complex, was a critical success, judged "stronger" than "Untitled" by *Women's Wear Daily*, the "breadth and depth" of his talent, according the *New York Times*, no longer in question. He showed ninety-one looks on models in white-caked faces and red contact lenses, medieval specters in hoods and chain mail. Writing in the *International Herald Tribune*, Suzy Menkes called the collection "mature and well-focused . . . Looking at the impeccable tailoring, it's hard to believe that a year ago the same designer sent out cavewoman goat skins in apocalyptic chaos."

McQueen didn't want to be mature, or a former punk provocateur. He posed for the cover of *The Face* as a male version of Joan, his head powdered and looped in what looked like barbed wire. He wrote a note explaining the image:

"Joan. Deep inside of me I have no regrets of the way I portray myself to the General Public. I will face fear head on if necessary, but will run from a fight if persuaded."

Within weeks of "Joan," McQueen staged his next show for Givenchy, and he really tried to please, with simple, well-cut suits and shift dresses in neutral palettes, plus a little leather and Lurex to give high society a thrill. Yet even though his personal collection had met with a rapturous reception, nothing he did for Givenchy seemed to satisfy anyone: not Arnault, not the critics, not the editors or buyers. He was only the second Englishman this century appointed head of a French couture house, and Anna Wintour had yet to attend a single show. Two years into his tenure at Givenchy, Amy Spindler at the *New York Times* tried to divine the problem: "He knows so much, he's so talented, and yet nothing about it looks easy or natural for him," she wrote.

Despite his difficulties, he re-upped with Givenchy for another two years. His clothes might not have been selling, but he brought the house more press than Arnault could have hoped. McQueen became the kind of fashion person he'd once loathed, demanding flights on the Concorde and suites at the Ritz, where he'd order mounds of caviar to use as ashtrays.

As John Galliano later said, each time he signed a contract, his life was suddenly mapped out to the second. "The pressure gets to you," says Julien Macdonald, McQueen's successor at Givenchy. But McQueen, he says, "had an addictive personality—whether it was drink or drugs or sex, he had a secret life that only his closest friends knew about." Catherine Brickhill, his design assistant, was one of those friends, but when she tried to talk to McQueen about his drug use, he fired her.

"Catherine is lovely and down-to-earth, and she was perhaps too honest, too truthful," says Simon Costin. "It wasn't what he was looking to hear at that time. I wasn't surprised that Catherine was off."

The message was clear: If Brickhill wasn't safe, no one was. McQueen was not to be challenged on anything. It was becoming common knowledge in the industry that McQueen's people, like Marc's beleaguered staff, were in chaos. "It was like, 'Can everybody not give Lee any drugs?'" Macdonald says. "He was completely off his head. He was like, taking coke, taking E—he was just uncontrollable. In a mad state, I think. The stories you used to find out . . . Oh God, that guy really needed help."

McQueen didn't see it that way: He needed the drugs to produce this endless number of collections. "I think what happens sometimes, drugs are your only true companion," Adrover says. "Without [them], I don't think he would have come up with the creativity." As far as McQueen was concerned, Givenchy was now a day job, his focus mainly on hitting deadlines. He would save his genius for his own shows, and his next one, "No. 13," would be a masterpiece. He knew it before he staged it.

McQueen had become obsessed with the idea of impairments and disability, and explored the theme when he guest-edited Jefferson Hack's *Dazed & Confused*, using the double amputee Aimee Mullins as a model. Once again, McQueen was accused of sensationalism, and once again he expressed moral outrage. "The idea is to show that beauty comes from within," McQueen said. "You look at all the mainstream magazines, and it's all about the beautiful people, all of the time." He called the issue "FASHION-ABLE" and wrote that it was a rebuke to an industry that still insisted beauty meant "you have to be young, you have to be thin, you should preferably be blond and, of course, pale skinned."

He later went on to speak the unspeakable. "The concept was that fashion should reach everybody," he said. "Magazines are afraid of fat people."

He hired Mullins to walk in "No. 13," on wooden prosthetics he commissioned from the artist Bob Watts. Two thousand people crammed into a disused Victoria bus station, where McQueen mounted his most ambitious, accomplished show yet. There were dresses and skirts made of balsa wood, a stitched-up leather breast-plate over lace, a model encased in a thin spiral of stiff Swarovski crystal chains. For the finale, Shalom Harlow stood on a rotating plat-form, swirling in white as two robot arms splattered her with spray paint. "The triumph of London's fashion week," Suzy Menkes said. "McQueen captured the raw aggression of Britpop and the swagger-ing showmanship of the art scene." McQueen agreed. "It was my best show," he said, "that moment with Shalom." He later said he was so moved by his own talent, he wept.

As usual, McQueen was working out his own demons on the

runway, and "No. 13" was a plain depiction of how he saw himself: hobbled, disabled, a puppet on a pedestal vandalized by automatons. "Anger in my work reflected angst in my personal life," he said. "People saw me coming to terms with what I was in life: my morbid side, my sexual side. It's always been about the human psyche. My work is like a biography of my own personality."

He wanted out of LVMH. He'd capped his teeth, gotten liposuction and lost weight, dyed his hair and rolled with rock stars and royalty, yet he was sure that the LVMH execs were mocking him, the fat East Ender who thought he was good enough for French couture. "I think he felt he was slightly disgusting to look at," says Alice Smith. "I think he felt that they were a bit scornful, called him names behind his back—and I suspect they did. I think he felt like, even though he was in this amazing position, looking after Givenchy— there were certain elements of society that laughed at him. He always had that impression." McQueen knew that he was undervalued; unlike Marc, he wasn't going to sit around waiting for Bernard Arnault to pat him on the head. He went to the press: "Fire me!" he said.

Issie took credit for what happened next: As she would tell it, she was seated next to Tom Ford at a dinner in May 1999 and told him to "take a look at Alexander." Ford was quite interested. Not only did he think McQueen was a genius, but poaching him would be the best revenge against Arnault, who'd recently attempted a hostile takeover of Gucci Group—one Ford successfully fought off by convincing French luxury company Pinault-Printemps-Redoute to inject $3 billion into the company, acquiring Yves Saint Laurent in the process.

McQueen met with Ford and his business partner Domenico De Sole and liked them both. LVMH, normally an iron fortress of brand management, let it leak that "the problem with Mr. McQueen is that he is always on drugs." Ford wasn't sure how much to believe; it was possible LVMH was trying to poison the deal. Besides, drug use in the industry was commonplace, and Ford himself liked to take the edge off each night with a vodka or three. So he made McQueen an attractive offer: For a 51 percent stake in his company, Gucci Group would ask that he produce only for the house of McQueen, slicing his workload in half. Ford's one caveat: McQueen had to make clothes that would sell. McQueen understood and respected Ford; he agreed, and in 2000 officially defected to Gucci Group.

"Talk about bite the hand that feeds you," McQueen said. "I bloody chewed it up and spat it out."

CHAPTER 21

# THESE PEOPLE ARE
# NOT YOUR FRIENDS

JUST LIKE MCQUEEN, MARC found himself in an impossible situation: He had been hired by one of the biggest luxury brands on the planet for his credibility and cool, and now that he was through the doors, Arnault and his team were attempting to defang him. It was as though the increasingly corporatized world of high fashion had a perpetual case of buyer's remorse.

Yet when it came to true danger, to the huge amounts of drugs and alcohol Marc and McQueen were consuming, LVMH didn't seem to care, as long as both designers were producing. "I kept looking over my shoulder and thinking, 'Well, this one does it, and that one does it, so I can too,'" Marc said. "Because all designers are like that, and we're creative people, and that's how artists are."

Marc was still grappling with his feelings of subpar treatment by Arnault and LVMH and couldn't help, once again, but compare himself to Tom Ford's relationship with PPR. "I think Gucci treated Tom Ford better than LVMH has treated me," he said. What he didn't know was that Ford also felt he'd been treated horribly; he just kept it to himself. It wasn't until years after his split from Gucci and YSL that

193

Ford spoke about it. "Being at Yves Saint Laurent was such a negative experience for me, even though the business boomed while I was there," Ford said. "Yves and his partner, Pierre Bergé, were so difficult and so evil and made my life such misery . . . It was an awful time for me . . . I have letters from Yves Saint Laurent that are so mean you cannot even believe such vitriol is possible."

Gucci also had it written into Ford's contract that he couldn't take the customary bow on the runway, and the man who saved the house now grappled with depression. He just hid it better. "I have a very dark side," Ford said. "I've never been one who showed that to the outside world."

Marc was like a teenager, all raw angst. "I'd walk in a room and all I'd think about is, 'How many people in this room hate me right now?'" Marc said. "They think I'm ugly, or whatever. It was the idea of . . . not feeling good-looking enough, not tall enough, not clever enough—I guess that's how I've felt pretty much most of my life."

Like McQueen, Marc found solace in his own brand. Here, he had a clear, confident approach: After the Kim Gordon test ad, Marc wanted to hire photographer Juergen Teller to do all his campaigns. He wanted the photos to have that same blown-out look, like Polaroids left to dry in the sun, and he wanted the same kinds of alt-celebrities to model, ones who looked a little off. He cast Harmony Korine, face bloated from self-abuse, posing with his arm around a young black girl; Pavement's Stephen Malkmus, hunched over a guitar in the back of a library, face obscured by shaggy hair; and, in 2001, Sofia Coppola, pronouncing her his muse in the wake of her well-reviewed feature debut, *The Virgin Suicides*.

Coppola had written an adapted screenplay after Sonic Youth's Thurston Moore had given her a copy of the book in 1995; her father produced the film, which was set in the 1970s and was most striking for its look. Coppola and her cinematographer Edward Lachman soaked the film in sun, her three backlit blond leads looking like girls in '70s shampoo ads. Sofia had located Marc's artistic marrow and produced a faithful interpretation; the appropriation of unstylish clothes, music, hair, all made improbably chic filtered through the soft pain of nostalgia. Coppola pulled from Corinne Day, whom she hired to do still photography, and Juergen Teller; from Beck videos and Bill Owens's *Suburbia*. Geoff McFetridge, former art director of the Beastie Boys' *Grand Royal*, did the title sequence, and would later work on Marc by Marc Jacobs. Sofia was the next face of his brand, shot by Teller on the lip of a pool. "She is young and sweet and beautiful," Marc said. "The epitome of the girl I fantasize of."

Marc dreaded going back to Paris. Like McQueen, he soon realized that his job entailed being a brand ambassador as much as being a designer. He was expected to do interviews, to attend store openings and launch parties and dinners, to juggle time zones and manage jet lag and produce six ready-to-wear collections a year plus accessories. In September of '98, he was the star of the launch of the Louis Vuitton store in New York City, flown in that morning from Paris. Kate Moss was there, as were Naomi Campbell, Steven Meisel, and Chloë Sevigny, and he veered from excitement to exhaustion.

"If I move, I'll fall over," he said.

He was spiraling downward, his trajectory near identical to McQueen's: the rent boys and porn stars, the drugs and chain-smoking. Marc was up to fifty Marlboro Lights a day. He'd get wasted and have bizarre endurance contests, seeing who could hold a lit cigarette against his skin the longest. Sometimes he'd nod off while smoking, waking up to burns on his skin, clothing, furniture.

"I don't have anger issues," he said. "I only hurt myself. I don't really hurt other people." That was not the case: He was hurting Robert Duffy, the houses of Vuitton and Marc Jacobs, and every member of his staff who cleaned up in his wake.

Marc didn't appear at the Vuitton show in Paris, nor did he show at New York Fashion Week. He was checking into hotels for days on end, bingeing on coke, vodka, heroin. Duffy was paralyzed. It was Anna Wintour who called and said enough—and this was a woman who'd seen Donatella Versace face-plant into her glass coffee table at *Vogue*. Naomi Campbell, herself an addict, also intervened, and Duffy finally confronted Marc, reminding him that to LVMH, he was just another acquisition.

"These people don't really love you or care about you," Duffy said. "They want you to work, and if you die, that's it."

Marc checked into rehab in spring 1999, and after Page Six broke the story, Duffy gave an interview to Bridget Foley at *Women's Wear Daily*, knowing she'd be sympathetic. (Foley went on to author a Jacobs monograph, and Jacobs would later hire Foley's daughter.)

"I didn't want to go to rehab at first, because I was high out of my mind," Marc said. "I'm sure the root of my problems goes much further back than before I was successful. When I was younger, all the kids I thought were cool smoked cigarettes, my favorite rock stars were heroin addicts, and my favorite writers were taking acid. As a kid, what I thought looked cool was very dark and drug-oriented."

It was one thing to love the way it looked but another to live it, and the culture had moved on. It was now five years since Kurt Cobain had killed himself, taking grunge with him. Now kids listened to scrubbed-up boy bands and the Spice Girls, Britney Spears and Ricky Martin. Lollapalooza, unable to sell enough tickets, had been canceled in 1997. *Friends*, *Frasier*, and *Who Wants to Be a Millionaire* were the top-rated TV shows, and the year's biggest movies were *Star Wars: Episode 1— The Phantom Menace*, *Toy Story 2*, and *The Mummy*. Gisele had deposed Kate Moss, with Anna Wintour dubbing Bündchen "the model of the millennium." No one was much interested in looking at waiflike androgynes anymore; they wanted Victoria's Secret models. There was a retreat to wholesomeness and predictability.

It was against this landscape that Marc had to reinvent himself. He was beginning to realize that so many of his famous friends didn't really care about him either. "All the friends he had weren't really friends," Duffy said. "When I made phone calls to his supposed best friends when he was in rehab, they were like, 'He's what?' These are not your best friends. There were the people he was honest with— which was zero except me—and the people he did drugs with. And then there were the people who sat in the front row. There was never any group that knew everything. The people he did drugs with didn't really know his personal life, that he had a boyfriend. The people who sat in the front row didn't know he did drugs, or simply thought he did [them] occasionally. One of the hardest things for me when I sent him away to rehab was to figure out, when he came out, where the safest place would be, who would be his support group."

When Marc got out of rehab, he regressed. Once so beautiful and charismatic, he stopped caring about his looks, replacing drugs and booze with carbs and Coca-Cola. He got fat, wore ungainly eyeglasses, and let his hair grow greasy and long. He'd once seemed to glow from within; now, his complexion was flat, his eyes dead. He developed ulcerative colitis, the same disease that had killed his father.

"I thought, Who cares about my appearance?" Marc said. "They only care about what I'm making."

For his own show that September, he reverted to the '70s chic that was becoming his hallmark: The girls he designed for had been little then, and no cohort had as much nostalgia for its collective childhood as Generation X. He showed denim jeans and skirts, A-line dresses and shifts and sandals in what the *New York Times* called "a qualified success." His recent stint in rehab went largely unmentioned: Fashion designers were still the province of the fashion world, not the tabloid stars they'd soon become. But Marc wanted that. He wanted to be as famous as the movie stars he designed for, to have the same name recognition as Brad Pitt or David Beckham. "I love attention," Marc said. "I'm a shameless human being."

It was that aspect of his personality, the part that operated without fear, that led to his two breakout moments, one for each house. In 2001, he and Duffy opened three Marc Jacobs stores on sleepy Bleecker Street in the West Village. It was a bold move: The only other foot traffic was generated by girls who were obsessed with *Sex and the City*, who wanted to see Carrie Bradshaw's apartment building and get cupcakes at Magnolia Bakery. Marc's girl was not an *SATC* girl, with her Cosmos and her credit card debt, but the *SATC* girl, consumed with bags and shoes and designer goods, was quite possibly a Marc girl. Those stores turned Bleecker Street into a Gold Coast to rival Madison Avenue and turned the West Village into Manhattan's coolest neighborhood.

That year, Marc, sick of the dump picked by LVMH, went looking for another apartment in Paris. One potential place belonged to Charlotte Gainsbourg, who was sort of a French Sofia Coppola: a subtly stylish girl with *jolie laide* appeal, the daughter of national icon Serge Gainsbourg and the Swinging '60s model Jane Birkin. While touring Gainsbourg's flat, Marc noticed a piece of Vuitton luggage, painted black and tossed on the floor. He'd been stymied by how to make the LV logo "more rebellious, more punk," and here was the answer.

He called Stephen Sprouse and talked out his idea, how he wanted to do something inspired by Sprouse's graffiti, how he'd been stuck trying "to create this sort of anti-snobbery snobbism." Sprouse was a hero to Marc, an artist and designer who ran with Basquiat, Haring, and Meisel in the '80s; when Sprouse showed his first collection at the Ritz in May 1984, Marc was among three thousand kids fighting their way in. "It was like a rock concert," he said—just as his fashion shows, and McQueen's, would become. "It was incredible decadence—dark, punky, edgy. And the audience was downtown club kids sitting next to *Vogue* and *New York Times* fashion editors. It was the first time that had happened in New York." Sprouse, too, had been tapped as the future of fashion and had been on the verge of complete failure several times, eventually wiping out in the crash of '87. There was a kinship.

After nearly four years of trying to please Mr. Arnault, following his sphinxlike directives to little effect, Marc just went for it. "I had been trying to follow the rules and do what everybody told me," Marc said, "until it got to the point where I realized that's not why I was brought in here. I'm here to do something to make this young and cool and contemporary and of the moment. I wanted to use Stephen's graffiti specifically because it meant something to me. Stephen as an artist, Stephen as a New York figure. It had the credibility of street, but also this sort of style of somebody who was a fashion designer."

The "fucked up" logo Sprouse designed for Vuitton, a graffiti-inspired font in neon colors, was an unprecedented success. For the first time in Vuitton's history, there were waiting lists for bags. Carcelle and Arnault had to concede that Marc's instincts were unassailable, and that, given enough freedom and encouragement, he could make the house billions. That collection cemented Marc as a genius, and the fuckup who'd been fired from Perry Ellis for grunge had his revenge: He'd designed a bag that cost more than a month's rent, and young girls didn't care.

CHAPTER 22

# A SUPERMODEL JUST
# LIKE MCDONALD'S

KATE, WITHOUT QUITE REALIZING it, was becoming a fashion icon all by herself, no campaigns or catwalks necessary. Thanks to her party-girl ways, she was both high-end and tabloid, one of the most photographed women in the world. And now with the Internet, girls were getting daily updates on what Kate Moss was wearing, and they wanted what she had: When Kate was shot in a pair of Vivienne Westwood pirate boots in January 2000, the boots promptly sold out, and one season later Chanel did a version. Kate would ultimately be credited with popularizing the skinny jean, the ballet flat, McQueen's skull-print scarf, Jacobs's Stephen Sprouse LV leopard-print scarf, and the return of the dress for day. Most famously, she influenced a generation of festival-goers when she was shot wearing a belted sweater over rolled-up men's shorts and muddy Wellies, causing a run on the formerly staid boot. "The demographic for this brand changed in 2005," said the *Guardian*, "when Kate Moss wore them at Glastonbury, and they became *the* VIP area-festival Wellie." Corinne wound up shooting a model inspired by Kate's off-duty look for the December 2001 issue of British *Vogue*, pairing scuffed-up boots with a vintage sequined 1920s dress.

This was the Kate Moss alchemy: tossing thrift in with high-end, wearing both with such élan it was impossible to tell which was which, and never wearing or carrying anything with a logo. "She subtly moves the goalposts, so you never figure out who she is," said Simon Doonan, then Barneys' creative director. "She's an amalgam of very different archetypes: She's a rock chick, a society girl, a bohemian." While fans began hunting down similar looks, fast-fashion chains like Topshop and Zara began knocking off Kate's clothes. Her good friend Bella Freud, who worked for such a company, said that mood boards often were covered with paparazzi shots of Kate. "Whole lines have been made out of one look she put on one morning," Freud said.

When Kate stumbled across the prototype of a bag that Balenciaga's Nicolas Ghesquière decided not to produce, he gave it to her, and within weeks his offices were inundated with calls. That bag, the Lariat, is a modern classic. "At that point, we realized, without a doubt, her influence is enormous and global," said Ghesquière. When Kate chopped her hair into a Jean Seberg pixie and dyed it platinum blond, Tom Ford used her as inspiration for his spring 2001 collection for Gucci.

"Like a good fashion designer, Kate anticipates what people want," Ford said. "Whether it is cerebral or intuitive, she manages to pull from the air the spirit of the moment and embody it."

Marc Jacobs agreed. "With Kate, the elements are not really important," he said. "It's the sum of them."

Carine Roitfeld, then editor-in-chief of Paris *Vogue*, agreed that her impact was unprecedented. "If Kate is seen wearing jeans and a white fur coat, all the kids want to be wearing jeans and white fur," Roitfeld said. "She must be the most copied person on the planet. She isn't too tall, she isn't too thin . . . she's the stuff of dreams, because she has imperfections like everyone else, even though she's perhaps the biggest fashion icon in the world."

Recently out of rehab, Kate was thinking about no longer modeling. Chopping off her hair was freeing, as was abandoning the Hollywood-sheen look she'd cultivated with Johnny. She was trying to find her own identity through these revolving looks, and in doing so was becoming more powerful and influential than ever. She transcended fashion and was part of pop culture. The art world took note.

In late 1999, British *Vogue* commissioned seven of the Young British Artists, including Tracey Emin, Sam Taylor-Wood, Jake and Dinos Chapman, and Marc Quinn to create pieces inspired by Kate, displayed at the Tate Modern in May 2000. Quinn did Kate as ice sculpture, dressed in McQueen. "It's a perfect metaphor for our consumption of beauty," he said. "As the ice evaporates . . . people will literally breathe her in."

A few years later, *W* magazine did the same thing, commissioning artists and photographers such as Chuck Close, Tom Sachs, Richard Prince, Alex Katz, Takashi Murakami, Steven Klein, Mario Sorrenti, Craig McDean, and Inez van Lamsweerde and Vinoodh Matadin to interpret Kate. Sachs saw her appeal as "universal, just like McDonald's." McDean was inspired by her imperfection: "She's kind of off-beauty," he said. "She's not a little cookie, but she's probably the most beautiful girl in the world." Katz felt the same. "She's completely ordinary," he said. "That's what makes her so extraordinary." "When she started, she was so different from everybody else in terms of size and body shape and attitude," said van Lamsweerde. "She's definitely a generation's muse. I can't think of anyone else from our generation whom you'd aspire to look like."

Maybe Kate had found her other career. She wasn't even thirty years old, but unlike any of her forebears, she'd been relevant for thirteen years, the only model who had as much, if not more, influence on what girls wanted to look like than any designer. "At the end of the '90s, she started to notice that women were starting to emulate her distinctive style—especially in France, people in the fashion industry," says a friend. "She doesn't like it when the tabloids use her image. She says it's because she's not getting paid: That's *her* image."

Kate had also begun dating Jefferson Hack, who'd started *Dazed & Confused* in the apartment below Corinne's on Brewer Street. Hack formally met Kate when he interviewed her for the magazine, and though some in the industry couldn't quite figure out his success—to them he wasn't that bright, and the magazine was impossible to read— he'd failed upward, surrounded by his gifted cofounders Rankin, the photographer, and Katie Grand. McQueen's future stylist, Katy England, was an early staffer.

Hack was a natural networker. In the magazine's infancy, "we were really actively going out a lot at that time," he said. "I mean, we met everybody through clubs or bars . . . everybody that became a part of the framework of what was to be *Dazed & Confused*." After the magazine shot Chloë Sevigny in 1996, she introduced Hack to the kids on the Lower East Side scene, including Harmony Korine, who became a collaborator. The magazine was as much a labor of love as a way for Hack to meet famous people.

So when he interviewed Kate, he took a clever tack, betting that by putting her down—something no one ever did—he'd get her attention. "You smell of pee," he told her, then asked why she had such problems settling down. "Is no one good enough for you?"

For Kate, it wasn't love at first sight, but she was trying to change, and in her circle, Jefferson was as stable as they came. "She likes him and thinks, 'Oh, what a charming man,'" says a friend. "He drinks a bit, likes a bit of marijuana and cocaine"—but he didn't have an addiction to either. "He courts her in a way that she likes, lots of dates and fashion parties. They have sex about two weeks in." But Jefferson was "always, always" more into Kate than she was into him. She quickly began treating him like the help, but having Kate Moss on his arm was worth it. He was now in a whole other echelon.

"When Jefferson turns up at a fashion designer's party with Kate Moss, he's not an editor, he's part of the gang," said the *Guardian*. The article went on to note that "the extended *Dazed* family includes the Chapman brothers, Alexander McQueen, Stella McCartney, Damien Hirst, Björk, Chloë Sevigny, and the filmmaker Harmony Korine," and quoted Rankin asserting that "at the end of the day, we're as creative as they are. They became our friends." It was arrogance masquerading as egalitarianism, star-fucking as socializing.

But there was something else appealing about Jefferson: Everyone around Kate was having a baby; maybe she should too. Sadie was pregnant, and so was Meg Mathews. Pearl Lowe had just had a baby. The actress Samantha Morton, a fairly recent member of the Primrose Hill set, had a daughter that February and named Kate the godmother. Jefferson would be a good dad.

So motherhood would be next, Kate announced, and within six months she was pregnant. Her friends whispered among themselves: Was Jude really the father? There were also rumors that Kate had been sleeping with the great octogenarian artist Lucian Freud, whom she'd been sitting for—could it be his? Kate ignored the gossip. She maintained that the baby was Jefferson's, and said she'd be staying clean throughout her pregnancy, which she did for about two weeks. At the least, "she drank and smoked like a chimney," says a friend. "It's more about what she wants." Jefferson was alarmed, "but he didn't really have the balls to stand up to her. He was more like her butler than her husband: '*Jefferson*, get my coat!' '*Jefferson*, where's this?' He would just roll his eyes and be exasperated."

*Diary* didn't receive the critical acclaim Corinne had expected: She thought it would make her a member of the art world, on par with her idols Nan Goldin and Larry Clark. Instead, she was greeted with confusion, if not outright repulsion. She decided to humble herself and go back to fashion photography, to the few editors who might still give her another chance. She and Mark needed the money; they were so broke that Mark was working across the street from their flat at Whole Foods. And people wanted to help; word had gotten around that Corinne was really sick, but no one knew how dire the prognosis was. Corinne didn't want people to treat her differently.

She was approached by the fashion magazine *Dutch*; her dream was to reunite with her favorite models from the '90s, Rosemary Ferguson and Kate Moss. Though Corinne and Kate never really had a rapprochement, Kate had heard Corinne was ill, and she said yes. So did Rosemary.

They took off for the seashore, where they spent a couple of days shooting in strip clubs and bedsits. It was as if Corinne wanted to recreate that Camber Sands shoot with Kate in 1990, but with a sleazier vibe, and Kate couldn't believe Corinne still romanticized this way of living. Corinne staged Rosemary sitting in a chair next to Kate with one breast hanging out of her sweater, staring off into space, looking vacant and high. Kate, sad and bored, sat next to her. It wasn't a pose.

"I looked at Kate's face, and it said it all," Corinne said. "She was quite horrified to go into this smelly old nasty room. She had definitely gone into another world." But at night, when they'd go out for drinks after a day of work, they all had a great time. Those were the only moments Corinne left her camera in her room, and all the while she kept thinking to herself, "I wish I had my camera." It was as if moments weren't real unless she was shooting them, but she couldn't see that these moments were probably lighter, more vibrant and true, for the absence of a lens.

"Bang into drugs" was the way Kate Moss once described herself, and the christening party for her daughter, Lila Grace, was no reason to stop. Lila's garden brunch became a hedonistic weekend that ended with guests strewn across other people's lawns. Still, there was no transgression that could dim Kate's allure.

For her thirtieth birthday, Kate threw a wild party themed to F. Scott Fitzgerald's *The Beautiful and Damned*, and the accounts that emerged remain the stuff of legend: Kate and Naomi Campbell disappearing together for forty minutes. Gwyneth Paltrow, scandalized, fleeing swiftly. The after-party in a suite at Claridge's, where there was champagne and cigarette smoke and group sex in the main bedroom. "Kate went in and out," says a friend who claims to have attended. "Sadie was in there, and models, and Ronnie Wood." As the night wound down, Kate began bellowing for her long-suffering boyfriend, who was waiting outside the door.

"All you can hear is, '*Jefferson!*'" says the friend. "And he's standing there drinking and smoking, like he's seen it all before." Yet the British press paid just as much attention to what Kate was wearing: a liquid blue-black sequined dress from the 1920s once owned by actress Britt Ekland. Within four weeks, a near replica of that dress was shown in the next Gucci collection.

Kate's drug and alcohol use didn't impair her ability to model; in fact, it seemed to help. There were stories that she was thoroughly wasted for her famous British *Vogue* 2001 cover—Kate sitting on the floor with a crown tied on her head, a scepter slung behind her back. That image was later short-listed for Cover of the Century by the Professional Publishers Association.

"The thing about Kate—and I think it's part of her longevity— she's quite an elusive girl," said Anna Wintour. "There's something quite hidden about her. And I think that's why so many photographers and editors—and, later on in her career, artists—were drawn to her. Because it was hard to say exactly what she was or who she was, and they could put their own fantasies onto her. At the same time, there was always something a little edgy about her. She was not in any way corporate. She was a little bit dangerous, and that made her exciting and interesting."

Kate's entourage began calling lost time with her "getting

Mossed." Her friend and employee Jess Hallett recalled Kate having her fly to Paris. "I came back two days later with a black eye, a broken finger, and I can't remember what else happened to me . . . It can be a nightmare if you're the only one there. 'Please can we go home?' 'No.'" It happened to Marc Jacobs, too, when Kate got married in 2011; he was supposed to be there only for the weekend and wound up partying for five days. "I couldn't even remember the name of the hotel," he said. Kate's father, on those rare occasions he saw her, began introducing her to friends with a wry disclaimer: "Welcome to our nightmare," he'd say.

Kate was so impervious that when she took up with the Libertines' Pete Doherty—a junkie, thief, and former gay hustler—it only burnished her brand. Her rock 'n' roll aura wasn't an affect: This girl was *living it*. No matter the self-abuse, she always looked great, turning Doherty into a fashion touchstone in the process. Hedi Slimane designed an entire collection inspired by Doherty's skinny suits and ties, and so would Gaultier. It was during her time with Pete, oddly enough, that she had the greatest sustained period of trickle-up influence on fashion.

In 2004, Kate was honored for her unique impact by the CFDA. By the time she took the podium, she was so out of it that she could barely pronounce "CFDA," yet her look that night—tumbled hair, smoky eyes, and a simple strapless Dior cocktail dress—inspired Galliano's next collection. Sofia Coppola hired Kate to star in the video she was directing for the White Stripes, as a stripper working a pole, because, she said, "I would like to see that." Paris *Vogue* hired Kate to guest-edit their December issue. Cheap-chic retailer H&M was reported to have approached Kate about designing a line.

And then that picture surfaced of Kate chopping up lines of coke in a recording studio, sitting on a couch, wearing shorts, a fitted vest, and knee-high boots, stylish as ever. Her drug use was no secret in the industry, but this was too public, and she lost nearly all her contracts.

She apologized, went to rehab, dumped Doherty, and stopped with the heroin, which she'd started again with him.

"Initially, it was about her career—she realized he was too much of a waste, even for her," says a friend. "Then she realized he was dysfunctional, and she was functional."

## CHAPTER 23

# PARIS FOR COUTURE, LONDON FOR SUITS, AMERICA FOR PSYCHIATRIC HOSPITALS

BEFORE LEAVING GIVENCHY AND going to Gucci Group, McQueen was producing some of the most striking work of his career. His autumn/winter 1999 collection, "The Overlook," was inspired by Stanley Kubrick's *The Shining*, an icy phantasmagoria in white. His models traipsed through falling snow in cloud-like furs, laser-cut lace, eyelids streaked in silver and white. "A spectacular, magical show," said the *New York Times*, consisting of clothes that were "both beautiful and imaginatively conceived." It was the first McQueen show Anna Wintour deigned to attend.

While he seemed to be stabilizing artistically, McQueen was a wreck in his personal life. He'd met a new man, George Forsyth, who, at twenty-two, was ten years younger than McQueen and had never been exposed to the fashion industry. He was saddened by what he saw. "The fashion world is the loneliest place on the face of the planet," Forsyth said. "It's a shallow world full of party people and party 'friends.' Lee knew that."

Forsyth thought the only two people in his famed circle who really cared about Lee were Isabella Blow and Naomi Campbell. The rest were there for the residual gold dust, and McQueen knew it. Part of him loved running around with Kate Moss and the Primrose Hill set, even though he thought they were fucked up and superficial. "There's no substance," Forsyth said. "Lee was sharp as a pin. He'd spot it. He explained it all to me, that he had this public persona, the 'bad boy of fashion.' There was Lee at home and Alexander McQueen, the outrageous nutter, in public."

But McQueen had lost almost all of his old friends by his own hand, and no one in his new circle would ever express concern, because they really didn't care. His escalating mood swings, which his old friends thought were a sign of mental illness, were shrugged off as fashion-world eccentricity: There was the night McQueen took Forsyth to drinks in Paris, dinner in Spain, then dancing in Amsterdam. There was the lounging at home, watching a documentary on Africa, with McQueen deciding that should be their next trip—and there they were, two days later. Two days more and McQueen was over it, calling Naomi Campbell to meet up for New Year's. McQueen and Forsyth "spent three days partying and taking drugs there," Forsyth said. "Naomi didn't do any coke even though she was surrounded by people who were." The couple flew to New York for a day of shopping, McQueen dropping hundreds of thousands on art and clothes, and flew right back to London. He took Forsyth to Paris for the shows, and one night, walking through the lobby of the Four Seasons, decided he loved their chandeliers so much he'd buy one, which he did, on the spot, for more than $50,000.

Issie was furious that McQueen was throwing around millions while paying her nothing, but she was more upset by his drug use. "This boy she loved—this is her creative genius, and what is he doing?" Detmar says. "He's shoveling it, he's destroying himself. She knew the destructive path; she'd gone through a heroin period herself.

And he's in it, and we just think it's stupid, because he's got talent. It suits him to hang out with the shovelers, because they've got money—they can get on a plane and fly to Mustique. Issie can't do that."

"The hedonistic parties would go on and on," Forsyth said. There was at least one a night, clichéd as it gets, "ice sculptures and expensive champagne and people jumping into swimming pools fully dressed, and drugs." McQueen and Forsyth were usually partying with Kate, Sadie, Jude, Annabelle Rothschild, and the heiress Davinia Taylor, and in that group the common denominator was the rapacious Kate.

"It was a very incestuous, cliquey world," said Forsyth. "They were hard-core—staying up for days, either drinking or taking drugs, in some cases both . . . People had a lot of money, so they never had to stop."

The two had been dating for six months when McQueen asked Forsyth to marry him. They planned on a small ceremony, but Kate and Annabelle took over, ferrying them to a massive yacht stocked with £40,000 worth of lobster and champagne. In attendance were Kate's friends: Sadie and Jude, Noel Gallagher's ex-wife Meg Mathews, and Patsy Kensit. The priest barely spoke English. The whole thing seemed less like a wedding than another excuse to party.

"Everyone was eating and drinking and taking drugs," Forsyth said. "There [was] no family. It was all party people . . . Everybody wanted to be with Lee. He was the hottest ticket in town. But I noticed that in the fashion world there were very few people who said, 'There's someone who needs looking after.' "

Isabella would have gladly looked after Lee, had she been welcome in his life and had she been capable. As it was, Issie was in the throes of a deep depression. She was trying antidepressants to no avail, and began talking openly about suicide. "My head will be severed and sent to my father's estate," she said. "My heart will be ripped out and put in a box to be buried with Detmar."

Doing herself in became a regular topic. "She said, 'Maybe it would be better if I just popped off,'" Philip Treacy says. "And we were like, 'What? You're joking.' But she was introducing the idea. And she would sit there and have conversations about it, and tell me what would be a good reason, and thought that she was convincing me of her point of view. It sounds completely wild, but it was very pragmatic."

She had days and weeks where she was still capable of functioning, and was gratified when the *New Yorker* asked to do a profile of her in late 2000. She was portrayed exactly as she'd hoped, as an eccentric power broker responsible for discovering McQueen, Treacy, Macdonald, Dahl. Issie, said the magazine, was an authority "with avant-garde credentials." She portrayed herself as still so close to McQueen that he'd be "hysterical" if she missed his show, yet she also let slip her great disappointment when he left her behind at Givenchy: "I was devastated. The other day, I got drunk and plucked up the courage to ask him, 'Why didn't you take me?' And he said, 'Because you're with so many other people.' I understand. He loves me, but he can't work with me. It's blood, sweat, and tears with us, because we're both really angry people and we both feel we've had a hard time. I think we would have made each other very, very ill. But the other day he rang me up and said, 'I miss you, I love you.' He knows that I'm absolutely obsessed by him." But she couldn't resist knocking him down a bit, noting that when she first took on McQueen, "they wouldn't allow him into the *Vogue* offices. His teeth looked like Stonehenge."

She was bitter about Treacy too, saying that she couldn't believe he hadn't mentioned her in a recent high-profile book about hats. "Boy George is there and not me," she said. "I resent it, really a lot. I asked Philip about it. I said, 'Why aren't I in the book? Why aren't I in your press releases?' No explanation. I might as well not even exist."

People were finally seeing what McQueen had been dealing with:

There was no satisfying Isabella. Treacy adored her and raved about Issie's importance to the *New Yorker*, while McQueen refused to play along: "She's like a disease," he told the magazine. "A terminal disease. Everything she does rubs off on you."

It sounded like black humor, but those who knew McQueen well knew how capable he was of being cruel, and this was cruel. Issie had been fired again, and though it was blamed on the departure of her boss, Issie's reputation as an unstable spendthrift preceded her. She got a few consulting jobs, spent more and more time in Paris—in McQueen's old flat in the Marais, spending hours in bed propped up on pillows, eating croissants and smoking cigarettes, cuddling with the assistants who were never allowed to leave her side. She and Detmar had separated.

"You know how hard it is to live with someone who's trying to commit suicide all the time?" Detmar says. "It's really fucking hard. I never gave up, I never broke down, I was always there for Issie." But he couldn't live with her anymore. "I was having a good time making love to all these girls," Detmar says. "I was having a ball."

Issie took comfort in the small things. Tom Ford gave her his private line to VIP cabs in Paris; she slept in a bed once owned by Freddie Mercury; she was still a front-row presence nonpareil, showing up at Julien Macdonald's show with a dead lobster on her head. But nothing and no one was as important as McQueen. And now his new best friend was Daphne Guinness, whom she didn't think was that great an influence. To Issie, their whole sudden relationship was based on the superficial. As Issie would say, "Daphne may have money, but she hasn't got a brain in her head." Still, when McQueen took Tom Ford up on his offer to join Gucci Group, Issie allowed herself to think that maybe now he'd pay her back somehow. That he didn't left her feeling doubly betrayed, and she was so bitter she told Detmar that when she died, it wasn't going to be in McQueen.

*       *       *

Madness was much with McQueen, and he followed up "Overlook" with the show now regarded as his career pinnacle. For "Voss," McQueen staggered the terror. He began by deliberately starting an hour late, forcing his audience to sit around an enormous reflective Perspex box: What better revenge than to make all these horrible people stare at themselves, compare their looks, maybe find themselves, as McQueen had, falling so short? Fashion critic Sarah Mower got it, calling the crowd "the prime arbiters of vanity."

"I was looking at it on the monitor, watching everyone trying not to look at themselves," McQueen said. It was his greatest retribution.

And then, suddenly, the lights went off and the giant box was lit from within, his models—who couldn't see out—going crazy against the glass, pleading and keening, gorgeous inmates with skulls sheathed in white caps, curved steel and stuffed birds in their faces. McQueen showed seventy-six looks, the most elaborate pieces made with feathers and shells, his half-cyborg women now crossbreeding with the animal kingdom. The show closed with the collapse of a wooden box-within-the-box, revealing a naked model, flesh spilling over, her head encased in a demonic gray mask. She was hooked up to a breathing tube and covered in moths, the tableau a replica of photographer Joel-Peter Witkin's *Sanitarium*.

The *Times*, the *Guardian*, the *International Herald Tribune* all raved. McQueen's show was peerless, and he knew it. "Voss" was a statement of intent: He was now the designer to beat.

"Up until Mr. McQueen's glorious crack-up, there was no discernable reason to get out of bed for the London shows," said the *New York Times*'s Cathy Horyn, who went on to call McQueen "a great designer who is not only making beautiful clothes, but also responding, like an artist, to the horror and insanity in contemporary culture."

McQueen was also working through personal traumas. His marriage to George didn't last long. He had recently been diagnosed as HIV-positive. Few people knew. He couldn't find happiness anywhere. The more successful he was, the more paranoid he became, convinced that everyone in his life was using him. "He was so obsessed with what he was doing that he couldn't see a bigger picture," says Andrew Groves. "At every level." Each triumph, in his mind, quickly plateaued. "Even if you're the hottest young thing, you want more. At Givenchy—did he get bigger and better than Galliano? And if he did, then what?"

Not long after he joined Gucci Group, rumors began circulating that PPR wanted McQueen to take over at either YSL or Gucci. McQueen shot them down. "I'd rather kill myself," he said. "I ended up designing fourteen collections a year, including stuff for my own house. I'm never going back to that."

Issie was another part of his life he'd pronounced over, but her bipolar disorder was so out of control that everyone who knew her, especially McQueen, was concerned. She'd miss flights while sitting at the airport terminal. She plopped her bare breasts on a table while having lunch with a Prada exec. Her underwear came off as she was walking to her seat at a couture show, so she stepped out of it and kept going. She introduced the Duchess of York to a photographer saying, "This is Donald. He has an enormous cock."

She was carrying on an affair with a gondolier she'd met in Venice. She called him Casanova; he took her money and broke her heart. Her depression became the only thing she could talk about. "The best thing you could do was listen," said Anna Wintour. "It didn't make sense from the outside, but that's the illness."

Desperate, Issie checked into the Priory in the summer of 2003. She had no money, so Daphne Guinness pitched in £5,000, McQueen the other £5,000. Her doctors there said she had to stop wearing Treacy's hats, because she was using them to hide her face, and she had to find a way to like herself. They put her on lithium, and when she was released in September, she was nearly catatonic. She began electroshock treatments, which only seemed to speed up the cycling of her mania and depression. Detmar, who had never really left Isabella, tried to convince her to go to the United States after a conversation with Andrew Solomon, who'd written *The Noonday Demon* about his own battles with depression.

"He said to me, 'Detmar, Paris for couture, London for suits, but America for psychiatric hospitals.'" But Issie didn't want to leave. London was where her friends and family were, and she couldn't get better without them. She never lost hope that McQueen would come back to her. She had no idea how depressed he was too.

McQueen was having unprotected sex with prostitutes—sometimes one, sometimes several at the same time. He began seeing an escort named Paul Stag regularly, but he'd never take Stag out of the house. He couldn't—LVMH wouldn't have it. Instead, Stag would wait in McQueen's luxury apartment in Mayfair; most nights, McQueen would get home at around eleven and have to be up at seven the next day, unless he was in the middle of a collection, which meant Stag would see him maybe five or ten minutes over three weeks.

On less stressful nights, McQueen would wait for his delivery of cocaine and talk shit about having to go to fashion parties with mindless celebrities. The two men weren't quite a couple, but they had been involved for nine months, and when Stag asked McQueen to donate something for an auction of porn star memorabilia, he agreed. Then, one night at the tail end of a seven-hour, coke-fueled orgy, McQueen turned to Stag. "He said to me, um, 'I want you to fuck this guy now.' And I said, 'I don't want to, I'm too tired, I've just ejaculated.' And he goes, 'Well, if you don't, say goodbye to that £10,000 dress for the charity.'" In the time they were together, McQueen never really struck Stag as depressed, just mean; on that night together, their last, Stag remembers thinking, "'You're a fucking shit.'"

\*　　\*　　\*

Issie reconciled with Detmar, though when her shrink asked her if she really wanted to be with him, she said, "At this point, I'd settle for a hamster.'" She began taking lunch in the park where she'd sit with the homeless and chain-smoke, going on about how she'd soon be joining them. "She was very determined in her depression," says her former assistant Brian O'Callaghan. "She wouldn't give up on it; she was constantly talking about it. Her favorite subject was death." O'Callaghan would talk with her for hours and try to reason with her.

"She said, 'Brian . . . unfortunately, you can get up on Monday, you can get up on Tuesday and feel good and look at the flowers and say they're beautiful and look at the sky and say it's amazing. But I can't. I feel like I'm fading in and out. I never thought this would happen to me, but it has.'"

"Being with Issie was like having someone around who was slightly drunk," said her friend Nicholas Coleridge. "Your heart went out to her, but as it went on longer and longer, it got harder." In April 2007, when Issie was scheduled for surgery to remove a mass on an ovary, McQueen came up to Hilles to spend the weekend with her. He hardly left his bedroom. "McQueen was unsettled by Issie's nervous, unconfident state," said Detmar, "and Issie was upset by Alexander's failure to appreciate the effort she had gone [to] to make his weekend enjoyable. It was the last time she saw him."

Her depression was killing her. As Issie decompensated, different doctors were called upon, different drugs tried, electroshock therapy resumed, yet nothing worked. She tried to kill herself four times in two months: overdoses on heroin, pills, vodka. Her sense of humor was the last to go: Early one morning in May 2006, Issie smashed her car into a delivery truck parked behind a Tesco; when Detmar asked her why she'd done it, she replied, "I always hated Tesco." Finally, on April 26, 2006, she threw herself off an overpass known as Suicide Bridge, breaking both feet. She was told she'd never wear heels again.

She was institutionalized and placed under the care of Dr. Stephen

Pereira, who would also treat McQueen for severe depression and suicidal tendencies. Issie was now burning her vagina with lit cigarettes, a literal form of self-abuse for someone who couldn't have the babies she so badly wanted. She felt useless in every way, convinced that she was irrelevant. She'd read comments online referring to her as "a figure from the past."

"Everyone knows I've fucked up," she'd say. She talked about her withering status in the fashion world incessantly. "She didn't want to be a joke," said Brian O'Callaghan. "Fashion is about looks, size, beauty, clothes. She didn't want to be stuck somewhere between kitsch and oblivion."

She kept those fears secret from the few friends she had left in the industry. "I'm fighting depression," she'd say, "and I can't beat it." Anna Wintour visited Issie in the hospital that summer and drew the same conclusion. "There was a saddening inevitability about what was going to happen," Wintour said. "She'd decided to embark on the journey, and she had every intention of taking it."

On May 5, 2007, Issie guzzled weed killer, the same way Detmar's father had committed suicide thirty years ago. She was rushed to the hospital, irritated that the nurses didn't recognize her: "Google me!" When her doctors came back with her test results and told her she'd be dead within twenty-four hours to two weeks, she was relieved; as she'd told her sister Lavinia, "I'm afraid I haven't taken enough." She'd ingested twenty times the amount needed to kill her. She sat in bed and waited to die, and though many stories circulated after her death about Issie in her gold lamé lingerie or her Giles Deacon, stacks of fashion magazines piled up, smoking cigarettes and wearing red lipstick, none of them were true. She sat up in bed in a public hospital, dressed in cotton, on a drip, nothing glamorous about it. "It's bullshit to pretend otherwise," Detmar says.

Only Issie's family knew she was dying. She called some friends from the hospital. McQueen was not among them.

He attended her funeral and looked so stricken that Detmar actually felt sorry for him. The sentiment didn't last long: After McQueen and Treacy mounted a tribute show to Issie later that year, Detmar made his true feelings known. "I said to Alexander, 'Beautiful tribute. Pity she can't wear the clothes.'"

# EPILOGUE

ON AUGUST 7, 2011, New York's Metropolitan Museum of Art took the unprecedented step of remaining open until midnight. Such was the response to "Alexander McQueen: Savage Beauty" that people lined up for hours, snaking down and around Fifth Avenue for the last chance to see his life's work on display. The exhibit became one of the museum's highest grossing ever, bringing in nearly $15 million over three months.

Left unsaid was a brutal truth: "Savage Beauty" would never have been mounted had Alexander McQueen not killed himself the year before, at age forty, on February 11, 2010, just weeks before his next show. The industry had long ago come to regard McQueen as an endless generator of fantastical clothes and shows, the sustained quality of his output having long ceased to amaze, his genius taken for granted. In so many ways, his suicide was almost inevitable. As Tom Ford said, "If you had written him as a character in a novel, the end would almost inevitably have been the same." Still, his death stunned the fashion world.

"Shocked and devastated," said Kate Moss.

"An insurmountable loss," said Anna Wintour.

"Immortal in the history of fashion," said Diane von Furstenberg.

He was the first fashion designer whose death felt like a larger cultural, generational loss, on the level of Kurt Cobain's suicide, or the accidental deaths of River Phoenix and Heath Ledger: These were originals all. That McQueen's fame was on par with that of actors and rock stars was as much due to his talent as to the acceleration of culture and technology. *Sex and the City* made household names of Manolo Blahnik, Fendi, and McQueen, and when he attended the Met Ball in 2006—now known as "Fashion's Oscars"—Sarah Jessica Parker was on his arm. McQueen hit his apex just as the Internet was creating more access to design, allowing hobbyists and obsessives to become bloggers. The appetite for behind-the-scenes drama grew, as the success of shows like *Project Runway* and movies like *The Devil Wears Prada* and the *Vogue* documentary *The September Issue* proved. The pace of technology has allowed cheap-chic chains such as H&M and Zara to knock off high-end collections as soon as they hit the runway, allowing rich and poor to dress alike and creating even more pressure on designers to produce, produce, produce. There is a through-line from the minimalism of Calvin Klein's early '90s ad campaign with Kate to the aesthetic Steve Jobs created at Apple, and the result is a general public more attuned to good design than ever. How ironic that it took the death of a maximalist like McQueen for us to see it.

Almost immediately after his suicide, the house of McQueen, owned by PPR, began distancing itself from the man who built it. Lee McQueen was an openly gay man who had group sex, dated escorts and porn stars, was fueled by amphetamines and coke, could be a monster to those who loved him best, and whose darkest sexual impulses inspired his greatest work. The moment McQueen went to LVMH—as with Marc—the walls came down around him, protecting him from the real world and isolating him from those who knew and loved him best. Now, in death, his biography needed to be kept clean by the estate and by PPR, to keep the house profitable and respectable, no matter the disservice to its founder. It's impossible to know whether the future Queen of England would have commissioned a McQueen for her wedding gown had he lived—"he would have put antlers on her head," says one friend—but it was a near certainty once he died.

In the year before his suicide, McQueen was thinking about leaving the industry. He told Simon Ungless that he was exhausted, that he had lined up his protégée Sarah Burton to take over for him, that he wanted to establish an "Alexander McQueen School of Design." In his way, he tried to make amends, showing up unannounced at a Christmas party Simon Costin threw in 2007. He saw his old friend Chris Bird, and in a rare moment of vulnerability revealed that he was HIV-positive. "I just sort of said to him, 'Well, that was bloody stupid, wasn't it?' And he just said, 'Yeah.'" He had a chat with Simon— "surface stuff"—and nodded a hello to Andrew Groves, and after about an hour and a half, he quietly left.

McQueen, like Issie, had been battling depression for some time, and had begun seeing Dr. Stephen Pereira, the same psychiatrist who'd treated her. Most everyone who knew Lee is convinced that his suicide was a rash impulse brought on by darkness and drugs, by the recent death of his beloved mother, but in truth McQueen had tried to kill himself twice before, in 2009. He had felt isolated by fame, let down by people he loved, existentially depressed after the triumph of a show, a failure in every other way except professionally. His mother's death, his psychiatrist said, left him feeling that "there was nothing else to live for."

On the night of February 10, McQueen snorted a small pile of cocaine and did an Internet search for the fastest ways to die. He did more coke, enough to kill himself three times over, swallowed some sleeping pills, then took a cord into the bathroom and tried to hang himself in the shower. He failed. He went into the kitchen and grabbed a cleaver, found one of his favorite daggers, then went into his closet. He looped his favorite brown belt around his neck, slashed his wrists, and hung himself, leaving behind a note that read in part:

*Please look after my dogs.*
*I'm sorry, I love you,*
*Lee.*
*PS: Bury me at the church.*

In his flat, in pride of place, were two portraits of Issie by Steven Meisel. "It was the most valuable thing I learned in fashion, her death," McQueen said in 2009, months after his own two failed suicide attempts. "Isabella was so strong in her public image but couldn't stand her ground in her personal life. I know the other side. She would say that fashion killed her, but she also allowed that to happen in a lot of ways."

Nearly twenty years after Corinne Day discovered Kate Moss, the two reunited for a show at the National Portrait Gallery, which had commissioned Day to shoot Moss for their permanent collection. "What she did to fashion photography is unparalleled," says Panos Yiàpanis, stylist, editor, and Day protégé. "She knew her legacy was set in stone."

The images were stark and solemn, Kate still beautiful but harder-looking now. The aesthetic was classic Corinne, and though Kate found the photos unflattering, she said nothing. On opening night, Kate posed in front of the portraits, arm around a beaming Corinne, whose face was swollen, the tumor growing rapidly. As Corinne ran out of money, Kate joined up with several friends for a fund-raiser called "Save the Day," autographing five hundred copies of a Corinne print to raise funds for her treatment. She visited Corinne in the hospital, bringing along an iPod she'd loaded up. Corinne still felt Kate could have done more—she was a multimillionaire who wouldn't have gotten where she was without Corinne; it was the sentiment shared by Isabella Blow about McQueen. Kate didn't think that was fair, and it remained an undercurrent throughout their rapprochement.

The sicker Corinne got, the more docile she became, the more interested in a kind of clean, perfect beauty that was a counterpoint to the revolution she'd started. She shot for Cacharel and Hermès, did portraits of designers like Stella McCartney, and became so obsessed with airbrushing and artifice that friends wondered if the tumor was clouding her judgment. Corinne insisted she was just being pragmatic; she needed to plan and provide for Mark, for after she'd gone. "I've actually come to a point in my life where I want to make money," she said. "I've realized that it can be quite useful! I'm enjoying it, but I'm also keeping within the boundaries."

As Corinne got sicker, she became kinder, and her friends could never figure out how much of her behavior—the drugs, the explosive rages, the excommunication of friends—had been caused by the tumor, which doctors said had been there for seven years before it was ever diagnosed. In total, she lived with it for twenty-one years. "I can't imagine that this tumor wouldn't affect her behavior," Neil Moodie says. "It must have. I think she always knew what she was doing, but I think sometimes she didn't know why she was doing it. She just did it. But I think she had so much more remorse, years later, about it all."

Toward the end of her life, Corinne was, by chance, in the same hospital as Tara St. Hill, the friend she'd betrayed with the publication of *Diary*. When Tara learned that Corinne was there, that she was dying, she got herself down to Corinne's room and sat by her bed. There was a lot of awkward silence, but they talked and cried; Tara still loved her, still considered Corinne her best friend. Corinne told her she felt real regret about *Diary* and had spent the past few years buying up every copy she could find.

Corinne died in a small rented cottage in the country, in a hospital bed in what had once been her dining room, on September 1, 2010. She was forty-eight. Her funeral was held in the backyard, and among her mourners was Kate. "Corinne's pictures, you might say, made Kate," said the *Evening Standard*, "and Kate made Corinne's reputation."

By now, Kate was a phenomenon in the industry: So desired was her personal style that she became the first model to resell slightly tweaked pieces from her own wardrobe. On May 1, 2007, she launched her line, Kate Moss for Topshop, posing in a window at the flagship store on Oxford Street; thousands of girls screamed and cried and snapped photos as if it were a rock show. In fall 2013, she was named Contributing Fashion Editor at British *Vogue*. She'd found a way to monetize her personal style, and her defiant silence amid all the scandals—the destruction, drugs, the orgies—were, in a post-confessional, reality-TV age, added value. She was a debauched libertine, superstylish but never perfect, and her appeal crossed generations. Teenage girls and their moms, who grew up with Kate, found her equally aspirational. So did her peers: Among the first to be shot wearing Kate Moss for Topshop were actresses Selma Blair and Cameron Diaz. Twenty years after her impish debut on the cover of a cult British magazine, Kate Moss has remained the longest-lasting, most influential model in history. "Years and years from now, when you look back on pictures of Kate, you'll get an idea of what our time was about," said stylist Brana Wolf. "You'll understand where fashion was at the time, because they all want to wear what Kate Moss wears."

By 2010, Marc Jacobs had established himself as a global superstar with brand recognition on par with Madonna's. He had appeared on *Oprah* and *Late Night with Jimmy Fallon* and been named one of *Time* magazine's 100 Most Influential People in the World. "I'd urge you to take a trip to China," Anna Wintour told him. "Everywhere I went, I heard the same thing: 'Ms. Wintour, do you know Marc Jacobs? Could you possibly get me Marc Jacobs's autograph?' "

"The two individuals perhaps most responsible for transforming the West Village from what it was ten years ago into what it is today are Carrie Bradshaw and Marc Jacobs," said the *New Yorker* in 2008, which went on to call the part of Bleecker Street clustered with his multiple shops "a kind of Marc Jacobs theme park." By the end of the decade, there were more than two hundred Marc Jacobs shops in eighty countries.

Yet he spent the first decade of the new millennium struggling to stay alive. After emerging from his first stint in rehab in 1999, Marc slowly began to let himself go, joining the ranks of the fat and unwashed who would never be worthy of wearing a Marc Jacobs design. By 2007, he'd relapsed again, and in February, after Marc failed to meet Robert Duffy right before his show, Duffy called him out. "Marc, I know what's going on," he said. The first four years at Vuitton had been a nightmare, Marc lost to drugs, Duffy doing all he could to cover it up. But Marc had turned himself into a tabloid fixture, and his exploits only added to his appeal, as Kate's did to hers. There was no use in lying about another prolonged absence; that would only undermine the brand's authenticity. "Marc is a gay man who is a drug addict, who hires hookers," Duffy said. "Why lie about it?"

When he emerged from rehab, Marc underwent another physical transformation: Like McQueen, he lost weight and had plastic surgery, broadening the bridge of his nose and getting hair transplants. Kim Gordon recommended her nutritionist, who cured his ulcerative colitis. He began going to the gym, covering his body with tattoos, and posing naked in his own ads. His true stroke of genius with the house of Vuitton was hiring Japanese artist Takashi Murakami in 2002; Murakami's reimagined handbag, featuring candy-colored LVs on white leather, became a blockbuster hit, earning the house $300 million in its first year on the market. It was the ultimate example of Marc's ability to balance high and low culture, and to hit an unforeseen sweet spot. It's a feat he's performed with his own label, selling everything from

$10 key chains to $5,000 bags, the accessibility of lower-priced kitsch not denigrating the high-end pieces but imbuing them with authenticity. Kate, Marc, and McQueen helped create a world where older women want the approval of younger women, while the younger women hope to become like the older ones, and where the lowbrow is as desirable as the high. Aspiration, now, goes both ways.

# ACKNOWLEDGMENTS

TO THOSE WHO SO generously shared their time and memories, especially Mark Szaszy, Hazel Day, Susie Babchick, Melanie Ward, Neil Moodie, Tara St. Hill, Panos Yiàpanis, Ally Coker, Detmar Blow, Andrew Groves, Julien Macdonald, Philip Treacy, Miguel Andover, Simon Ungless, Simon Costin, Chris Bird, and Jeff and Louise Weisbord.

My deep thanks also to Diane von Furstenberg, Anna Sui, Tracy Reese, Todd Oldham, Daryl K, Sue Stemp, Isaac Mizrahi, Fern Mallis, Tom Sykes, Plum Sykes, Robin Givhan, Valerie Steele, Louise Osmond, Sheryl Garratt, Daisy von Furth, Mark Lewman, Mary Clarke, Andrea Linett, Christina Kelly, Jane Pratt, Jackie Farry, Imogen Edwards-Jones, Rosemarie Terenzio, Madonna Badger, and Glenn O'Brien.

Thanks to Molly Wicka and Keshida Layone at Condé Nast for providing access to their archives, and to Sarah Marland at Blast Films, Jackie Haliday at Gimpel Fils, Sarah Morton at the 92nd St. Y, Whitney Kuhn at CBS News, and Rosie Guerin at Bloomberg News.

Michelle Howry was a gift of an editor. My great thanks as well to David Kuhn, Nicole Tourtelot, all at Touchstone and Kuhn Projects, and to photo editor Carter Love.

And thanks to those who read, listened, advised, and encouraged throughout: William and Mary Callahan, Bill Callahan, James Iha, Marc Spitz, Steve Lynch at the *New York Post*, Susannah Cahalan, Sarah Mullins, Phaeleau Cunneen, Lizzy Goodman, Serena French, Lara Behnert, William van Meter, Annette Witheredge, and Preston Browning at Wellspring House.

# NOTES

## INTRODUCTION

xv "Was I going to be used?": Unpublished portions of interview conducted by Mary Clarke with Marc Jacobs for *Index Magazine*, 2001

## CHAPTER 1: THE MAYBE DRAWER

1 "an ethereal quality about her": Fred Vormel, *Kate Moss: Addicted to Love* (London: Omnibus Press, 2006), 21.

2 Things were much darker: Laura Collins, *Kate Moss: The Complete Picture* (London: Sidgwick & Jackson, 2008), 16.

2 "At the end of that first day": Vormel, *Kate Moss*, 22.

3 "I went to this guy's house": Vormel, *Kate Moss*, 22.

5 "I wanted to get out the concept": Terry Jones, *Smile i-D Fashion and Style: The Best from 20 Years of i-D* (New York: Taschen, 2001), 10.

10 "What we were doing": Calvin Klein and Melanie Ward, *Interview Magazine*, March 2010.

11 "I see a sixteen-year-old now": James Fox, "The Riddle of Kate Moss," *Vanity Fair*, December 2012.

## CHAPTER 2: THE PINK SHEEP OF THE FAMILY

15 Cinderella: *Telegraph*, Alexander McQueen obituary, February 11, 2010.

16 "I always, always wanted": Susannah Frankel, introduction to *Alexander*

233

*McQueen: Savage Beauty* by Andrew Bolton (New Haven: Yale University Press, 2011), 17.

18 Jock Delves Broughton and murder: Detmar Blow with Tom Sykes, "The Curse of the Delves Broughtons," in *Blow by Blow: The Story of Isabella Blow* (London: HarperCollins Publishers, 2010), 9–16 and Lauren Goldstein Crowe, "The Stately Homes of England Are Mortgaged to the Hilt" in *Isabella Blow: A Life in Fashion* (New York: Thomas Dunne Books, 2010), 23–36.

19 "That explains my obsession": Blow with Sykes, *Blow by Blow*, 4.

28 "sabotage and tradition": Louise Osmond, *McQueen and I*, documentary, 2011.

## CHAPTER 3: FIFTEEN-YEAR-OLDS DON'T GO TO NIGHTCLUBS

33 "When I went to sleepaway camp": Lucy Kaylin, "Marc Jacobs Doesn't Give a F," *GQ*, May 2008.

35 "No one ever said 'no' to me": Dan Shaw, "To Make His Own Marc," *New York Times*, February 28, 1993.

36 "I was so dazzled": Bridget Foley, "Tom Pumps Up," *W* magazine, July 2000.

36 "suburban refugees": Ann Magnuson, "The East Village 1979–1989 A Chronology: Ann Magnuson on Club 57," Artforum, October 1999.

37 "I like romantic allusions": Amy Larocca, "Marc Jacobs: Lost and Found," *New York* Magazine, September 5, 2005.

37 "So I went to Parsons": Fern Mallis with Marc Jacobs at the 92nd St. Y, January 9, 2013.

## CHAPTER 4: JUST ANOTHER COMMON BITCH

41 "We were looking for new girls": Fox, 'The Riddle of Kate Moss."

41 "feral . . . when I used to come back": Fox, "The Riddle of Kate Moss."

43 "It wasn't about 1980s glamour": Vormel, *Kate Moss*, 32.

43 "just as exciting": Mark Szaszy, *Corinne Day Diary*.

43 "The images of Kate Moss": Marc Karimzadeh, "Costume Institute Looks at the Model as Muse," *WWD*, October 29, 2008.

43 "If I had been a teenager": Mary Clarke, unpublished portion of interview with Marc Jacobs for *Index* magazine, 2001.

44 "an aesthetic shock": Angela Buttolph, *Kate Moss Style: Inside the World's Most Famous Wardrobe* (London: Century, Random House, 2008), 26.

44 "just another": Collins, *Kate Moss*, 61.

### CHAPTER 5: I AM THE '90S

47 "I'm marrying a house": Crowe, *Isabella Blow*, 113.

47 "It was like Issie having two lovers": Blow with Sykes, *Blow by Blow*, 160–1.

48 "fashion desperados": Caroline Evans, *Fashion at the Edge* (New Haven: Yale University Press, 2009), 70.

51 "zero talent": Charlie Porter, "Stitched Up," *Guardian*, November 17, 2000.

51 "John was the '80s": Christa D'Souza, "McQueen and Country," *Guardian*, March 3, 2001.

52 "I want people to fear": Katherine Betts, "McCabre McQueen," *Vogue*, October 1997.

### CHAPTER 6: A CULTURE PERSON IN THE FASHION WORLD

53 "Domesday Book": Eleanor Lambert, "School Produces Designers," *News and Courier*, February 3, 1974.

54 "He didn't wear a suit": Carol Mongo, "Marc Jacobs," http://www.parisvoice.com /style-and-shopping/142-marc-jacobs. 2013.

55 "I ended up on someone's boat": Mongo, "Marc Jacobs."

55 "sort of the beginning": Clarke, *Index*, 2001.

56 "I saw Marc's three sweaters": Sally Singer, "Robert Duffy," *032c*, Summer 2008.

56 "We literally shook hands": Meenal Mistry, "Fashion's Better Halves," *Wall Street Journal*, August 21, 2011.

58 "Actually intelligent": Karen Bizer, "Marc Jacobs," *W*, June 30, 1986.

59 "the next time": Bridget Foley, "Hard Acts to Follow," *Women's Wear Daily*, October 24, 1994.

59 "Everyone I knew at that time": Singer, *032c*, 2008

60 "interviewed with Calvin nine times": Foley, *W*, July 2000.

61 "I remember the printers": Amy Wicks, "Anna Wintour set for *CBS Sunday Morning*," *Women's Wear Daily*, December 9, 2011.

62 "The most painful": Mallis with Jacobs, 92nd St. Y, January 9, 2013.

### CHAPTER 7: WHY CAN'T I HAVE FUN ALL THE TIME?

65 "They wanted to prove themselves": Buttolph, *Kate Moss Style*, 26.

66 "I was always on my own": Fox, "The Riddle of Kate Moss."

67 "she's really little": Fox, "The Riddle of Kate Moss."

67 "Moss and only Moss": Fox, "The Riddle of Kate Moss."

67 "I hate talking about her": Vormel, *Kate Moss*, 49.

68 "Corinne would make me cry": Fox, "The Riddle of Kate Moss."

68 "South Boston version of ebonics": Glenn O'Brien, GQ.co.uk, November 7, 2012.

68 "I wasn't into the waif thing": Tim Nixon, UK *Sun*, November 11, 2008.

68 "It didn't feel like me at all": Fox, "The Riddle of Kate Moss."

69 "Kate's body represented closing the door": James Kaplan, "The Triumph of Calvinism," *New York* Magazine, September 18, 1995.

69 "I was thin": Fox, 'The Riddle of Kate Moss."

70 "Suddenly this little unknown": Fox, "The Riddle of Kate Moss."

71 "In photographs, it doesn't matter": Vormel, *Kate Moss*, 50.

71 "She's very sensual": Kaplan, "The Triumph of Calvinism."

### CHAPTER 8: A CATALOG OF HORRORS

74 "If you're beautiful": Blow with Sykes, *Blow by Blow*, 171.

74 "I would get to the office": Blow with Sykes, *Blow by Blow*, 142.

75 "London Babes" shoot: Blow with Sykes, *Blow by Blow*, 142.

75 "I was expecting": Crowe, *Isabella Blow*, 135.

### CHAPTER 9: GRUNGE R.I.P

80 "Maybe everybody's insecure": Hadley Freeman, "Outside In," *Guardian*, February 16, 2007.

83 "It made me happy": Michael Gross, "Fun and Color by Marc Jacobs," *New York Times*, November 6, 1987.

83 "Tom was a different person then": Leisa Barnett, "Marc On . . . Hiring Tom Ford," Vogue.co.uk, May 20, 2008.

84 "That place was '90s New York": Aaron Rose and Carlo McCormack, *Young, Sleek and Full of Hell: Ten Years of New York's Alleged Gallery*, (Rome: Drago, 2005).

86 "I didn't set out": Clarke, *Index*, 2001.

88 "Punk was anti-fashion": Rick Marin, "Grunge: A Success Story," *New York Times*, November 15, 1992.

88 "You don't know what to do": Singer, *032c*, 2008.

### CHAPTER 10: A NICE GIRL FROM CROYDON

92 "I wanted the ordinary person": Mark Szaszy, *Corinne Day Diary* documentary, first aired on BBC4 on January 28, 2004.

93 "We thought": Fox, "The Riddle of Kate Moss."

94 "It wasn't very *Vogue*": Szaszy, *Corinne Day Diary*.

94 "It seemed strange to object": Charlotte Higgins, "Corinne Day: Raw Genius," the *Guardian*, August 31, 2010.

94 "It was really strange, the way I felt": Szaszy, *Corinne Day Diary*.

96 "She did feel kind of lonely": "Fox, "The Riddle of Kate Moss."

96 "The supermodel thing is over": Bridget Foley, "Calvin's Year," *W*, January 1996.

96 "I knew from the first moment": Buttolph, *Kate Moss Style*, 60.

97 "What would those twelve-year-old girls think?" Tad Friend, "The Short, Happy Life of River Phoenix," *Esquire*, March 1994.

97 "When River passed away": Vormel, *Kate Moss*, 70.

98 "Johnny invented grunge": Stephen Dalton, "Cooler Than You," *UnCut*, December 2004.

98 three different jail cells: Margaret Moser, Michael Bertin, and Bill Crawford, *Movie Stars Do the Dumbest Things*, (London: Renaissance Books, 2000), 69.

98 "Kerouac": Vormel, *Kate Moss*, 79.

98 "It must make you feel secure": Collins, *Kate Moss*, 122.

CHAPTER 11: FASHION PEOPLE HAVEN'T GOT ANY BRAINS

102 "As my therapist says": Tamsin Blanchard, "Blow by Blow," *Guardian*, June 22, 2002.

103 "We literally took the tire": Cathy Horyn, "McQueen: The Backstory and Beyond," On the Runway, *New York Times*, April 5, 2010.

103 "In its discipline": Kin Woo, "Insiders No. 50: Mr. Pearl," *AnOther Magazine*, September 24, 2012.

106 "I saw my own sisters being beaten": Jane Fryer, "A Life in Fashion," *Daily Mail*, February 12, 2010.

106 "A wild bird": Osmond, *McQueen and I*.

106 "Everyone gets frustrated": Crowe, *Isabella Blow*, 138.

CHAPTER 12: A HANDBAG THAT COSTS AS MUCH AS A MONTH'S RENT

109 "Marc's way of dealing": Singer, *032c*, 2008.

113 "We had this simple ambition": Adam Clarke Estes, "Remembering *Grand Royal*, the Beastie Boys' Brief, Brilliant Magazine," *Atlantic Wire*, May 4, 2012.

113 "I think X-Large and X-Girl": Elizabeth Thompson and Alexis Swerdloff, "An Oral History of X-Girl," Papermag.com, August 28, 2012.

115 "I thought it would be the worst thing": Singer, *032c*, 2008.

### CHAPTER 13: COOL BRITANNIA

117 "I never liked it": Guy Trebay, "The Garbo of Fashion," *New York Times*, November 4, 2012.

117 "She never fixed anything": Trebay, "The Garbo of Fashion."

118 "When I met Marlon": Fox, "The Riddle of Kate Moss."

118 "never complain": Trebay, "The Garbo of Fashion."

118 "Kate's look really reflects": Buttolph, *Kate Moss Style*, 46.

119 "The pendulum has swung": "Superslump?" *Entertainment Weekly*, October 27, 1995.

120 "all of a sudden middle America knows what Prada is": Amy M. Spindler, "Fashion Hitches a Ride with Hollywood's Shining Stars," *New York Times*, August 29,1995.

120 "It's not like I was dying": "Superslump?" *Entertainment Weekly*, October 27, 1995.

120 Adair and "death of the author": Vormel, *Kate Moss*, 80.

120 "I just did not have time": Michael Humphrey, "Great Moments in Publishing: Celebs Turned Novelists," *Salon*, October 1, 2010.

121 "It's easy to do other things": Lisa Birnbach, "How Long Must I Waif?" *New York* Magazine, September 18, 1995.

123 "I realized the importance": Buttolph, *Kate Moss Style*, 86.


### CHAPTER 14: THOSE SKINNY FASHION BITCHES IN THE FRONT ROW

128 "That was the end": Watt, *Alexander McQueen*, 88.

129 "She would say": Amy Larocca, "The Sad Hatter," *New York* Magazine, July 15, 2007.

129 "I didn't get it": Crowe, *Isabella Blow*, 136.

130 "What attracted me to Alexander": *Alison Bancroft, Fashion and Psychoanalysis: Styling the Self* (London: I.B. Tauris, 2012), 97.


### CHAPTER 15: THE DECADE OF THE DILETTANTE

133 "I thought that at the time": "Isaac Mizrahi on 'Unzipped,'" *The Huffington Post*, March 14, 2012.

134 "Everyone is tired of restraint": Amy M. Spindler, "In Milan, Brazen Men Parading," *New York Times*, January 19,1995.

135 "I had connections": Melina Gerosa, "Goddaughter," *Entertainment Weekly*, January 25, 1991.

139 "People still complain": Bridget Foley, "Jacobs' Ladder," *W*, August 1996.

140 "Maybe five girls own his stuff": Zoë Heller, "Jacobs' Ladder," *New Yorker*, September 22, 1997.

## CHAPTER 16: THE QUEEN OF PRIMROSE HILL

143 "I felt hurt": Szaszy, *Corinne Day Diary*.

145 Vodka for looks: Katherine Kendall, *Kate Moss: Model of Imperfection* (London: Penguin Books, 2005), 88.

146 "It's more fun getting dressed up": Buttolph, *Kate Moss Style*, 73.

147 "She was going in the complete opposite direction": Buttolph, *Kate Moss Style*, 75.

148 "It's been used as an accessory": Amy M. Spindler, "A Death Tarnishes Fashion's 'Heroin Look,' " *New York Times*, May 20, 1997.

148 "If a girl becomes a star": Catherine Wilson, "The Dark Side of Modeling," Tripod.com, 1997.

150 "It wasn't so much the friendships": Hadley Freeman, "My Wasted Years," the *Guardian*, July 8, 2007.

151 "she doesn't know what time zone she's in": Alex Tresniowski, "Out of Fashion," *People*, November 23, 1998.

152 "We both know": Collins, *Kate Moss*, 187.

152 "We'd both get really pissed": Collins, *Kate Moss*, 198.

152 "Sleep? Why?": Collins, *Kate Moss*, 199.

153 "I'm not even going to ask you": Tony Parsons, "Rock 'n' roll Tsars," *GQ*, February 2000.

153 "There are some things I can never discuss": Vormel, *Kate Moss*, 188.

153 "This is not a sad story": Tresniowski, *People*.

## CHAPTER 17: PARIS DOES NOTHING FOR ME

156 "I don't agree": Bridget Foley, "Ford Drives," *W*, August 1996

157 "The man is most concerned": Amy M. Spindler, "Zut! British Infiltrate French Fashion," *New York Times*, October 15, 1996.

157 "He's a really nice guy": Lynn Barber, "Alexander McQueen: Emperor of Bare Bottoms," the *Observer*, December 15, 1996.

158 "I didn't like the way LVMH": "Fashion's Hard Case," *Forbes*, September 16, 2001.

158 "total disaster": Cayte Williams, "Intelligent Consumer: The Fashion Month," the Independent, January 25, 1998.

158 "I don't know whether I can survive": Colin McDowell, "Shock Treatment," the *Sunday Times of London*, March 17, 1996.

159 "If she talked out of turn": Crowe, *Isabella Blow*, 145.

166 "I didn't want to be a groupie": Cator Sparks, "Daphne Guinness at FIT," *W*, August 2011.

166 "She had a childlike perception: Larocca, "The Sad Hatter."

167 "Fashion is a vampiric thing": Bibby Sowray, "Who's Who: Isabella Blow," Vogue.co.uk biography.

170 "He needed cocaine": Osmond, *McQueen and I*.

### CHAPTER 18: IT'S THE GIRL, NOT THE CLOTHES

173 "She pointed us toward": Joshua Levine, "Brand Anna," *Wall Street Journal*, March 23, 2011.

174 "I knew he was the one": Heller, *New Yorker*, 1997.

174 "contract was 500 pages long": George Wayne, "Marc Jacobs," *Vogue*, February 1997.

176 "all this palace intrigue": Mallis with Jacobs, 92nd St. Y, 2013.

178 "He could be so mean": Singer, *032c*, 2008.

### CHAPTER 19: WHEN THE LITTLE GLOW IN YOUR FACE GOES

181 "Skin up!": Collins, *Kate Moss*, 205.

182 Creating a monster: Collins, *Kate Moss*, 224.

### CHAPTER 20: CAN EVERYBODY NOT GIVE LEE ANY DRUGS?

187 "All of a sudden": Hilton Als, "Gear," *New Yorker*, March 17, 1997.

187 "I never smoked in my life": Crowe, *Isabella Blow*, 77.

190 "The concept": Bridget Foley, "King McQueen," *W*, September 1999.

190 "he wept": Watt, *Alexander McQueen*, 153.

191 "Anger in my work": Suzy Menkes, "Mr. Letterhead: McQueen Shows a Corporate Side," *New York Times*, September 18, 2001.

191 "Fire me!": Hillary Alexander, "Rival Left Fuming as Gucci Sews Up McQueen Deal," the *Telegraph*, December 5, 2000.

### CHAPTER 21: THESE PEOPLE ARE NOT YOUR FRIENDS

193 "I kept looking over my shoulder": Evgenia Peretz, "There's Something About Marc," *Vanity Fair*, April 2004.

193 "I think Gucci treated Tom Ford better": Teri Agins, "For Marc Jacobs, a Hot Partnership Needs Alterations," *Wall Street Journal*, February 9, 2004.

194 "such a negative experience": Kevin Sessums, "Tom Ford Tells All," the *Advocate*, November 2009.

194 "I'd walk in a room": Kaylin, *GQ*, 2008.

195 "She is young and sweet": Larocca, "Marc Jacobs, Lost and Found," *New York*, August 21, 2005.

195 "If I move": Monique P. Yazigi, "A Night Out With: Marc Jacobs; Even Steamier Than Paris," *New York Times*, September 20, 1998.

196 "These people don't really love you": Mallis with Jacobs, 92nd St. Y, 2013.

196 "I didn't want to go to rehab": Vanessa Grigoriadis, "The Deep Shallowness of Marc Jacobs," *New York*, November 27, 2008.

197 "All the friends he had": Singer, *032c*, 2008.

198 "It was like a rock concert": Sarah Mower, "The Man Who Put Marc in the Pink," *Guardian*, February 7, 2009.

### CHAPTER 22: A SUPERMODEL JUST LIKE MCDONALD'S

202 "She subtly moves the goalposts": Maureen Callahan, "Repli-Kate," *New York Post*, November 14, 2005.

202 "Whole lines have been made out of one look": Fox, "The Riddle of Kate Moss."

202 "Like a good fashion designer": Buttolph, *Kate Moss Style*, 106.

202 "elements are not really important": Buttolph, *Kate Moss Style*, 99.

206 "Kate's face . . . said it all": Szaszy, *Corinne Day Diary*.

206 "Bang into drugs": Collins, *Kate Moss*, 263.

207 "The thing about Kate": Fox, "The Riddle of Kate Moss."

207 "getting Mossed": Fox, "The Riddle of Kate Moss."

208 "Welcome to our nightmare": Collins, *Kate Moss*, 243.

## CHAPTER 23: PARIS FOR COUTURE, LONDON FOR SUITS, AMERICA FOR PSYCHIATRIC HOSPITALS

211 George Forsyth: Laura Collins, "Alexander McQueen's ex-partner throws a disturbing light on the 'hangers-on' who lionized him, but never truly knew him," *Daily Mail*, February 14, 2010.

217 "I'd rather kill myself": Lisa Armstrong, "Go to Gucci . . . I'd Rather Die," *Times of London*, March 3, 2003.

217 "The best thing you could do": Larocca, "The Sad Hatter."

219 "I'd settle for a hamster": Crowe, *Isabella Blow*, 221.

219 "Being with Issie": Crowe, *Isabella Blow*, 223.

219 "McQueen was unsettled": Blow with Sykes, *Blow by Blow*, 262.

220 "Everyone knows I've fucked up": Osmond, *McQueen and I*.

## EPILOGUE

223 "If you had written him": Paula Reed, "Tom Ford Talks McQueen and Galliano," *Grazia*, July 26, 2011.

225 "there was nothing else to live for": Sam Jones, "Alexander McQueen Hanged Himself After Taking Drugs," *Guardian*, April 27, 2010.

226 "the most valuable thing I learned": Cathy Horyn, "General Lee," *T Magazine*, September 11, 2009.

227 "I want to make money": Sheryl Garratt, "Corinne Day: Pioneer of a New Kind of Beauty," *Guardian*, September 3, 2010.

228 "Years and years": Buttolph, *Kate Moss Style*, 198.

228 "I'd urge you": Gregory Delli Caprini, Jr., "Anna Wintour Thinks Marc Jacobs Should Go to China," Fullfrontalfashion.com, December 14, 2010.

229 "hires hookers": Singer, *032c*, 2008.

# INDEX

Ford, Tom:
  awards and honors to, 134
  early years of, 60
  and Gucci, 84, 133–34, 156, 174, 176,
    191–92, 193–94, 202, 215
  and Issie, 215
  and McQueen, 191–92, 215, 223
  and Parsons, 53
  and Perry Ellis, 83–84
  and Studio 54, 36
  and YSL, 122, 193–94
Ford Models, Supermodel of the Year,
  119
Forsyth, George, 211–13, 216
Forsythe, Robert, 82–83
*48 Hours* (CBS), 79, 80
Fox, James, *White Mischief,* 18
Frank, Andy, 144, 151
Franks, Milton, 33–34
Fraser, Honor, 75, 162
Freud, Bella, 75, 161, 202
Freud, Lucian, 205
Frey, Mary, 111
Friel, Anna, 182
Frischmann, Justine, 122
Fritz, Scott, 77, 78–79, 81–82
Frost, Sadie, 149, 150, 182, 205, 207,
  213
Funky Bunch, 68
Furstenberg, Diane von, 36, 109, 224
Furth, Daisy von, 87, 113, 114, 135,
  137–38

Gainsbourg, Charlotte, 198
Gainsbourg, Serge, 198
Gainsbury, Sam, 170

Gallagher, Liam, 122, 150
Gallagher, Noel, 118, 139, 152–53
Galliano, John, 73, 166, 167
  and Arnault, 128, 174
  and bankruptcy, 40
  and Central Saint Martins, 25, 40, 51
  and Dior, 155
  and Givenchy, 128, 155, 156, 189,
    217
  and *i-D,* 6
  and Kate, 40–42, 96, 208
  and McQueen, 51–52, 157, 162
Gallo, Vincent, 43, 111
Garratt, Sheryl, 6, 8, 9–10, 11
Gaultier, Jean-Paul, xv, 51, 156, 208
Geffen, David, 68, 70, 96
Gen-X, 85–86, 121, 134, 197
Ghesquière, Nicolas, 202
Gieves & Hawkes, 21–22
Gigli, Romeo, 23–24, 173
Gili, Oberto, 47
Gimpel Fils gallery, Mayfair, 185
Girl, 112
Giuliani, Rudy, 61
Givenchy, 128, 130, 167
  and McQueen, 155–56, 158, 159–65,
    169–70, 173, 174, 182, 187–90, 191,
    211, 214, 217
Givenchy, Hubert de, 158, 164, 168
Godard, Jean-Luc, 113
Goffey, Danny, 150
Goldie, 128
Goldin, Nan, 205
  *The Ballad of Sexual Dependency,*
    92, 184
Gorbachev, Mikhail, 20

"Nihilism," 73–74

"No. 13," 190–91

as outsider, 14–15, 16–17, 21–22, 46,
    105, 167, 191

"The Overlook," 211, 216

persecution complex of, 164, 217

personal collections by, 188, 190, 192,
    224

physical appearance of, 14, 20–21,
    229

public persona of, 212, 216, 224

as Savile Row apprentice, 20–22

self-mythologizing by, 13, 29, 45, 76,
    157

self-punishment of, 168, 217

stresses on, 163–65, 168, 170, 187–89,
    217, 225

substance abuse of, 159, 163, 165,
    168, 170, 183–84, 187–88, 189, 191,
    193, 212–13, 218, 224, 225–26

and success, 74, 102, 105, 106,
    125–26, 127, 128, 134, 156, 166,
    198, 216–17, 224, 230

suicide of, 20, 223–26

as sui generis, xix–xx

"Taxi Driver," 48–49

"Untitled," 170, 188

"Voss," 216

wedding of, 213, 216

McQueen, Janet (sister), 26

McQueen, Joyce (mother), 16, 17, 160,
    225

McQueen, Ronald (father), 15–16

Meisel, Steven, 35, 195, 198

    and Issie, 74–75, 226

    and Kate, 70

and *Vogue*, 74–75, 87, 175

    and X-Girl, 114, 137

Mello, Dawn, 84

Menkes, Suzy, 110, 188, 190

Mercury, Freddie, 215

Mercury Lounge, 84

Metropolitan Museum of Art:

    "Alexander McQueen: Savage
        Beauty," 223–26

    Costume Archive, 53

    Met Ball (Fashion's Oscars),
        224

Miceli, Camille, 179

Michael, George, 4

Mike D, 113

Milk Fed, 138

Mills, Mike, 84, 111, 113, 135

Minogue, Kylie, 24, 25

*Miss London*, 7

*Miss Saigon*, 22

Mitsubishi, 59, 135

Miu Miu, 92, 175

Miyake, Issey, 58

Mizrahi, Isaac, 53, 112, 174

    and Perry Ellis, 54, 82, 110

    and Studio 54, 36

    and *Unzipped*, 133

models:

    Amazonian, 10, 40, 182

    and beauty, 91

    and body image, 69–70, 71, 93,
        117

    celebrity of, xx, 119, 197

    expanding the brand, 120

    remoteness of, 46

Montana, Claude, 51, 58

# ABOUT THE AUTHOR

Maureen Callahan got her start at *Sassy* magazine. Her work has appeared in *Vanity Fair*, and she has worked as an editor and writer at *New York* magazine, *Spin* and the *New York Post*, where she has covered everything from the subcultures of the Lower East Side to politics to fashion. She lives in Brooklyn, New York.